Interest Groups, Lobbying and Policymaking

POLITICS AND PUBLIC POLICY SERIES

Advisory Editor

Robert L. Peabody

Johns Hopkins University

*Financing Politics: Money, Elections
and Political Reform*
Herbert E. Alexander

*Congressional Procedures and
the Policy Process*
Walter J. Oleszek

Interest Groups, Lobbying and Policymaking

NORMAN J. ORNSTEIN

SHIRLEY ELDER

Congressional Quarterly Press

A DIVISION OF CONGRESSIONAL QUARTERLY INC.
1414 22nd Street, N.W., Washington, D.C. 20037

Fifth Printing

Library of Congress Cataloging in Publication Data

Ornstein, Norman J.
  Interest groups, lobbying, and policymaking.

  Bibliography: p.
  Includes index.
  1. Lobbying — United States. 2. Pressure groups — United States. 3. Pressure groups — United States — Case studies. I. Elder, Shirley, 1931- II. Title.

JK1118.075   328.73'07'8   78-17492
ISBN 0-87187-143-3

To Judy
and
To Richard

Foreword

"Groups," argued Arthur F. Bentley, "are the raw material of politics." Bentley published his classic demand for research on interest groups in *The Process of Government* (1908). Almost 50 years would pass before David B. Truman would respond with his major contribution to the understanding of these phenomena in *The Governmental Process* (1955). Although there have been several important case studies of interest groups, before and especially since Truman's work, our knowledge of how such groups are organized, how they operate, and with what range of effectiveness and responsibility, is still surprisingly limited.

Interest Groups, Lobbying and Policymaking goes a long way toward explaining and illustrating what we do know about the organization and operation of interest groups. Its authors — Norman J. Ornstein and Shirley Elder — wisely attempt few definitions and do not distinguish between "interest groups" and their more pejorative cousins, "pressure groups" and "lobbies." They generally adopt, instead, Truman's definition of an interest group as "a shared-attitude group that makes certain claims upon other groups in society." If and when, Truman continued, the group "makes claims through or upon any of the institutions of government, it becomes a political interest group." Ornstein and Elder concentrate primarily on classifying interest groups, describing their operation and evaluating their effectiveness and responsibility.

This book appears at a particularly opportune time, as Congress attempts to design and implement new regulations covering lobbying activity. It comes, moreover, during a period in which new types of lobbies and changes in Congress have combined to make a fresh look at interest groups not only useful, but necessary.

Although primarily designed as a textbook, Ornstein's and Elder's study is a valuable addition to an otherwise thin, uneven and somewhat dated literature. Their collaborative effort successfully combines the trained analytical skills and familiarity with the literature of a political scientist with the seasoned insights of a knowledgeable Washington journalist.

Both Ornstein and Elder have had a rich and varied exposure to Washington and especially Capitol Hill politics. Prior to obtaining his Ph.D. in political science from the University of Michigan in 1972, Ornstein spent a year as an American Political Science Association Congressional Fellow. After teaching at the International Center of Johns Hopkins University in Bologna, Italy, he joined the faculty of The Catholic University of America in Washington, D.C., in 1972. He subsequently worked as a staff assistant and later staff director for Senator Adlai Stevenson's committee on Senate committee reorganization.

After graduating with a B.A. degree from Stanford University, Elder has held a series of newspaper jobs in the Washington metropolitan area, including a decade's experience as a congressional correspondent for *The Washington Star*. Currently, she is working as a free-lance political writer in Washington, D.C.

Interest Groups, Lobbying and Policymaking begins with four theoretical and background chapters, primarily conceptualized and drafted by Ornstein. Chapter 1 traces "Theories about Groups" from Madison through Bentley and Truman to more contemporary treatments by Milbrath, Mills, Bauer, Pool and Dexter, and Olson. Chapter 2 provides an inventory of group functions, a typology of groups, and a discussion of how lobbyists relate to the more formal institutions of government — the legislative, executive, and judicial branches. Chapter 3 examines the principal resources available to different kinds of political interest groups, including a close look at their strategies and tactics.

Chapter 4 consists of a review of various attempts to regulate the activities of interest groups, including a discussion of reforms pending in recent Congresses.

The three case studies, researched and drafted by Elder, were selected not only because of their importance, but also because they illustrate a range of successful and not-so-successful interest group activities. Chapter 5 analyzes the defeat of the common-site picketing bill in the House of Representatives in 1977. Chapter 6 consists of a study of how the Clean Air Act Amendments of 1977 were pushed through the House and Senate after an earlier version of the bill had been killed by a Senate filibuster in the closing hours of the 94th Congress. Chapter 7 explores the many forces at work in the B-1 bomber controversy that ended in a presidential decision to forego a continuing or expanded program. The primary focus of these studies is on the involvement of contending interest groups rather than a stage-by-stage analysis of the passage or defeat of particular legislation.

In a concluding chapter, Ornstein returns to an examination of some of the broader questions posed by interest groups in our society. How responsible have interest groups been? To what extent do they contribute to the workings of the national government? What can be done to curb their excesses? "Here, Sir, the people govern," Alexander Hamilton once argued. Have interest groups largely taken their place? *Interest Groups, Lobbying and Policymaking* cannot answer all of these questions, but it is a valuable and insightful contribution to these enduring problems of a democracy.

Robert L. Peabody

Preface

This book arose in part out of frustration — the frustration of a university professor who could find no adequate books on interest groups to use in his college courses on American Government, Congressional Politics, and Political Parties and Pressure Groups. The existing literature was either too detailed, too complex, or too outdated. He thus decided to write one himself, and joined with a veteran Washington journalist to do so.

Interest Groups, Lobbying and Policymaking is designed to be a concise (and, we hope, lively) overview of interest groups and American politics, useful in particular to the undergraduate student. The book surveys the theories that have been suggested about groups; develops a framework for understanding the internal dynamics and characteristics of groups and their political behavior; examines the development of government regulation of groups and lobbying; and provides three in-depth case studies of groups lobbying on issues in Congress and the executive branch. Along with the specific knowledge about groups and issues described in this book, we hope that the reader will come away better able to understand the role interest groups and lobbies should play, have played, and will play in the American policy process.

The profession of lobbying changes constantly to reflect evolving public attitudes and to respond to new conditions. We have seen in the last 15 years the growth of both public interest lobbies and of business-oriented groups. Tactics have also changed, to include more grass-roots work and to respond to the reforms in Congress.

To us, lobbying is an important part of the democratic system and one of the least understood professions. Lobbyists are plagued by a stereotype of the shifty-eyed bag man, slipping envelopes of cash to dishonest politicians. As in all professions, there are bad apples among lobbyists, but the vast majority are skilled, hard-working men and women, neither as glamorous nor as disreputable as popular myth would have them.

Several people deserve acknowledgement for assistance on this book. First and foremost, our thanks go to Margaret Thompson, whose prodigious research efforts and concise editing skills were crucial to the completion of the manuscript. Editor Robert A. Diamond was unstinting in his devotion to making this book a quality product; so too was political science editor Jean L. Woy. Executive editor Wayne Kelley and CQ research director Robert Cuthriell helped get the book project focused and off the ground. Michael J. Robinson of The Catholic University of America and Robert L. Peabody of The Johns Hopkins University (also the advisory editor to this series of books on Politics and Public Policy) provided insight and suggestions on earlier drafts of the manuscript. James S. Coleman and Zdzislawa Walaszek of the University of Chicago's National Opinion Research Center assisted Norman Ornstein in conducting a variety of interviews with interest group representatives and lobbyists between 1974 and 1976. We also thank the lobbyists themselves, along with the representatives, senators, and congressional staff to whom we talked, for their candor, insights, and time.

Norman J. Ornstein
Shirley Elder

Contents

PART I

Groups in the American Political Process

Perhaps the only conclusion that observers of groups in America might agree upon is that there are a lot of groups attempting to influence the political process and policy outcomes. But the variety of observers could not so easily agree on the role interest groups generally *should* play and *do* play in the policy process: whether group involvement, overall, biases policy outcomes or approximates the aggregation of all interests in the society; and what factors determine a group's ability to influence outcomes in politics.

In Part I of this book, we will address these and related areas of concern and controversy. To begin, we will examine the scope and variety of theories that have developed over the years about group involvement and importance in America. A simple glance at the various group theories shows the wide range of opinion that has existed about the proper and actual roles groups play in American political life. To many, interest groups are an evil (albeit a necessary one in a democracy), with the potential to corrupt the process and distort policy away from the popular will. To others, groups express the best features of democracy; they are both necessary and useful in translating the myriad opinions and interests in the society into representative policy. Taken together, these divergent opinions reflect a deep and persistent ambivalence about the role of groups in American politics and society. Widespread belief in their necessity and efficacy — underscored in the Constitution itself — is often accompanied by a distrust of their motives and actions.

Several theories of groups focus on their alleged upper-class bias. To many observers, groups with money and an ability to organize — both characteristics of upper-class, business-oriented interests — will have access to policymakers, and hence power. To others, the range of effective and active groups is much broader; groups without monied credentials and with noneconomic resources can and do compete on an equal footing in the policy arena.

To address this question adequately, we need to look at the factors that enable a group to organize and persist, and to become involved in the political process. Thus, in chapter 2, we begin our examination of the Washington-based interest groups that attempt to influence national policy. The functions groups may provide for their members are considered, as well as the types of groups that exist in contemporary America. In chapter 3, we examine the variety of resources, monetary and other, that groups can bring to bear on the policy process.

But a mere cataloguing of groups by function and subject, and by the resources they possess, does not tell us when, how, or why groups do have impact on policy; influence in an area is not wholly determined by the number of groups involved, or by an audit of the resources they own. At least of equal importance is the *manner* in which groups try to influence policy, that is, their lobbying and strategic abilities. As we move through chapters 2 and 3, the focus shifts from the internal organization of groups to their political behavior. We look at what groups can do to affect the political process, from monitoring political activity to initiating government action to blocking a policy initiative, and at what groups can do to gain easy access to policymakers. Further, we examine the range of strategies that can be adopted by groups in their political endeavors. These chapters will demonstrate the great complexity of groups and lobbying. Many factors, including money, size and geographical distribution of membership, group cohesiveness, leadership abilities, the availability and use of information, political and parliamentary savvy, group intensity, and others, can contribute to a group's success in the governmental process. As we will see in Part II, each of these factors comes to the fore at some point in the case studies we have chosen.

Chapter 4 shifts the focus from interest group political activity to government response, by regulation, to groups and their lobbying efforts. This subject is especially topical since, as this book is written, Congress is in the midst of structuring a new comprehensive lobbying disclosure bill, which, if passed, will be the first legislation of this kind in more than 30 years. As chapter 4 indicates, lobby regulation and disclosure efforts were intermittent and ineffective in the nineteenth century and were limited in the twentieth until the passage, in 1946, of the first comprehensive lobby disclosure law.

Congress' views on lobbying, as expressed in its legislative efforts, reflect the ambivalence towards groups that we have mentioned. While congressmen support lobbyists for the benefits they provide, there is enough distrust of their actions to inspire efforts to regulate. Acknowledging the constitutional protection of freedom of speech, however, regulations have emphasized disclosure, providing few direct and real restrictions on group political activity. In the past few years, pressure has increased to expand the scope of disclosure required to include the membership, financial contributors, leadership activities, and types of lobbying behavior of groups who attempt to influence the policy process. This has been the major area of controversy, dividing groups and politicians alike, in the contemporary debates over government regulation of groups and lobbying.

Overall, Part I of *Interest Groups, Lobbying and Policymaking* is intended to provide the reader with a framework for understanding the role of interest groups generally in American political life, and for analyzing the roles of particular groups involved in influencing specific issues in the policy arena, focusing on Congress. The reader should also recognize that, as the society, the political system, and its institutions have changed in the past and will change in the future, the nature, role, and behavior of groups will also change.

Both chapters 2 and 3 emphasize important political and systemic changes, especially those of the past decade, and relate them to group behavior. In the 1970s, as a result of the turmoil of Vietnam, Watergate, and other political upheavals, the American political process became more decentralized, more active, more open to public scrutiny and pressure, and more diffused generally. Interest groups responded with a concomitant increase in numbers, as well as in the scope and intensity of political activity. The effects of these interrelated changes are only now being assessed. As the reader finishes Part I and moves on to the case studies in Part II and to the concluding observations, he or she should keep in mind this dynamic relationship of groups, lobbying, and politics.

1

Theories About Groups

From the eighteenth century onward, observers of America have noted its group orientation: America, more than most, is a society of joiners and of groups. From childhood — through the Cub Scouts, Boy Scouts, Girl Scouts, and Campfire Girls; the YM and YWCA; Little League, church, and synagogue youth groups, and so on — Americans are encouraged to join and to identify with organizations and associations. It is not surprising, then, that American politics would have a significant group dimension.

Nor is it surprising that many theories have been propounded about the impact and desirability of groups in the American political system — some positive and some negative. Public attention towards groups has tended to focus on the episodic bouts of corruption in lobbying, but scholars and political theorists have grappled with the broader questions surrounding the intended and real impact of groups on politics and policy.

In general, the various theories about groups that have been offered through the years have centered on three questions:

1. Most broadly, are interest groups good or bad forces in American politics and society?

2. Do groups, in the sum of their actions and interactions, provide some approximation of the "public interest," or is

the public interest ignored or shortchanged by group behavior in the political process?

3. Do interest groups reflect a basic bias in favor of monied, upper-class or business-oriented segments of the society, or are they a fair cross-section of all interests in the society?

Each of these questions has received attention over the 200 years of thought and writing on groups in America, but the predominant concern has been whether groups are noble or evil. These views have coexisted for some time, reflecting in large measure a deep and persistent ambivalence that Americans — group members and joiners all — feel toward interest groups and lobbying, an ambivalence shared by the mass media and by Congress.

The American press has historically emphasized lobbying scandals and the insidious influence of groups over politicians, and the main reaction of Congress as an institution has been to generate investigation after investigation of lobby corruption and illegality. But at the same time, publishers, editors, and reporters have not hesitated to lobby Congress themselves (or through their group representatives) on matters that concern them, ranging from postal rates to First Amendment guarantees, and Congress remains notably open to the entreaties and information of groups and lobbyists (many of whom are former representatives and senators). The group theorists that we will mention, who range from polemical ideologists to quantitative social scientists, tend to reinforce this ambivalent position toward groups in American politics and society. It should be clear by the end of this chapter that the debate goes on largely unresolved.

Theories about groups in American politics go back at least to James Madison, one of the principal authors of *The Federalist Papers*, written in support of ratification of the Constitution. Since Madison's time, the prevailing opinion about groups has changed several times, most frequently in the mid-twentieth century, when the role of groups in contemporary American politics has been most intensively debated. Because "lobbying" as we know it today did not develop until the 1820s or later, and widespread organized group activities in Washington were not apparent until the turn of the century, the term "group" has meant different things to different people at different times. Nevertheless, themes recur, and the reader can readily compare the various theories about groups. Although society has changed and groups have changed, these theorists are basically looking at the same activity.

MADISON: GROUPS AS INHERENTLY BAD

James Madison was the first prominent American to emphasize the group connection to American politics; he was also the first important American theorist about groups. In several of *The Federalist Papers*, written pseudonymously in 1788, Madison discussed the importance of groups, which he called "factions." Madison defined a faction as "a number of citizens, whether amounting to a majority or a minority of the whole, who are united and actuated by some common impulse of passion, or of interest, adverse to the rights of citizens, or to the permanent and aggregate interests of the community."[1] As the definition makes clear, Madison felt that factions, or interest groups, were *inherently* bad: They worked *against* the rights of others, or of the community as a whole. To Madison, however, the emergence of factions resulted from human nature, and their development and activity could not be naturally checked, nor should it be eliminated by force. Rather, the "mischiefs of faction" must be contained, by setting the "ambition" of one faction against the selfish tendencies of other factions.

Thus, Madison expressed the concept of checks and balances that underlies the American governmental structure. The large and diverse American Republic could encompass and contain a wide variety of factions, and the system of numerous and divided powers would act to prevent any of the narrow factional interests from gaining a position of dominance in government and the society.

Madison's discussion of factions (which takes in our modern concepts of both interest groups and political parties) centered in *The Federalist Papers*, numbers 10 and 51, and contains perhaps the best-known passages in America's constitutional debate. Although Madison's main thrust was to justify the constitutional framework to the populace to ensure the Constitution's ratification, his theory of factions was itself widely appreciated in early America. But it underscored the deep ambivalence toward groups that we have mentioned. Interest groups are inevitably selfish, narrow, and bad, said Madison — but they are also part of man's nature, and should by no means be forcibly eradicated or made illegal. The Constitution reflects both these themes, in checks and balances and in First Amendment protections of citizens' freedom of speech and right to petition the government for redress of grievances.

CALHOUN'S "CONCURRENT MAJORITY" THEORY

In the 1840s, the Madisonian notion of factional checks and balances was turned around to become the basis of John C. Calhoun's defense of southern states' rights. In a pair of "disquisitions" on American government, Calhoun set forth his theory of "the concurrent majority."[2] Calhoun agreed with Madison that interests were destined to be varied and diverse in society, and he shared Madison's fear of a potential "tyranny of the majority." Calhoun, however, did not label factions as selfish by definition and contrary to the society's needs and views; he saw the existence of varying group views and positions as vital to the nation. Thus he argued that *each* of the various interest groups of the society should be allowed a veto power over any major policy proposal that affected them. Conversely, a "concurrent majority" of all interest groups would have to support a policy proposal for it to be adopted.

Calhoun's theory (published after his death in 1850) was treated by many as an argument for slavery, and was naturally caught up in that controversy, but he raised many interesting points about the nature of society and its interests, and his writings continue to receive attention. Most significantly, perhaps, Calhoun focused attention on the Madisonian notion that a broad community interest — what we would call today the "public interest" — exists and is independent of the views of particular factions. To Calhoun, the various factions *were* the community interest, and should be treated as such by allowing them veto powers.

THE BENTLEY-TRUMAN THEORY

In the early twentieth century, the debate over the role of groups in American politics took on a new coloration, as political science entered the arena. Before the turn of the century, the predominant legal-institutional framework of nineteenth-century academic political science focused on the formal branches of government — the presidency, Congress and the judiciary. Political science basically ignored the interplay of groups — nongovernmental forces — in American politics. But Arthur F. Bentley (a sociologist by training), shifted the focus, in a rather dramatic fashion. In his book *The Process of Government*, published in 1908, Bentley not only discussed the impact of groups on politics, but he also developed a portrait of the entire American political scene in group terms. Bentley said of governmental institutions:

> We shall have to take all these political groups, and get them stated with their meaning, with their value, with their representative quality. We shall have to get hold of political institutions, legislatures, courts, executive officers, and get them stated as groups, and in terms of groups.[3]

Bentley was scornful of the concept of an overall public interest. To him, government and policy were merely the result of the interactions of groups within and outside government; "Government by the people" was basically "a slogan and a rallying cry for some particular groups at special stages of their development."[4] In Bentley's view, the society is "nothing other than the complex of the groups that compose it."

Bentley's analysis was a departure from the past and from the prevailing wisdom — so much so that it was all but ignored for decades after its publication. But it served as the catalyst for an ambitious expansion of group theory presented in 1951 by David B. Truman. Truman's book, *The Governmental Process*, was not ignored; rather, it was received immediately by political scientists as an important and significant breakthrough. Truman exhaustively described the institutions of government as aggregations of groups, interacting with one another and with the variety of outside groups. Truman also saw individual citizens in terms of their group identification and membership. He pointed out that an individual is normally a member of several groups, each of which makes claims on him; this overlapping group membership helps to control the "mischiefs of faction." In his political analysis of groups in the policy process, he focused on the importance for groups of access to political decisionmakers. Much of his book looked at how and why access is obtained.

Although *The Governmental Process* was in many ways a restatement of Bentley's thesis, it expanded and updated Bentley, adding many contemporary examples. Truman's book was framed as an objective and empirical examination of groups in society. Truman did not label groups as good or bad; he concentrated on their existence and place in the political system. But, as political scientist George McKenna notes, the book nevertheless tends to portray groups in a rather favorable light — favorable certainly in contrast to Madison.[5] Whereas Madison saw factions as a reflection of the selfish side of human nature, Truman viewed groups as a necessary and vital component of the democratic governmental process. McKenna writes, "For Madison, the ultimate aim of government was to achieve justice ('Justice is the end of government. It is the end of civil society.')"[6] But Truman and other modern group theorists "were satisfied with 'consensus' and 'mutual adjustment' " of the many and varied group interests.[7]

Truman's book fit in well with the emerging stream of political science research in the 1950s and early 1960s, which emphasized "objective" analysis of how things worked in the political arena, not how they ought to work. In part because this period was one of relative political and economic stability and prosperity, the research tended to show the governmental process working rather well. With some notable exceptions, theories of group involvement developed in this period, whether they looked at groups in Washington or at groups and individuals in the society, tended to view groups positively.

The major study of lobbyists done during this time, Lester Milbrath's *The Washington Lobbyists* (1963), suggested that the influence of groups and their lobbyist representatives were greatly constrained by the multitude of other forces pressing on public officials. Milbrath wrote:

Lobbyist and lobbying groups have a very limited ability to control the selection of officials or to affect the likelihood that an official can keep or enhance his position.... They also find it difficult and very expensive to try to manipulate public opinion.... This is not the same as saying that groups have little influence on politics; they obviously do have considerable influence; however, the influence of groups is derived from the fact that members of groups are citizens and the political system is designed to respond to the influence of their votes.[8]

Milbrath suggested that the public's negative image of groups and lobbyists was in large part the result of press distortion of group behavior:

The press plays up the unsavory and sensational aspects of lobbying, printing very few stories about the ordinary, honest lobbyist and his workaday activities — presumably because they would not "sell"...it is simple and believable to place the blame on the unsavory activities of lobbyists; it is difficult to search out the true complexities of the situation.[9]

This last sentence suggests a major underlying belief of the Truman-era group theorists — that theories of groups and lobbying were simplistic. They regarded their own research and theories as "realistic," reflecting better the actual complexities of governmental and political behavior.

Truman's conclusions about group impact on the governmental process were also largely corroborated and reaffirmed in much research done on individual political behavior and public opinion. The 1954 study *Voting*, by Berelson, Lazarsfeld, and McPhee, concluded by suggesting that individual political participation, mediated through groups, basically served the political system very well, supporting stability and continuity.[10] *The Civic Culture,* a multination study of democracy written by Gabriel Almond and Sidney Verba and published in 1963, noted approvingly the support provided by voluntary associations for individual citizens and for the democratic political culture. They commented:

> ...Voluntary associations do play a major role in a democratic political culture. The organizational member, compared with the nonmember, is likely to consider himself more competent as a citizen, to be a more active participant in politics, and to know and care more about politics. He is, therefore, more likely to be close to the model of the democratic citizen.... Membership in some association, even if the individual does not consider the membership politically relevant and even if it does not involve his active participation, does lead to a more competent citizenry. Pluralism [the existence of many groups], even if not explicitly political pluralism, may indeed be one of the most important foundations of political democracy.[11]

THE "UPPER CLASS BIAS" THEORY

Even as the conventional wisdom of political science research moved toward a "groups as benign" or "groups as beneficial" position, dissident voices were raised. One of the most prominent was E. E. Schattschneider, who, beginning in the 1930s, forcefully articulated his views about democracy, public opinion, interest groups, and political parties. His theories about groups appear particularly in two classic books, *Politics, Pressures and the Tariff* (1935) and *The Semisovereign People* (1961).[12] In his study of the tariff, Schattschneider observed that groups able to afford to maintain experienced lobbyists in Washington had great advantages in influencing Congress. He noted that groups achieved access through campaign contributions and "inside" connections, not because of the size of their memberships. To Schattschneider, this pattern of influence badly distorted the process of representation. These conclusions were not unknown, especially in the press, but Schattschneider was among the first to suggest them after a systematic study, and to put them into a theoretical context.

In a broader sense, Schattschneider attacked the operation of groups in the American political process on the basis of what he regarded as a profound upper-class bias and a distortion by groups of the "public interest." The interest group-oriented political system in America meant not just that very small groups would be important actors in the process, but more importantly that *particular* interests would dominate. The interest group system was narrow in scope, with few real participants, and with a definite upper-class and pro-business bias. Schattschneider felt that not only was business far better organized than other segments of the American population, but that other groups in the society would also "reflect an upper-class tendency" because participation in these groups would be much greater among upper-income, educated, and high-status individuals.[13]

Schattschneider was anything but a Marxist (he believed passionately, for example, in the need for democratic majority rule through a responsible party system in America), but his views about the biased nature of group representation have been shared by many Marxists, and by those who propound an "elite" theory of American politics. C. Wright Mills articulated this view in *The Power Elite*, published in 1959.[14] Mills perceived a narrow elite of individuals in American society, having common social and educational backgrounds, who dominate economic, political, and military circles — and thus power in America. Mills extended his analysis to the role of interest groups and lobbying, stating at one point:

> There are, in fact, cliques of corporate executives who are more important as informal opinion leaders in the top echelons of corporate, military and political power than as actual participants in military and political circles and on the sidelines in the economic area, these circles and cliques of corporation executives are in on almost all major decisions regardless of topic. And what is important about all this high-level lobbying is that it is done within the confines of that elite.[15]

Many recent analysts have repeated these views. For example, Robert Paul Wolff in his 1965 essay "Beyond Tolerance" criticized the favorable theories of groups for failing to take into account the upper-class bias, and he added a

15

broader criticism: He stated that group theories ignored the national interest. In suggesting that contemporary interest group politics inevitably shortchange the general interest to favor the particularized interests of the upper classes, Wolff underscored Schattschneider's viewpoint that there *is* a public interest transcending the aggregation or sum of the various private interests. That is, those who accept the view that varying group interests combine to approximate the public interest are accepting a profoundly upper-class biased political system.[16]

GROUPS ERODING GOVERNMENT AUTHORITY

In a broad-ranging and provocative book published in 1969, Theodore Lowi took the criticism of interest groups in contemporary America in yet another direction. Lowi suggested that the prevailing ideology of "interest groups as legitimate and good" — what he called "interest group liberalism" — had, over time, resulted in a very dangerous situation in American society, in which government had lost its basic sense of legitimacy and authority. Government had constantly expanded its role and impact in the society, while simultaneously and systematically abdicating to private groups its powers over the *direction* of public policies. The result had been distorted and ineffective policies and a "corruption of modern democratic government."[17] Lowi offered four major criticisms of interest-group liberalism:

1. It deranges and confuses expectations about democratic institutions and reveals a basic disrespect for democracy;

2. It renders government impotent, unable to plan;

3. It demoralizes government, by replacing concern for justice (doing the "right thing") with concern for jurisdiction (which actors make the decisions);

4. It weakens democratic institutions by opposing formal procedure with informal bargaining.[18]

Lowi's solution is a set of reform proposals for a new order, which are at the same time radical and a harkening back to government in an earlier era. Lowi's theory, which he called "juridical democracy," would strengthen governmental authority, through clearly defined legislative delegation of authority, broadened administrative rule-making power, and strengthened regional government. Lowi's sweeping attack on liberalism and his emphasis on the rule of law place him closer to the conservative camp than to the "New Left" perspective of Wolff, but they share a dislike for the contemporary role of interest groups in American politics.

INDIVIDUAL MOTIVATION

Modern social science has increasingly emphasized formal and systematic techniques of investigation and models of behavior, and these approaches have not been ignored by group theorists. Although the more formal and scientific models of group behavior are not as intense or ideological as, say, the theories of Schattschneider or Wolff, they nevertheless grapple with the same types of issues — and they contain some significant insights and criticisms of groups in America. The two most important of these theories are the "collective action" theory of Mancur Olson, and the "exchange" theory of Robert Salisbury.

"Collective Action" Theory

In a 1965 book entitled *The Logic of Collective Action,*[19] Mancur Olson, an economist, laid out a theory that focused on the decisions of individuals about whether or not to join a given interest group. Olson suggested that, rationally, individuals have little real incentive to participate in large interest groups, because the costs of membership and participation usually seem to exceed any tangible payoffs to the individual. Olson suggested that individuals joined in "collective," or group, activity only when membership provided selective benefits (for example, recreational, social, or economic); when membership is compulsory (for example, a labor union "closed shop"); or when the group is small enough that an individual feels he or she is vital to the group's success.

Implicit in Olson's argument is that broad "public interest" groups will rarely succeed, because there are few incentives for individuals to join and participate. Trade associa-

17

tions, however, with a relatively small number of firms and a set of specific material interests, are perfectly suited to organizational activity. Olson notes that trade associations:

> ...have not only the advantage of being composed of rather small numbers of rather substantial or well-to-do business members, but in addition all the opportunities that other organizations have to provide a non-collective good to attract members. Many trade associations distribute trade statistics, provide credit references on customers, help collect bills, provide technical research and advisory services, and so on.[20]

Thus, though he wrote without rhetorical flourishes, Olson supplied corroboration for Schattschneider's thesis about group bias and Wolff's argument about the inattention, in group behavior, to the broader public interest.

The "Exchange Theory"

In 1969, Robert H. Salisbury offered a carefully reasoned and broad-ranging framework for the study of group formation and activity, based on exchange theory — the various mutual incentives that might exist between the members and leaders of groups.[21] Salisbury thus focused not only on the members of organizations, but also on their leaders, or entrepreneurs. He worked with three basic types of incentives: *material* (related to tangible rewards, such as money, jobs, taxes); *solidary* (the socialization and friendship of group involvement); and *purposive* (ideological satisfaction). To Salisbury, politically-oriented groups trade mainly in purposive and material incentives. While purposive incentives are "cheap" — rhetoric does not cost much — groups that are solely purposive-oriented are by nature unstable. They attract splinter groups and have difficulty maintaining membership interest. He notes:

> The benefits derived from value expression are seldom of great intrinsic worth. Consequently, even if civil liberties remain equally endangered, a slight change in the member's resources or social pressures may lead to his failure to renew his membership.[22]

To use a contemporary example, Common Cause, an interest group devoted to broad governmental reform, saw its membership (with $15 annual dues), which had skyrocketed during the Nixon impeachment proceeding, fall back considerably after the Nixon resignation.

On the other hand, material benefit groups are costly to establish, but once established, they tend to be stable, and to be able to offer reasonable incentives to members and leaders alike. Salisbury's framework, then, underscores the inherent advantages of materially-oriented groups, including business *and* labor, and the inherent drawbacks of "public interest" or ideologically-motivated organizations.

CONCLUSION

Salisbury's exchange theory attempts to develop a systematic and general framework for understanding groups in American politics and society. But like all other theorists, Salisbury was writing at a particular point in history, and to some extent the theory reflects the group situation in America at that time. Since the appearance of all the theories we have discussed in this chapter, there has been a major development in groups in the United States — a marked growth in the number and influence of so-called "public interest" groups — organizations that deny most material or particularized interests and claim instead to represent the society as a whole. There are consumer groups, environmental groups, and more general organizations, the most prominent being Common Cause and Ralph Nader's Public Citizen conglomerate. Political scientists are now paying considerable attention to this phenomenon.[23]

This development has had a definite impact on contemporary group theories and theorists. Many would continue to assert that regardless of the developments of the 1970s, groups remain upper-class biased and unrepresentative — Common Cause, for example, is overwhelmingly and unabashedly upper-middle class in its membership. Others would say that the political system has changed, and previously unrepresented elements in the society now have organized voices as a result of the growth of public interest groups.

The case studies in this book provide some additional perspective on the roles of the newer, public interest-oriented groups. You will want to consider whether there have been or are today voices representing the broader society in the political process; whether the newer groups are indeed public interest groups, or simply represent other sets of particularized interests; and the larger question, whether interest groups as a whole are a beneficial or detrimental force in the American political system.

NOTES

1. *The Federalist Papers,* No. 10 (New York: New American Library, 1961), pp. 77-84.
2. See John C. Calhoun, "A Disquisition on Government," *Source Book of American Political Theory,* Benjamin F. Wright, ed. (New York: Macmillan, 1929).
3. Arthur F. Bentley, *The Process of Government* (San Antonio, Texas: Principia Press, 1949), p. 210.
4. *Ibid.,* p. 455.
5. George McKenna, *American Politics: Ideals and Realities* (New York: McGraw Hill, 1976).
6. *Ibid.,* p. 143.
7. *Ibid.*
8. Lester Milbrath, *The Washington Lobbyists* (Chicago: Rand McNally, 1963), p. 342.
9. *Ibid.,* p. 298.
10. Bernard Berelson, Paul Lazarsfeld, and William McPhee, *Voting* (Chicago: University of Chicago Press, 1954).
11. Gabriel Almond and Sidney Verba, *The Civic Culture* (Boston: Little, Brown, 1965), p. 265.
12. E. E. Schattschneider, *Politics, Pressures and the Tariff* (New York: Prentice-Hall, 1935) and *The Semisovereign People* (New York: Holt, Rinehart and Winston, 1960).
13. Schattschneider, *The Semisovereign People,* p. 33.
14. C. Wright Mills, *The Power Elite* (New York: Oxford University Press, 1959).
15. *Ibid.,* p. 292.
16. Robert Paul Wolff, *et al.,* "Beyond Tolerance," *A Critique of Pure Tolerance* (Boston: Beacon Press, 1965).
17. Theodore Lowi, *The End of Liberalism* (New York: W. W. Norton, 1969), p. 287.
18. *Ibid.,* pp. 288-91.

19. Mancur Olson, *The Logic of Collective Action: Public Good and The Theory of Groups* (Cambridge, Mass.: Harvard University Press, 1965).
20. *Ibid.,* p. 145.
21. Robert H. Salisbury, "An Exchange Theory of Interest Groups," *Midwest Journal of Political Science* (February 1969), pp. 1-32.
22. *Ibid.,* p. 19.
23. See, for example, Andrew S. MacFarland, *Public Interest Lobbies* (Washington, D.C.: American Enterprise Institute, 1976), and Jeffrey M. Berry, *Lobbying For the People* (Princeton, N.J.: Princeton University Press, 1977).

2

Interest Groups and Lobbies

To some observers, American politics is best understood in terms of group actions and conflicts. Although group influence can be exaggerated, there is no question that virtually every decision made in American politics, whether it is on a legislative committee bill, a congressional floor amendment, a public law, a presidential policy announcement, judicial opinion or a bureaucratic regulation, affects one or more groups in American society. Increasingly, the affected groups are becoming aware of the whole range of important governmental decisions and are endeavoring to have an input into them.

In this chapter, we will discuss groups in America and their involvement in political decisions. This is an intricate and multifaceted subject. The array of groups — from corporations and unions to associations and neighborhood clubs — in the United States is dizzying; handbooks of associations alone catalogue well over 10,000 separate groups, with innumerable chapters, which vary according to type, motivations, size and nature of membership, length of existence, degree of direct political involvement, resources, and level and scope of activity. Groups may expand, overlap, fragment, disappear, or multiply. Moreover, to understand the *political* impact of groups, one must further distinguish between the overall group and its operations or involvement in Washington (or in state capitals).

As an example of the complexity in a single interest group, consider the AFL-CIO. The AFL-CIO, or American Federation of Labor/Congress of Industrial Organizations, is an umbrella organization consisting of 106 separate affiliate unions ranging from teachers and plumbers to meat cutters and government employees. There are nearly 14 million dues-paying members of the AFL-CIO, which means, including spouses and children, approximately 50 million Americans in the AFL-CIO "family." The AFL-CIO in return is but one part of "organized labor," which also includes, among other individual groups, the United Auto Workers, United Mine Workers, and the Teamsters. Organized labor is not monolithic or unified; neither is the AFL-CIO. Each of its affiliate unions has its own members and interests.

But the AFL-CIO also is more than a simple collection of diverse affiliate unions, and more than a conglomeration of 14 million union members whose dominant common interest is their economic well-being. It is a powerful political entity, with a variety of interrelated internal components, operating through a large and hierarchical organization. It is headed by its famous and crusty president, George Meany. Its Washington headquarters, housed in a large marble building two blocks from the White House, includes a separate legislative department, with eight professional lobbyists led by Andrew J. Biemiller, a former representative from Wisconsin. The AFL-CIO's legislative department coordinates its own efforts with those of a large number of lobbyists employed separately by the affiliate unions, and it implements policy made by the AFL-CIO's executive council, composed of Meany and the presidents of the affiliates. Also in the Washington office is a political department, known as COPE (the Committee on Political Education), under the direction of Al Barkan, with a staff of seven professionals and 15 assistants, as well as 18 field representatives. COPE engages in campaign efforts, fund-raising, political organizing, polling, political research, political party activity, voter registration drives and other grass-roots political activity.[1]

When legislators or other politicians speak of the AFL-CIO, they may mean George Meany; they may also possibly be referring to Biemiller, Ken Young (a key lobbyist), or chief political operative Barkan. In addition, the AFL-CIO may to politicians connote other lobbyists: Evelyn Dubrow, lobbyist for and vice president of the affiliate International Ladies' Garment Workers Union; Arnold Mayer, lobbyist for the Amalgamated Meat Cutters and Butcher Workmen of North America, or other noted affiliate lobbyists. More than likely, members of Congress will also think of the shop stewards and local union officials in their districts or states.

The AFL-CIO is as big, complex, and important as any other single interest group in America, but even taken as an example, it clearly demonstrates the complexities of defining and understanding what "groups" are and what they do. The AFL-CIO is at the same time a part of organized labor, a union group, 106 affiliate unions, eight lobbyists, 60-plus affiliate lobbyists, a large political organization, and hundreds of local pressure groups in all 50 states and 435 congressional districts. Any one segment of the group described above might singly and separately have major impact on the political process. On issues that are deemed crucial to labor, such as the minimum wage or repeal of "right-to-work" provisions, *every* element of the AFL-CIO catalogued above will be mobilized.

While the *structure* of the AFL-CIO is complicated, its group *behavior* may be even more so. As mentioned earlier, the AFL-CIO has a hierarchical organization, ranging from a president and executive council to 14 million rank-and-file members. Occasionally on important issues, the viewpoints of the executive council and the rank-and-file membership may clash. One example, a major legislative surprise in 1977, was the defeat in the House of Representatives of the common site picketing bill, which would have allowed one small group of tradesmen, for example, electricians, to picket an entire construction site. The picketing could lead to work stoppages by non-striking plumbers, carpenters and masons — and thus shut down the entire site. The common site bill was vigorously pushed by the AFL-CIO executive council and its lobbyists. (A similar bill had been passed by Congress and vetoed by President Ford in 1976; however, Jimmy Carter promised to sign the bill into law if it reached his desk.) But many rank-and-file union members opposed the common-site concept for construction areas; they were mobilized by business groups to write to Congress. The split in union ranks defused the AFL-CIO's Washington lobby effort, and was one factor responsible for the bill's defeat. *(See chapter 5)*

In other cases, there have been splits within the ranks of the executive council. In 1972, many affiliate unions broke with George Meany's "official" position of neutrality in the presidential campaign and actively supported the Democratic nominee, George McGovern. That election also underscored the overall lack of cohesiveness and uniformity in the ranks of organized labor; along with Meany's neutrality and the McGovern support from some AFL-CIO affiliates, a handful of affiliates joined with other unions such as the Teamsters to back Richard M. Nixon.

As this example demonstrates, evaluating the role or impact of groups in the American political process is no easy task. Even after categorizing a group according to its goals, membership, resources, and activities, one must distinguish the overall group from its official leadership, evaluate both its Washington behavior and its grass-roots activities, and allow for internal schisms.

Many groups act individually as well as within the framework of a broader "umbrella" organization, or even a number of broader groupings. The affiliates of the AFL-CIO are one such example. In addition, corporations may belong to trade associations like the American Petroleum Institute or the Associated Milk Producers Inc., as well as to broad groups like the Chamber of Commerce or the National Association of Manufacturers. Moreover, groups may also join short-term coalitions to pursue common interests; for example, a broad working committee composed of labor, civil rights, church, and social groups coalesced to oppose President Nixon's 1969 nomination of G. Harrold Carswell to the Supreme Court, and a similar coalition was set up to oppose the B-1 bomber. Some such coalitions begin as short-term or one-shot projects, and end up persisting indefinitely. An example is the Committee for Full Funding of Education Programs, formed in 1970 to combat Nixon vetoes of education appropriations bills, and continuing in 1978 to push for higher federal education funding.

Thus, at the same time, a group may act alone and as part of one or several larger groups or coalitions of interests, both permanent and ad hoc.

CATALOGUING INTEREST GROUPS

Understanding interest group political behavior begins with distinguishing the types of groups that exist in America and that attempt in one way or another to influence the political process. However, as David Truman observed, cataloguing groups by type has many potential pitfalls. Groups change in nature, focus, or membership over time. Groups may have a *primary* reason for being, but under some circumstances may alter their political behavior, temporarily, as an issue flares, or permanently. A group may change as it achieves its major goals. Groups' professed reasons for existing may not coincide with their *real* purposes: A group may be a "front" for another organization. For example, Truman noted, "One who tried to reconcile the Farmers' State Rights League of the early 1920s with other 'farm' organizations would have been dealing in fact largely with a group of cotton mill operators who assumed this guise to work against the proposed child labor amendment to the Constitution."[2]

Despite its pitfalls, classifying groups can be a useful step towards understanding them. It does, however, require that we examine groups from a variety of intersecting perspectives. To begin, we must look at why groups organize and persist. To form a group takes energy, time, money, and other resources from the organizers. To maintain a group requires some kind of organization and leadership, and probably a supporting staff. Simply to join a group may require payment of dues, expenditure of time, and other efforts by members. Good reasons must exist before people devote their valuable time or money to form, maintain or join a group. Groups must perform some function or functions for their members if they are to persist. The services groups provide for their members may or may not be identical to the group's overall goals, or range of activities; a group's elite may gain freedom to use the group's resources for many peripheral activities as long as it fulfills the major, but more narrowly focused, needs of its members. For example, a labor union, if it continues to enlarge the wage base and protect the working conditions of its members, can safely involve itself in a host of foreign and domestic policy issues that go far beyond the immediate needs of the membership, without an internal protest.

In spite of these complexities, knowing the various motivations for group formation and the functions that groups perform for their members tells us much about the anatomy of group behavior and activity. For purposes of classification and examination, we will make no fine distinctions here between group motivations and group functions; we will use the terms interchangeably as the underlying roots of group behavior.

Once we have examined some of the major factors that motivate groups to form and to engage in political activity, we can begin the task of classifying groups according to type and breadth of policy focus. This will be followed by an examination of groups in the political process. In this chapter, we look at groups in an overall sense — their functions, their types, and the methods by which they seek to influence the political process. In chapter 3, we will look more directly at the political component of interest groups, including the various resources available to groups to promote their interests, and the strategies and tactics employed by groups to attempt to influence governmental decisions.

GROUP FUNCTIONS: REASONS FOR FORMATION AND ACTION

Groups can serve several functions for members, ranging from psychological (symbolic or ideological) to concrete (economic, informative, and instrumental). Each of the functions may involve a political element and require group involvement in the political arena. As we shall see, the type of political action — and the types of resources available to a group for its political activities — may depend on its motivations.

Symbolic Functions

Groups may provide a variety of symbolic benefits for their members. Political scientist Robert Salisbury has referred to these functions as "expressive." He notes, "Expressive actions are those where the action involved gives expression to the interests or values of a person or groups rather than instrumentally [or concretely] pursuing interests or values."[3] Religious or ethnic groups, racial groups, professional associations, pro- or anti-abortion groups, veterans' associations all have expressive value for their members to greater or lesser degrees. Membership or activity in a religious-based group, for example, may be undertaken to reinforce one's identification in that group rather than to promote a particular goal or policy. Members may join such groups, pay dues to them, and participate in their activities to express their group identifications. Ethnic cultural groups such as AHEPA (the Greek-American cultural association), the Italian-American Foundation, and the Polish American Congress, as well as groups like B'nai Brith, the Knights of Columbus, and the National Association for the Advancement of Colored People (NAACP), serve in part to reinforce their members' identification with ethnic, religious, or racial backgrounds. Similarly, professional associations such as the American Bar Association, the American Medical Association, and the American Political Science Association carry out symbolic functions for their members that underscore their self-identification as lawyers, doctors, or political scientists.

Organizations may be motivated to promote or solidify the *visibility* of a group, or to promote the *legitimacy* of a group. The National Welfare Rights Organization (NWRO), which was formed in the 1960s, actively lobbied for increased federal welfare programs, and simultaneously fulfilled symbolic functions for its members — it let citizens and policymakers know that individuals on welfare existed as a relevant and important group in society, that they had potential political influence and power; and that they, like other groups, had needs and legitimate demands. NWRO also provided psychological and emotional support for welfare recipients themselves. The Veterans of Foreign Wars (VFW) and the American Legion provide similar symbolic side-benefits.

These examples illustrate that groups can simultaneously perform symbolic and concrete (often economic) functions. In the act of pushing Congress to increase veterans' benefits, the VFW reinforces in its members, Congressmen, and the public the unique qualities and national importance of veterans, and also strengthens the group identification of veterans themselves.

Similarly, much of the concrete activity of a group such as the National Right to Life Committee is also expressive — actions taken by Right to Life in pursuit of a specific legislative goal such as a constitutional amendment outlawing abortions also serves to allow members to express their deeply-felt values about life and morality. Indeed, individuals may join such groups primarily to express their solidarity with these values. Many instrumental policy goals of groups may have primarily symbolic purposes — examples are drives by Italian-American and Black American groups to have Columbus Day and Martin Luther King's birthday, respectively, declared national holidays.

Economic Functions

Most people, when they think of interest groups, would view them in economic terms. Groups can and do promote the economic, or self-interest of their members; the primary distinction made between public interest groups and private interest groups is usually along economic self-interest lines. (Not everybody accepts this distinction. Frank Ikard, past president of the American Petroleum Institute, referred to Common Cause, described by its members as a public interest group, as a "special interest." Ikard added: "So are we, but we make no apologies for it."[4])

Maintaining the activities, personnel, and structure of organized groups, especially if they participate in the political process, requires money. While groups exist for a variety of reasons and engage in a variety of activities, a great deal of interest group involvement has an economic basis: People will commit their resources to a group in the hopes that they will receive an economic return on their investment. Groups may function to advance the economic interests of a broad class of individuals or institutions, or they may act more narrowly, to protect an individual entity. In the former category would fall most trade associations, and to a slightly lesser extent, professional societies and organizations; in the latter class would be single firms or corporations. There may be much overlap, of course. The American Petroleum Institute is an umbrella organization of oil producers and refiners. Individual API members like Mobil or Texaco will participate in its affairs but will also function separately, to protect their own particular interests.

Group activities with a direct economic basis — or what many observers perceive as economic — will range from the American Trial Lawyers Association vigorously opposing federal no-fault automobile insurance, the American Association of State Colleges and Universities lobbying for increased federal aid for higher education, and the American Medical Association opposing national health insurance, to aerospace manufacturer Rockwell International lobbying for continued production of the B-1 bomber, General Motors pushing for weakened automobile emission standards in the Clean Air Act, and publishers of the magazines *The New Republic* and *National Review* pushing for continued low second-class postage rates that apply to magazine subscriptions, to a lobbyist representing H. Ross Perot (an individual businessman) influencing Congress to enact an amendment to the Internal Revenue Code that would have the effect of reducing Perot's tax liability.[5]

Many groups function also to provide personal benefits, material and otherwise, to their members. These benefits may be the primary or the secondary functions of the groups. Many "travel groups" in the 1960s formed to take advantage of low charter flight prices (as well as the fun and companionship of group travel). On the other hand, many so-called public interest groups with primarily noneconomic goals do provide direct economic or social benefits to members:

> Anyone with an upper middle-class income will surely save many times the $11 price of membership in Consumers Union if he pays attention to the product information reported in that group's journal. The outdoorsman and conservationist can easily recover his $15 Sierra Club dues through reduced-fare travel, hikes, and social get-togethers arranged by the club, to say nothing of the fact that the dues include a sub-scription to the monthly magazine.[6]

Ideological Functions

Groups may perform broad or narrow ideological functions for their members. Groups may adopt far-reaching political ideologies covering all policy areas — liberal, conservative, socialist, communist, or other — that reflect the overall beliefs of their members. Americans for Democratic Action (ADA) and Americans for Constitutional Action (ACA) are examples, respectively, of durable and important liberal and conservative ideological interest groups. Other types of broad ideology may be reflected; Common Cause expresses a "citizens" and reformist philosophy promoting openness in government and institutional reform. The Consumer Federation of America reflects an ideological viewpoint that might be termed "consumerism," favoring the protection of the rights of individual consumers through regulation of corporate activities. The U.S. Chamber of Commerce reflects a strong belief in the character of the American free enterprise system, opposing excessive government regulation of business.

Other ideological functions are narrower, reflecting deep feelings about single issues. The National Rifle Association has a strong ideological belief in the American citizen's unrestricted right to bear arms; the World Federalists Association believes in the necessity for a world government transcending national governments; the National Right to Life Committee believes in the sanctity of the fetus; the various anti-Vietnam War groups believed that American participation in the conflict in Vietnam was immoral and misguided.

While some interest group activity is undertaken directly (and solely) for economic motives, or to promote an organization's self-interest, such group activity has at least a gloss of ideology, or an appeal to principle. The oil industry's "information" campaign cautioning against the breakup of large oil companies included in virtually every advertisement a defense of the free enterprise system and a castigation of government intervention in business affairs. Defense contractors have usually based their appeals for increased defense spending on the need to protect America against a foreign communist threat. Labor unions speak of the natural rights of the American worker when they campaign for repeal of right-to-work laws (which discourage union organization).

Information Functions

Groups often provide valuable substantive information or data to members of Congress and the broader public on their subject area, membership or other related topics. Some groups, like those composed of collectors of stamps, coins, beer cans and antique cars, are primarily information collectors and disseminators, exchanging information through newsletters and conventions. Professional associations have as one function the distribution of information; the American Political Science Association, for example, publishes a professional journal (the *American Political Science Review*) containing scholarly articles; a quarterly magazine *(PS)* giving information on the profession, announcements of conferences and promotions of members; an educational information magazine, *NEWS for Teachers of Political Science*; and a variety of publications for political scientists and for the lay public about the political science field. The American Petroleum Institute collects information on available oil reserves in the United States. Common Cause collects and analyzes the mass of data filed on campaign contributions to political candidates for use by its members, the press, and the public.

Collecting, analyzing and disseminating information is a function performed to some degree by most groups in America. For some, it may be a primary reason for being, while for other groups information may serve other ends. As we will see when we analyze specific lobbying efforts, the quantity and quality of information are frequently key elements in lobby political behavior.

Instrumental Functions

Thus far, we have discussed four primary functions, motivations, or goals of groups: symbolic, economic, ideological, and informational. There are other goals, of course, that cut across the ones above. We can call these instrumental functions — other concrete goals that are not economic. For example, antiwar groups sought to end American participation in Vietnam; right-to-life groups seek to outlaw abortions; the Committee of One Million fought to bar Communist China's admission into the United Nations; the March of Dimes aimed to find a cure for polio.

People may join such groups for a variety of reasons — expressive, economic, ideological or other — or may have a combination of motivations for group membership and activity. But a direct, narrowly focused instrumental goal can be important to sustaining a group, and such goals, as they often involve legislative or government decisions, lead frequently to lobbying activity.

Groups formed around narrowly focused instrumental goals will often face a crossroads when their goal is either achieved or permanently blocked. The Vietnam War ended, and a multitude of antiwar groups disbanded; but many of their organizers and active participants, using the organizational skills and political expertise they had gained in the antiwar movement, moved on to other instrumental groups, such as environmental organizations and groups set up to campaign for human rights in American foreign policy or for reduced federal spending on defense. After an effective polio vaccine was developed, the March of Dimes remained in existence (it continues to thrive) as an organization battling to conquer birth defects. The China Lobby, having lost its battle to keep the People's Republic of China out of the U.N., fights on to keep the United States from jettisoning Taiwan as a condition of full diplomatic ties with Peking.

TYPES OF GROUPS

Groups can be classified according to their primary functions, type of membership, subject area, and in countless other fashions. Our discussion of group motivations touches on the variety of primary functions groups may fulfill. But some additional comments are necessary for the interpretation of the political behavior of groups. It doesn't always help one's understanding of a group's political actions to know its overall primary function. While the primary function of a group may be inspirational, educational, economic or purposive, its *political* function may be quite different. For example, the AFL-CIO's primary function is clearly the economic well-being, through collective bargaining, of its labor union members; its political function extends well beyond directly labor-related issues, to include civil rights, national health insurance, foreign trade, foreign policy, and the full gamut of domestic policy questions. Scarcely an issue comes up for a vote in Congress that the AFL-CIO has not taken a position on. Other labor groups (the United Mine Workers, for example), have the same primary function as the AFL-CIO, but restrict their political and legislative efforts to the narrow range of issues that affect the well-being of union members (such as wages, mine safety, strike benefits, or regulations to prevent black lung disease). Thus, a simple and single typing of groups according to primary motivations or functions will not tell us all we need to know about groups and the political process. We also need some understanding of the nature, size, and characteristics of the memberships of groups, their subject areas, and their resources. These broad topics may be approached by focusing on groups according to subject area. Most classifications or typologies of groups are done according to subjects[7] and subjects like "labor," "business," and "public interest" are commonly-used references in the mass media and among lobbyists themselves.

Business Groups

Corporations and business groups have numerous representatives in Washington. Many firms or corporations will also belong to a trade association, and possibly to umbrella groups like the National Association of Manufacturers. Business group representation will range from a small local firm seeking a federal subcontract or a Small Business Administration (SBA) loan to a national business interest seeking a particular government contract, benefit, or tax break, to a large multinational corporation which maintains permanent representation in Washington to protect its range of interests. Business groups generally focus their lobbying activity as much towards regulatory agencies and the federal bureaucracy as toward Congress. In this regard, many businesses, rather than set up a Washington office or use their own personnel, will hire Washington law firms for their representation and lobbying.[8] The published lists of lobbyists who are registered with the clerk of the House of Representatives are filled with names of members of law firms representing a variety of corporate clients.

In 1978, businesses registered as lobbyists included large corporations such as Union Carbide, Kimberly-Clark, Dupont, Republic Steel, and Sears, Roebuck, as well as other mid-size and small business interests, including Battles Farm Co., Cook Industries, Nokota Co. of Bismarck, North Dakota, Ocean Spray Cranberries, Uncle Ben's, Wometco Enterprises, and Powell Lumber Co.

U.S. Chamber of Commerce. The largest and best known business group in America is the U.S. Chamber of Commerce. The chamber was founded in 1912, partly at the instigation of President Taft, who felt there should be a single voice for business interests in America. The chamber "grew out of the insecurity which pervaded the business world in the period immediately preceding World War I. Businessmen saw themselves threatened not only by labor but also by the federal government. Instances of such presumably hostile attitudes were the passage of the Sherman and Clayton [Antitrust] Acts, the vigorous prosecution of trusts [large corporations controlling certain industries] by the Theodore Roosevelt administration, and the growing demands of disadvantaged groups for increased regulation of business."[9]

As of April 1, 1978, the chamber had more than 70,000 firms and individuals as "business and professional" members, along with more than 2,500 local, state, and regional chambers of commerce, and more than 1,000 trade and professional associations.[10] More than 18,000 of its members were manufacturers. The chamber's annual budget of roughly $16 million (in 1978) comes almost exclusively from membership dues, ranging from $100 a year for the smallest firms to .01 percent of invested capital for the largest.

Besides regional offices in six cities, the chamber has Washington headquarters in a large office building on Lafayette Park, across from the White House. The Washington office, with a staff of 400, has four administrative divisions, responsible to President Richard Lesher, and five areas under vice presidents — program development and implementation, economic policy, public affairs and federation development, legislative action, and communications.

The legislative action department has a director and four legislative counsel; all five are registered lobbyists. Other divisions, including the general counsel, the membership office, and the public affairs office, will frequently work on legislative matters. In addition, the chamber's experts — economists, accountants, and other specialists — provide help for testimony before congressional committees or for prepared materials, such as pamphlets, speeches or documents.

The chamber has about 30 standing committees and special committees that initiate policy positions, in general areas including agribusiness, taxation, antitrust, consumer affairs, education, environment, and labor relations. The committees are composed largely of professionals and corporate executives, who work with the chamber's staff experts. Their recommendations are generally taken up at quarterly meetings of the chamber's 65-member board of directors. The board, also primarily high-ranking corporate executives, has the final say on any issue. The Chamber of Commerce takes positions on about 60 issues each year, and lobbies, selectively, on a number of those issues. Recent issues have included common site picketing, the Consumer Protection Agency, and investment incentives in the tax codes.

National Association of Manufacturers. The National Association of Manufacturers (NAM) was organized in January 1895, when 583 business leaders, mostly owners of small firms, gathered in Cincinnati to promote American commerce, especially international trade. The NAM remained relatively small and dormant for about eight years until, in 1903, it became involved in labor issues. From that point on, it began to expand, until the great depression brought about a precipitous decline in membership in the late 1920s and early 1930s. The association was reorganized in 1933, and it moved from representing mainly small firms to being primarily an organization of "big business." The NAM's membership, as *National Journal* has noted, "peaked during the Korean War era at around 22,000 members. Since then it has dwindled to 13,000, in part because of the rash of corporate mergers that caught the fancy of business in the sixties."[11] However, a diminishing membership has been accompanied by a growing aggressiveness in political affairs.

The organization's headquarters moved from New York to Washington in 1973. NAM has a staff of about 100 in Washington, including 13 full-time lobbyists, and a budget of more than $8 million. The NAM and the U.S. Chamber of Commerce, the two most prominent overall business organizations, have discussed plans for a merger into a new "Association of Commerce and Industry."

Business Roundtable. The Business Roundtable, a group of the chief executive officers of approximately 190 major companies, was set up in the fall of 1972 to provide an active and effective voice for big business. To some extent, the Roundtable was formed in response to dissatisfaction with the performance of the other business-oriented groups in Washington. One official of the Roundtable has noted that the Chamber of Commerce and the NAM "can't function for all business because there are too many interests involved."[12]

The Roundtable's 190 members pay from about $2,500 to more than $40,000 in annual dues, depending on the gross revenues and stockholder equity of the various companies. Members include such giant corporations as ALCOA, AT&T, Procter & Gamble, General Motors, General Electric, Kennecott Copper, U.S. Steel, IBM, Continental Can Co., Federated Department Stores, Standard Oil of Indiana, Sears, Roebuck, and Citibank. The Business Roundtable's chairman is Irving S. Shapiro, chairman of E. I. du Pont de Nemours & Co.[13]

The Roundtable has a small Washington office headed by executive director John Post. According to its lobby registration form, the Roundtable "seeks to strengthen the economy and make clear the role of business in our society." To accomplish this goal, the organization has focused on a handful of major issues, including the proposed Consumer Protection Agency (defeated in 1978), antitrust measures, and the Arab economic boycott. The Roundtable frequently disdains the use of hired lobbyists and works directly through its members — the presidents and board chairmen of corporations — which gives it increased influence. As one Senate staff aide has commented, "If a corporation sends its Washington representative to our office, he's probably going to be shunted over to a legislative assistant. But the chairman of the board is going to get to see the senator."[14] Chairman Shapiro has noted, "The advantage of the Roundtable's approach is fundamental. If the CEO [chief executive officer] is involved, he knows the issue, its impact on his business. If it's government policy, he's in a position to express his opinion to policy makers. He has access."[15]

Oil Lobbies. Included in the broad category of "business" lobby groups are of course the varied groups involved in specific areas of business — for example, aerospace contractors, auto companies, bankers, energy producers, and chemical industries. One of the most prominent and topical areas is that of oil, which we will use as an example of a more specific business interest. Oil lobby groups are led by the major umbrella trade association, the American Petroleum Institute, but also include a set of other major trade groups — the Independent Petroleum Association of America, the American Gas Association, the Association of Oil Pipe Lines, the Interstate Natural Gas Association of America, National Oil Jobbers Council, and the American Petroleum Refiners Association. In addition, major individual companies —

Exxon, Texaco, Mobil, and Amoco — are also independent lobby groups.

Founded in 1919, the American Petroleum Institute (API) is the giant of the energy lobbies. It has a membership of more than 350 oil and gas companies and associations, plus 7,000 individual members, who together account for better than 85 percent of the total business volume in the oil and gas industry.[16] Many oil and gas producers, however, also simultaneously belong to three or four other industry associations. Since it has an almost universal membership, API is generally viewed as the spokesman for the major oil companies. API has a yearly budget of about $30 million, financed by membership dues scaled to the size of its member companies. Some corporations pay in excess of $1 million per year, while individual dues are $25 annually. API is a nonprofit, tax-exempt organization.

API has a board of directors (composed of oil company executives and independent producers), a chairman and a president. The board of directors also has an executive committee. In addition, there are three major institute committees: industry affairs, public affairs, and industry development. Lobbying is done through the public affairs committee; there are five full-time lobbyists who receive assistance from other top executives of API.

API's president until his retirement in 1978 was Frank Ikard, who served as a member of Congress from Texas for ten years before leaving the House to join the institute at an annual salary in excess of $100,000.

The Independent Petroleum Association of America (IPAA) is an association of the smaller oil and gas producers founded in 1929. IPAA has about 5,000 members, or 50 percent of the independent producers. Financed through membership dues, the association has a small lobby operation, headed by Harold B. (Bud) Scoggins Jr., its general counsel. The American Gas Association (AGA) has 5,000 members, including natural gas pipeline and distribution companies. Founded in 1918, the organization is headed by President George H. Lawrence, who is a registered lobbyist for the AGA. The Association of Oil Pipe Lines is an organization that represents all the pipeline companies in the United States; it was set up in 1947 and has a small Washington staff with a general counsel registered as lobbyist. The International Natural Gas Association of America (INGAA) was founded in 1944 and represents 29 interstate natural gas pipeline companies, most of the natural gas transport industry. Its president is Jerome J. McGrath, a Washington, D.C., lawyer who has previously served as general counsel, vice president, secretary, and executive vice president of INGAA. The National Oil Jobbers Council (NOJC) is a federation of 43 regional and state petroleum marketing associations; it has approximately 13,000 members, all independent wholesale petroleum marketers who buy fuel from refineries and sell it at wholesale and retail levels. The American Petroleum Refiners Association represents refiners processing fewer than 50,000 barrels a day. It has fewer than 100 members.

Small Business Groups. Major corporations and "big business" generally tend to dominate and define business interests in Washington, but small business has considerable and vocal representation.[17] The largest group representing small business is the National Federation of Independent Business (NFIB). With a membership of more than 530,000 business proprietors, NFIB has 600 employees overall, including a large headquarters in California, 450 field agents around the nation, and a Washington staff numbering 14. The Washington counsel is James D. (Mike) McKevitt, a former one-term Republican congressman from Denver who joined NFIB in 1973. Three additional staff members also lobby for NFIB. The National Small Business Association (NSB) has 50,000 members. Led by an executive committee, the group's lobbying efforts are in the hands of President John Lewis and governmental affairs Vice President Herbert Liebenson. The National Association of Small Business Investment Companies (NASBIC) represents about 300 companies that issue loans guaranteed by the Small Business Administration. NASBIC has the smallest Washington lobbying operation of the three groups, with only five people engaged in lobbying. The Chamber of Commerce recently set up a center for small business to service its smaller members.

Directed by Ivan Elmer, the chamber's center has been criticized by the other small business groups, who say that the
Chamber of Commerce represents big business and is not a
legitimate spokesman for small business. The Council of
Small and Independent Business Associations represents the
three major small business groups — NFIB, NSB, and NAS-
BIC — as an informal coordinating mechanism to increase
small business effectiveness on Capitol Hill.

Labor Groups

As shown earlier in the discussion of the AFL-CIO, many
unions within organized labor maintain substantial lobbying
operations. Some unions have their main headquarters in
Washington, D.C.; others have established legislative offices
in the capital whose sole purpose is to represent the views of
the union's members on Capitol Hill.

The United Automobile, Aerospace and Agricultural
Implement Workers of America, International (UAW) has
more than 1.5 million members. Headquartered in Detroit,
Mich., the union maintains a staff of eight persons in
Washington that includes a legislative director, Howard Paster, and two other lobbyists. Founded in 1935, the UAW
spends more than $500,000 annually on its lobbying office.

The United Mine Workers of America (UMW), led by its
president, Arnold Miller, represents 220,000 members. Its national staff with headquarters in Washington, D.C., includes
five employees in the legislative department. The UMW
employs three lobbyists and spends approximately $100,000
annually to support its legislative efforts.

The International Brotherhood of Teamsters, Chauf-
feurs, Warehousemen and Helpers of America is one of the
largest and best known of the unions. Headquartered in a
large building at the foot of Capitol Hill, the Teamsters have
a membership that approaches two million. The president of
the Teamsters in 1978 was Frank Fitzsimmons.

Education Groups

Education policy is the concern of numerous interest
groups represented in Washington, including a variety of or-

ganizations representing teachers, students, school officers, higher education institutions, adult and vocational education, and libraries. The largest group is the National Education Association (NEA), an organization of 1.8 million teachers founded in 1857. NEA is the largest professional organization in the world. It operates out of a large multistory office building in downtown Washington. NEA has an annual budget exceeding $48 million, raised mainly through membership dues of $35 annually. NEA has a president (who serves a one-year term), a board of directors, and a 10-member executive committee. The Washington staff exceeds 500. NEA's Washington operation includes a political action committee, NEA-PAC, and a large and active governmental relations office, with 18 registered lobbyists. Chief lobbyist in 1978 was Stanley J. McFarland.

The second largest teachers' group is the American Federation of Teachers (AFT), which was founded in 1916 and includes 445,000 classroom teachers. AFT is an affiliate union of the AFL-CIO (NEA does not consider itself a teachers' union, but rather a professional association). AFT's lobbying operation is small and coordinated with the overall efforts of the AFL-CIO.

A representative list of the other education groups which have some Washington ties includes the American Association of University Professors (AAUP), the major unit representing college and university faculty members, with a membership of more than 75,000 professors; the National Student Association, founded in 1947, a confederation of student government associations from more than 500 colleges and universities; the National Student Lobby, representing students and student groups from about 250 institutions; the National Congress of Parents and Teachers (PTA), founded in 1897, representing more than seven million parents, teachers, and school administrators from approximately 33,000 local PTA's; the National Association of Secondary School Principals, dating from 1916, representing 35,000 principals and other school administrators; the Council of Chief State School Officers, established in 1928, including 56 state and territorial commissioners of education; the American Association of School Administrators (AASA), founded in 1865, with a membership of 20,000 school superintendents, assistant superintendents, principals, and deans; and the National School Boards Association (NSBA), composed of 90,000 school board members from 16,000 local school districts.

There are also numerous groups representing institutions of higher education. The American Council on Education (ACE) includes nearly 200 national and regional associations and 1,400 institutions. Colleges and universities are also represented by, among others, the Association of American Colleges (600 private liberal arts colleges); the American Association of State Colleges and Universities (351 state colleges); the National Association of State Universities and Land Grant Colleges (133 major state universities); Association of American Universities (50 major universities); American Association of Community and Junior Colleges (918 junior and community colleges). In addition, there is an Association of American Law Schools (132 law schools), Association of American Medical Colleges (117 medical schools), and a Council of Graduate Schools in the United States (343 graduate schools).

Vocational and adult education have representation, also, through the American Vocational Association (50,000 vocational education teachers), the Adult Education Association of the U.S.A. (6,000 teachers of continuing education), and the National University Extension Association (228 universities with extension or continuing education divisions). In addition, the American Library Association represents more than 30,000 libraries, librarians, publishers, and businesses. Finally, the umbrella Committee for Full Funding of Education Programs, created in 1969, represents the above groups and others (90 groups in all) from diverse areas of education, and from labor, civil rights, and other social welfare groups, and is a major force lobbying for education appropriations.

Farm Groups

A wide variety of interest groups represent the agricultural sector, including broad farm groups and groups that represent particular commodities. Just as different crops are grown in different regions, many farm groups have regional hues. Three major farm organizations with Washington operations are the American Farm Bureau Federation, the National Grange, and the National Farmers Union. The Farm Bureau was founded in 1920, and has grown to include some 2.8 million farm families, with particular strength in the Midwest. The National Grange, with 600,000 families, was founded in 1867 and has membership strength particularly in the Northeast. The Farmers Union is strongest in the Upper Midwest and the West, and has a membership of about 250,000 farm families.

In addition, dairy farming is represented by three major associations of cooperatives: the Associated Milk Producers Inc. (AMPI) (with 40,000 members in 21 states); Mid-American Dairies (with 20,000 members in the Midwest); and Dairymen Inc. (10,000 members in the Southeast). Other agricultural groups include the National Cotton Council, the American Meat Institute, the National Wool Growers Association, the National Livestock Feeders Association, the American Cattlemen's Association, and many others. Large farm groups — agribusinesses, as they are often called — and commodity wholesaler and distributors, such as Cargill, Inc., also have Washington representation, and could be classified as agricultural groups.

Environmental Groups

Environmental groups include several older, established conservation groups, and a set of newer groups, organized in the late 1960s and early 1970s when "ecology" became a common term in the political lexicon. Among the former are the Sierra Club, founded in 1892 and with a membership exceeding 180,000 and a budget exceeding $5 million (with approximately $250,000 devoted to lobbying); the National Parks and Conservation Association (founded in 1919, with 50,000 members); the National Wildlife Federation, with 3.5 million members and a budget of more than $24 million. The newer groups include Environmental Action, Inc., founded on Earth Day, 1970, and currently with 15,000 dues-paying members; Friends of the Earth, Inc., with 25,000 members and seven Washington lobbyists; the Wilderness Society, 75,-000 members, a staff of 40 and a $1-million annual budget; the Environmental Defense Fund, a tax exempt organization which does limited lobbying, with 45,000 members, including economists, scientists, and lawyers, and a budget exceeding $1 million; and the Environmental Policy Center, a six-year-old group relying on non-membership contributions, with 10 lobbyists and a $230,000 budget.

Senior Citizens

In the past decade, a set of groups has become active on the part of the elderly in America, led by the National Council of Senior Citizens and the American Association of Retired Persons (AARP). The council, founded in 1961, has a membership of three million citizens over 55, organized into 3,500 local clubs. It has close ties to organized labor. AARP was formed in 1958 and has 7.5 million dues-paying members. Largely oriented toward middle income retired professionals, AARP is affiliated with the 500,000-member National Retired Teachers Association (NRTA). Other senior citizens groups include the activist Gray Panthers; the conservative National Alliance of Senior Citizens; the Gerontological Society (representing academicians in the aging field); the National Council on the Aging (NCOA), an organization of professionals, such as social workers and nurses; the National Caucus on the Black Aged, with 1,200 members; and the American Association of Homes for the Aging (AAHA), which represents residents of 1,400 nonprofit homes run by religious, civic, and charitable groups.

"Public Interest" Groups

During the decade of the 1970s, one of the most interesting developments has been the growth of groups which consider themselves to represent the public interest. Jeffrey Berry defines a public interest group as "one that seeks a collective good, the achievement of which will not selectively and materially benefit the membership or activists of the organization."[18] Berry identified 83 such groups in 1973-74 (he does not claim his list is exhaustive), including 21 environmental groups, 13 consumer, 11 general politics, nine church, five civil rights/poverty, 16 peace/arms, and eight miscellaneous.[19] Environmental groups have been dealt with separately. The 60-plus other groups listed by Berry will not be catalogued. Rather, the focus will be on a handful of prominent public interest groups in various areas.

Common Cause. Perhaps the most prominent public interest group operating in Washington in the 1970s is Common Cause, formed in mid-1970 by John Gardner, a former secretary of Health, Education and Welfare (1965-68). Gardner used his great public prestige to sponsor a mass-membership solicitation drive, through mailings and newspaper ads, with membership offered at $15. Common Cause was an immediate success, attracting 100,000 members in six months. Membership has since fluctuated between 200,000 and 320,000, reaching that peak in mid-1974, as impeachment proceedings began against former President Nixon. Membership in 1978 was 232,000, while Common Cause's annual budget stood at $5 million. Gardner stepped down as chairman of the board in 1978. Nearly a third of the budget goes for membership solicitation. Common Cause occupies a floor of a modern office building in downtown Washington. Key personnel include president David Cohen, chairman Nan Waterman, vice president Fred Wertheimer, and chief lobbyist Mike Cole. There is a large national staff including attorneys, field organizers, data analysts, public relations experts, and lobbyists. Common Cause also makes use of literally hundreds of volunteers in its Washington headquarters. Common Cause has focused its efforts on governmental and institutional reform including reform of the seniority system in Congress, opening meetings and hearings in Congress and executive agencies, public financing of political campaigns, and reform of lobbying disclosure laws.

The Nader Conglomerate. Ralph Nader, one of the most well-known, controversial, and remarkable Americans, heads a range of about 15 public interest groups. Nader's groups include consumer, environmental, health, science, regulatory reform, energy, and other orientations. Funds for Nader-based organizations come from a variety of sources, the most prominent being Public Citizen, a mass-membership organization modeled on the lines of Common Cause, which contributes nearly $1 million a year. It has been estimated that Nader's public speaking adds $400,000 per year, while book royalties, newspaper columns, grants, and gifts contribute another half-million dollars, for a total budget approaching $2 million.[20]

Nader's groups, which research issues, lobby, write books and reports, and attempt generally to influence the course of public policy, include Public Citizen, Inc.; Congress Watch, the lobbying arm; the Tax Reform Research Group; Critical Mass, which lobbies on nuclear power issues; Public Citizen Litigation Group, which does the Nader group advocacy before the courts; Center for the Study of Responsive Law; and the national Public Interest Research Group (PIRG). Nader has about 75 full-time staff members working for his groups in Washington,[21] along with numerous volunteers.

League of Women Voters. Founded in 1920, the League of Women Voters focused originally on the women's suffrage movement. The league directs its attention to public political education (for example, it sponsored the 1976 presidential debates), but it also lobbies on issues such as governmental reform and the Equal Rights Amendment. The league currently has about 140,000 members, 3,000 of them men. The league has 1,300 local chapters and a Washington office with 90 employees, supplemented with volunteers. Its annual income is roughly $1 million.

Consumer Federation of America. The Consumer Federation of America, established in 1968, is the most prominent of the consumer-oriented groups. It is a confederation of about 200 member organizations, including 150 local organizations (consumer groups, public power companies, rural electric cooperatives) and 50 national organizations, mostly national labor unions.[22] Former CFA Executive Director Carol Tucker Foreman was named assistant secretary of agriculture for food and consumer service in 1977. The director in 1978 was Kathleen O'Reilly. The Consumer Federation of America's Washington office has 15 employees, including three lobbyists. The group has been involved in a variety of issues, ranging from farm bills to the unfulfilled attempt to create a Consumer Protection Agency.

Americans for Democratic Action. Americans for Democratic Action (ADA) was founded in 1947 as "an organization of progressives, dedicated to the achievement of freedom and economic security for all people everywhere, through education and democratic political action."[23] ADA was a New Deal-oriented organization; Eleanor Roosevelt was active in its organization and served as honorary chairman for its first 15 years of existence. ADA has a rotating national chairmanship (chairman in 1977 was Senator George S. McGovern, D-S.D.). Leon Shull has been the executive director since 1964. There is a professional staff of eight, including two full-time Washington lobbyists, one on domestic and one on foreign policy issues. ADA has roughly 75,000 members in state-based chapters. Perhaps its best-known activity is the annual compilation of vote ratings of members of Congress, based on a selected list of key votes. ADA scores range from 0 to 100, with 0 considered to be a "conservative" rating, and 100 to be "liberal."

Americans for Constitutional Action. Americans for Constitutional Action (ACA) was founded in 1958 by former Admiral Ben Moreell, to support "constitutional conservatism," as a counter-thrust to ADA.[24] Its chief backers included Senator Karl Mundt, R-S.D., and former Senator Owen Brewster, R-Maine. ACA has a small Washington staff, with only five members, and does little lobbying on issues. It hires consultants for public relations, speech-writing, campaign work, and other political activities.[25] ACA does not have a large mass membership; it relies heavily on contributions from a range of benefactors in industry. ACA, like ADA, is known for its annual voting indexes, which measure conservatism of members of Congress, ranging from 0 ("liberal") to 100 ("conservative"). ACA selects its votes independently of ADA, but the scores for individual members of Congress are close to being opposites of one another.

The American Civil Liberties Union. The ACLU was founded in 1917 as the National Civil Liberties Bureau to defend conscientious objectors during World War I. It took on its current name in 1920 and began to establish a reputation for defending free speech rights for a wide variety of groups. ACLU's Washington legislative office employs 14 persons and is under the direction of John Shattuck. The annual budget for the ACLU is approximately $7.5 million, about $200,000 of which supports lobbying activities.

Civil Rights Groups

The three major civil rights groups are the National Association for the Advancement of Colored People (NAACP), the Leadership Conference on Civil Rights, and the National Urban League. The NAACP, founded in 1910 to promote the interests of black Americans, has a legislative office with one lobbyist and three staffers. The director of the legislative office is Clarence Mitchell. Benjamin A. Hooks is the president of the 450,000-member organization that employs 150 people. NAACP also has 1,700 local chapters nationwide.

The Leadership Conference on Civil Rights, located in Washington, is a coalition of 147 national civil rights, labor, business, religious, civic, fraternal, Spanish-speaking, and women's organizations. Director Marvin Caplan leads a staff of six that includes two lobbyists. Annual dues for member groups range from $150 to $20,000.

The National Urban League maintains a staff of nine people in Washington, none of whom is a registered lobbyist. The Washington bureau is headed by Ronald H. Brown, a vice president of the league. From the headquarters in New York, league president Vernon E. Jordan Jr. directs the operations of 107 local groups and 2,000 national staff members. The operating budget of the organization exceeds $4 million annually; the National Urban League also participates in numerous projects funded by outside sources that expand its total budget to almost $20 million.

Women's Groups

In the wake of the modern feminist movement, several groups have emerged to promote women's political, economic, and social equality. They include, among others, the National Organization for Women (NOW), led by president Eleanor Smeal, with a Washington staff of 15 and a national membership of 88,000; the National Women's Political Caucus, which promotes women's participation in politics, has 12 people in its Washington office and a total membership of 35,000; and the Women's Equity Action League, which has a Washington staff of five, including one lobbyist, and a membership of nearly 10,000.

Foreign Lobbying

The Tongsun Park scandal of 1977-78, in which a South Korean businessman was involved with spreading cash and favors around Congress in exchange for legislative support of his government, focused public attention on lobbying by groups to influence American foreign policy. This can include lobbying by agents of foreign governments and interests (regulated, as we will see in chapter 4, by a separate act of Congress, the Foreign Agent Registration Act of 1938), or by American groups with their own concerns about foreign policy. Perhaps the most famous foreign lobby is one which is now defunct, The Committee of One Million, which lobbied actively in the 1950s and 1960s against the admission of Communist China to the United Nations.[26]

Today, virtually every foreign nation of significant size has a lobbying agent or agents operating in Washington. Many foreign agents are prominent political figures. They lobby Congress and the State Department on such diverse issues as military aid, most-favored-nation trade status, and allowing the Concorde supersonic airplane to land and take off in the United States.

In recent years, lobbying by domestic groups on foreign policy has clearly increased. Business and labor groups lobby frequently for tariff protection or trade contracts. For example, the AFL-CIO has lobbied for imposing tariffs on Italian shoes to protect the American shoe industry; Zenith Corporation has argued before Congress and the executive branch that the American color television industry, weakened by Japanese imports, needs a protective tariff barrier.

Lobbying by American ethnic groups has also increased in the 1970s, among Jews, Greek-Americans, Irish-Americans, and Cuban-Americans, lobbying respectively for aid to Israel, blockage of aid to Turkey, American support for or opposition to the Irish Republican Army, and continuation of the trade embargo of Castro's Cuba. Arab-Americans operating through the National Association of Arab Americans map strategy to counter Jewish-American lobbying.[27]

Executive Branch Lobbyists

When individuals think of interest groups, they tend to think of private groups lobbying public officials (members of Congress and staff, or executive branch employees). However, a good deal of lobbying activity in Washington is *intra*-governmental — that is, one branch of government lobbying another. This has always been the case; presidents and their appointees have attempted to influence Congress since George Washington's days, and elements within the bureaucracy have presented their particular cases to Congress when the president did not heed them. But in the post-World War II period, the lobbying ties between Congress and the executive branch have been *formalized*.

The Eisenhower administration created the first office of liaison with Congress, headed by Jerry Persons; however, both Franklin D. Roosevelt and Harry S. Truman assigned key aides (Thomas G. Corcoran, Benjamin V. Cohen and James Rowe for FDR, and Charles Murphy, Clark Clifford and Donald Dawson for Truman) to "peddle influence" with congressional leaders.[28] Eisenhower used his small liaison office sparingly. During the Kennedy-Johnson years, the president's congressional liaison staff was both enlarged and institutionalized. Under Jimmy Carter, the formal liaison staff, headed by close Carter aide Frank Moore, also included four "lobbyists" to cover the House of Representatives and two to cover the Senate, as well as a considerable support operation. By mid-1978, some additional enlargement was contemplated.

In a parallel fashion, liaison with Congress has extended and expanded in every executive agency. Each cabinet department has a top congressional liaison person, of assistant secretary rank, with several subordinates to assist in lobbying efforts. The same format (though with fewer individuals) applies to regulatory agencies and executive bureaus, offices, and administrations. Many of these executive branch lobbyists were once private interest group lobbyists — a good example is Carter's assistant secretary of HEW for legislation, Richard Warden, who previously served as chief lobbyist for the United Auto Workers. Many others have had extensive staff experience on Capitol Hill; for example, Douglas J. Bennet, assistant secretary of state for congressional relations, had been staff director of the Senate Budget Committee before coming to the State Department.

Government lobbyists go to Congress to advance the interests of their particular agencies (we will see examples of this in the case studies), coordinating their efforts with the White House liaison staff. Agency lobbyists meet weekly with President Carter, Frank Moore, and the White House congressional liaison team, to exchange information and map strategy.

LOBBYING GROUPS AND
THE POLITICAL PROCESS

Groups and associations in our society have many functions and engage in many activities, but our prime concern here is group behavior vis a vis the political process. Groups have been an integral component of American politics since the founding of the Republic; one veteran observer noted, "Lobbying is as old as legislation and pressure groups are as old as politics."[29] In the twentieth century, as government's role and activity have expanded, so too have lobbying groups in numbers and scope of involvement. In the previous section, we have catalogued some of the myriad groups in America that have Washington offices and, to one degree or another, lobbying operations. Many groups target all or most of their efforts toward the executive branch of government, including the presidency, cabinet departments, and regulatory agencies such as the Food and Drug Administration (FDA) and the Federal Communications Commission (FCC).

Groups, in addition, may lobby the judicial branch, through direct litigation, "friend of the court" briefs, or other means.

Most lobbying activity, however, is targeted toward Congress, through its 535 members (100 in the Senate, 435 in the House of Representatives), its numerous committees and subcommittees, and its thousands of professional staffers. The initial discussion will focus on groups and Congress, followed by a brief discussion of groups and the executive, and groups and the courts.

Groups attempt to monitor governmental activity that might affect them, initiate governmental action to promote their interests, and block action that would work to their detriment. Each of these areas of activity requires, above all else, *access* — access to information on what the government is doing or is about to do, and access to key decisionmakers. One political scientist has commented, "All political interest groups seek access to public decisionmakers as a precondition to any other policy role."[30] For a group to pursue its goals and promote its interests in the political arena, it must have access to decisionmakers. As we will see, this access can be direct, through such means as conversations with legislators, or testimony before a congressional committee; semi-direct, through communications with staffs of legislators or other policymakers; or indirect, through, for example, advertisements designed to reach and influence the public.

Regardless of the type of group, access to political decisionmakers is the key to group activity, and the nature of that access — the number of points of access, the ability to reach the "right" people, the type of reception from the decisionmakers — is directly related to the resources of the group and its ability to utilize them.

Monitoring Political Activity

With several hundred executive agencies and congressional panels continually formulating regulations, provisions, and laws that affect individuals and groups, the job of simply keeping up with political activity relevant to a group's interests can be a massive one, even for a group with relatively narrow interests. For a group representing dairy farmers, for example, the important units of the federal government include the U.S. Department of Agriculture (with an Agricultural Marketing Service, an Animal and Plant Inspection Service, a Commodity Exchange Authority, a Food and Nutrition Service, and at least 20 other services); the Department of Health, Education & Welfare (with the Food and Drug Administration); the Small Business Administration (agricultural loan programs and disaster relief); the Department of Commerce (Industry and Trade Administration); and dozens of other agencies, administrations, and panels. For a dairy group, the federal government can take actions ranging from the USDA changing labeling or marketing standards, to the Commodities Futures Trading Commission altering trading regulations, to the International Trade Commission recommending the easing of import restrictions on foreign cheese, to the FDA issuing regulations reducing the milk content necessary for a food product to be labeled "ice cream," to the Food and Nutrition Service curtailing distribution of milk through the School Milk Nutrition Programs. Any or all of these actions (some are hypothetical, others have actually occurred) could have major impact on the economic health of dairy farmers or distributors.

In a parallel fashion, in Congress a dairy group must deal with House and Senate Agriculture Committees, each with several relevant subcommittees; a Senate Governmental Affairs and House Government Operations Committee, which oversee the activities of the Food and Drug Administration; House and Senate Appropriations Committees, with agriculture subcommittees; House Ways and Means and Senate Finance Committees, with tax responsibilities; House Education and Labor and Senate Human Resources Committees, with oversight authority for school nutrition programs; and various important jurisdictions in over a dozen other congressional panels.

While these governmental units do not work full-time on dairy-related matters, they each retain the potential authority to make decisions affecting the dairy industry. If a group representing some segment of that industry is to have an input into a government decision, it first must know that an

55

important decision is contemplated, when, and by whom. Then, of course, the group must assemble the data necessary to support its position, compile it into a usable and readable form, and see that it becomes a part of the governmental record, read and used by the relevant decisionmakers.

To monitor political activity, groups rely upon daily newspapers like *The Washington Post*, *The New York Times*, and *The Wall Street Journal*; specialized publications like the Congressional Quarterly *Weekly Report* and the *National Journal*, as well as various computerized information services; trade publications and newsletters (health groups, for example, follow *The Blue Sheet*, a weekly newsletter on political developments in the health area); and governmental publications, including especially the *Federal Register* and the *Congressional Record*. Groups will use other methods too. One business group representative commented,

> It's impossible to follow everything, or to read everything that might be relevant. Just the *Congressional Record* and the *Federal Register* take all day to read. We have one person who follows the Record, the Register, CQ and things like that, and I'll spend a lot of time on the Hill, talking to members and staff about what's going on. I learn more from gossip and idle chatter about what might happen than from anything else.[31]

Clearly, the more advance notice a group has of a contemplated government action, the more ability it will have to mobilize to affect that action. To have a good "early warning system," as one lobbyist dubbed it, requires a lot of resources, both to purchase information services, and to monitor activity. The more wide-ranging a group's policy interests, the more areas it has to cover, and the greater the resources necessary to follow the government's actions.

In order to have a political effect, however, a group must usually go beyond monitoring to take action, such as testifying at congressional hearings, preparing amendments to legislation, notifying congressmen of the support or opposition of the group to a bill or amendment, or petitioning a regulatory agency for a favorable ruling. Immediately upon hearing about the FDA's decision to allow a lower milk content in ice cream, dairy groups mobilized and advanced on the House

Agriculture Committee; soon after, a congressional directive to the FDA ordering them to rescind their ruling was included in an omnibus farm bill. Subsequently, the FDA revoked the ruling.

Initiating Government Action

Groups which are active in the political process seek avenues for promoting their interests through governmental action. This might mean passage through Congress of a new program, alteration of an existing program, increased appropriations in a policy area, implementation, removal, strengthening, or weakening of a regulatory limitation, alteration of an agency rule, awarding of a government contract, or a favorable presidential decision or expression of support. Consumer groups, for example, pushed unsuccessfully for Congress to create a new Consumer Protection Agency. Business groups seek to have Congress alter the tax codes to include additional incentives for investment. Education groups push Congress to increase federal aid to education. Labor groups urge Congress to remove limitations on the right to bargain collectively. Charter airline representatives petition the Civil Aeronautics Board to ease restrictions to allow lower transatlantic air fares. Aerospace groups battle over government contracts for the right to build an Air Force fighter plane. Dairy groups push the president to back increased government support payments for milk.

To petition Congress, agencies, or the White House, a group must know what it wants and how to achieve it legislatively or administratively (no mean feat, given the tangle of complex laws and regulations), must translate its desires into legislative or legal language, develop supporting materials, and find a way to have its initiative routed onto a path where it will have a chance of legislative adoption or administrative approval.

This means, once again, access, both to relevant decisionmakers and to the important units of decision. One lobbyist has said,

> You have to have lines into the right committee, and the right subcommittee. I always make sure I have a friend on the

subcommittee, someone who will look after my interests, who will introduce and push bills or amendments for me. If you don't have a friend on the inside, then you're really on the outside looking in.

Opposing Governmental Action

Many groups spend the majority of their time opposing proposed government action. Indeed, in a political system geared toward slow change and with numerous decision points and checks and balances, a group's likelihood of success is enhanced if it focuses on blocking rather than initiating action. Business groups, led by the Business Roundtable, vigorously opposed and defeated the formation of a consumer agency. American commercial airlines fought regulations which would alter the structure of air fares between New York and London (and also opposed unsuccessfully the secretary of transportation's decision to allow the Anglo-French Concorde SST to land at Washington's Dulles Airport.) Soft-drink manufacturers and chemical companies lined up to oppose the FDA's ruling to ban saccharine. Veterans groups fought the Senate's proposal to merge the Veterans' Affairs Committee with another Senate panel. Labor groups opposed the Senate's attempts to ban unions in the military.

One business executive explained his group's actions:

> Our position is that most of what government will do to us will be bad for us. It will mean more and more regulation. So it's only natural that we are oriented more toward stopping them from taking additional steps towards overregulation.

Opposition to legislation or regulation may require a different strategy by a group from that used in initiation, but, like initiation, it requires data, alternative approaches, and inside advocacy.

Groups and Congress

The nature of group involvement in the political process depends not only on groups; it is dependent as well on the needs, motivations, and constraints of the political actors. Why do politicians allow or encourage groups to have input into their decisions? Groups have incentives to offer politicians, and sanctions to use against them. It is true that group involvement per se has a constitutional basis of legitimacy in the First Amendment's right "to petition Government for redress of grievances," but political figures nevertheless have limited time and attention; their openness to groups is limited and selective. Lobby groups are important to political figures, especially legislators, because:

1. *They can provide important information to support a legislator's policy positions, or to help him or her make a policy decision.* "Information is our biggest problem around here," said one representative. "Lobbyists are one of my major sources of information," said another. One Senate staff aide explained: "There are hundreds of things happening here at any given time, including committee hearings, roll-call votes on the floor, and meetings. Senators run from meeting to hearing to the floor and back again all day long. There's not time to think, and they need information in a condensed and easily digestible form. Staff provide some of this, but lobbyists are indispensible sources, both to us [the staff] and to the senators."

2. *They can assist a legislator with political strategy.* As a legislator attempts to build a legislative coalition to pass or block a bill or amendment or other proposal, a lobby group can help by surveying other members and identifying potential allies, contributing parliamentary strategy, and coordinating the legislative effort. For legislators, who must be simultaneously active in a variety of policy areas, and who have limited staff assistance, such aid can be invaluable. In 1970, as Senator Birch Bayh, D-Ind., and others struggled against heavy odds to block the Senate confirmation of G. Harrold Carswell to the Supreme Court, the strategy to do so (which was ultimately successful), was developed and implemented by a group of labor and civil rights lobbyists.[32]

3. *They can provide legislators with ideas and innovative proposals.* Members are always on the lookout for new ideas and ways to promote their political viewpoints and their individual careers. One health lobbyist commented, "With the prospects dim for national health [insurance],

congressmen want other alternatives, more innovative ways of delivering health services, as substitutes. If our people can develop good group health plans, or paramedical service proposals, there are a lot of members out there eager to call them their own."

4. *Their lobbyists are often long-time friends.* Lobbyists tend to be gregarious, interesting, and engaging individuals. Many entertain lavishly. Legislators will attend parties, receptions, or dinners sponsored by groups, might play golf or tennis at a country club as the guest of a group or its lobbyist, might travel as a guest on the private plane of a group or corporation. Moreover, because of common interests, common backgrounds, or, in some cases, common service in Congress, lobbyists often become close personal friends of representatives and senators. From his days in the House of Representatives through his White House service, Gerald R. Ford counted William Whyte, vice president and Washington lobbyist for U.S. Steel, as a close friend, golfing companion, and adviser. Former legislators who become lobbyists or group representatives also maintain their friendships and ties with their former colleagues.

5. *They can provide campaign or electoral assistance.* Through endorsements, assistance in voter registration and get-out-the-vote drives, and campaign contributions, groups can provide important help to legislators in their bids for office and for their reelection efforts. Group donations, or money that can be tied to groups, make up the vast bulk of the campaign funds collected by most representatives and senators. In addition, of course, a group with internal cohesion and discipline, and with geographically concentrated membership, can provide a substantial base of votes for a political figure.

The other side of this coin is the *sanctions* groups can employ against members if the legislators fail to provide assistance or to vote for positions favored by the group. Interest groups can:

1. *Urge the party leadership of Congress to deny a member a committee assignment or other political benefits.* During the 1950s and 1960s, for example, the oil industry, which

had close ties to congressional party leaders, was noted for its successful efforts in blackballing from assignment to the prestigious House Ways and Means Committee members who might vote to eliminate the 27.5 percent depletion allowance on taxes for oil exploration. Similarly, Democratic members who fail to support labor on important issues rarely win seats on the Education and Labor Committee.

2. *Apply pressure to legislators in Congress and in their home district or state.* One conservative congressman lamented his fate after opposing labor on a set of key issues:

> They [the labor unions, especially the AFL-CIO] make life very difficult for me, especially back home. I can't give a speech without taking hostile questions from some labor guys.

Another House member discussed the reaction of the right-to-life lobby after he had voted in favor of federal funding for abortions.

> Instead of writing me off as a lost cause, these people seem to have redoubled their efforts. The mail keeps flooding in, and everywhere I go there are Right-to-Lifers handing me roses and literature.

3. *Offer "negative endorsements" of candidates.* A few groups single out their most prominent opponents, and actively campaign against them. Environmental Action regularly names a "dirty dozen," a list of legislators with the allegedly worst records on environmental issues, and urges their defeat. Their tactic of the past several elections has been quite effective but has met with annoyance and outrage on the part of some of the targets, including House Minority Leader John Rhodes, R-Ariz., and Representative James Cleveland, R-N.H., who threatened the group with a lawsuit. The National Rifle Association also pinpoints legislators who have voted for gun control and helps to organize for their defeat. Senator Joseph Tydings, D-Md., who lost his seat in the 1970 election, credited the anti-gun-control forces with major responsibility for his defeat.

4. *Offer campaign assistance and contributions to legislators' opponents.* Groups that disapprove of the voting

patterns of a legislator can go further than a negative endorsement or denial of campaign support; they can actively pursue his defeat by backing his rivals. One member commented:

> The AMA (American Medical Association) is especially aggressive that way. Although I'm generally sympathetic to their views, if I seem to be straying from their line in their view, they will let me know that they can always support another candidate in the primary.

Groups and the Executive Branch

As we have indicated, group activity in the political process is not limited to Congress. Indeed, the various decision points in the executive branch — the presidency and the White House, the various levels of the bureaucracy, and independent regulatory commissions — are monitored and pressured in the same fashion that members of Congress and congressional committees are.

Group involvement at the White House focuses on the president and on the variety of offices and special assistants that make up the White House staff and the executive office of the presidency. The president receives dozens of requests weekly from groups or group representatives for photos, interviews, or meetings, often seeking support or endorsement for a group position. Farm leaders met with President Carter in March 1978 to push for higher farm price supports; a group of Jewish leaders met with Carter in April 1978 to attempt to convince him to withdraw his proposal to sell jets to Saudi Arabia. Conversely, the president will often solicit group support for a proposed action. For example, during the 1978 coal strike, President Carter met with numerous business and labor leaders first to attempt to gain their support for a settlement, then to solicit backing for his move to invoke the Taft-Hartley Act to keep the coal mines open.

The White House also has a number of staff positions and offices, many of which were set up during the 1960s and 1970s "explicitly to serve as brokerages or clearinghouses to provide greater access to presidential attention for professional, demographic or specialized organizations."[33] Thomas

Cronin suggests that "presidents have appointed either an aide or an office for every American dilemma."[34] Among others, there are offices on domestic policy, economic policy, science and technology, the environment, consumer problems, and drug abuse prevention; special assistants for such matters as energy, the District of Columbia, civil rights, and cultural affairs and the arts, and White House staff members who informally handle liaison with such groups as blacks, Jews, hispanics, bankers, women, and party officials. When consumer groups pushed in 1977-78 for establishment of a consumer agency, they worked closely with Esther Peterson, Carter's consumer representative. Spanish-speaking American groups consult with Joseph Aragon in Carter's White House. For many months in 1977-78, the American Jewish community communicated with Carter political aide Mark Siegel, who informally assumed that portfolio, until his resignation in March 1978 over the administration's Middle East policy. Liaison with the Jewish community was then taken over by White House counsel Robert Lipschutz and domestic policy adviser Stuart Eizenstat.

In addition to communicating with the White House, groups also interact with the various executive agencies, from the top political appointees — the Cabinet officers, assistant secretaries, and administrators down to the career civil servants. Many federal agencies and departments are oriented toward clientele groups — the Agriculture Department toward farmers, the Commerce Department toward business, and the Veterans Administration toward veterans — and the interest groups follow agency activities closely, often utilizing their influence over the selection of top agency officials and in the formulation and implementation of government regulations.

Much lobbying is concentrated on independent regulatory commissions, which regulate different industries and policy areas.[35] The independent regulatory commissions include the Federal Trade Commision (FTC), Federal Communications Commission (FCC), Interstate Commerce Commission (ICC), Civil Aeronautics Board (CAB), Securities and Exchange Commission (SEC) and others. Airline lobbyists

63

concerned about rates and routes will divide their time between Congress and the CAB; broadcast industry representatives will spend a good deal of time monitoring the activities and hearings of the FCC; Wall Street representatives follow the SEC, and so forth. Many groups retain Washington attorneys (many of whom have worked for the regulatory agencies) to follow relevant commission activities and to lobby the commissioners and their staff where necessary.

Groups and the Courts

The involvement of interest groups in the political process does not stop simply with the so-called "political institutions." Groups frequently turn to the courts when their policy objectives have not been reached through Congress or the executive branch. Indeed, several groups have specific subunits whose primary activity is engaging in litigation to achieve the group's goals. One of Ralph Nader's subsidiaries is the Public Citizen Litigation Group, which among other activities has sued the Agriculture Department over its beef upgrading regulations. The NAACP's Legal Defense and Education Fund, created in 1939, has used the courts frequently and with great success to achieve its aim of eliminating racial discrimination. Other groups, including the American Civil Liberties Union, Common Cause, the Sierra Club, Natural Resources Defense Council, and the Environmental Defense Fund, have actively pursued their goals through the courts. Where groups do not initiate lawsuits, they will often join in the efforts of others to attempt to influence the courts through supplementary arguments called *amicus curiae* ("friend of the court") briefs. When the Supreme Court considered the Bakke case (regarding preferential admission of minority groups to medical school) in 1978, more than 40 *amicus curiae* briefs were filed with the court by interested groups on both sides of the issue. Groups may also attempt to influence court decisions more indirectly, by sponsoring or researching law review articles to build particular cases.

Groups' involvement with the courts extends as well to the appointment and confirmation of justices. The American Bar Association (ABA) rates nominees to federal courts, and other groups will get actively involved in the confirmation process if they approve or disapprove of the character, ability or ideology of the nominees. For example, we have mentioned the coalition of labor, civil rights, and public interest groups that joined together with key Senate Judiciary Committee members to block the confirmation of Nixon's Supreme Court nominee G. Harrold Carswell.[36]

While in the past the court was a "last resort" for interest groups, in recent times groups have turned more readily and more aggressively to the courts. Many groups now regularly use litigation and the judicial process to further their political goals.

CONCLUSION

This chapter has described the wide range of interest groups that lobby in contemporary America. We have catalogued groups according to their functions and their types, listing some of the groups currently involved in the political process. Finally, we have outlined generally the political activities of groups and their relationship to political actors. This chapter and the following one focus largely on contemporary groups and group behavior.

Although groups have always been a part of American society and politics, and many were active on the Washington scene in the nineteenth century *(see chapter 4)*, there has been a consistent growth over time in the number of groups and their political activity. Most particularly, the past two decades have seen a "veritable explosion" (in the words of a veteran legislator) in the number of groups lobbying in Washington. Many of the groups we have mentioned — educational, environmental, public interest, civil rights, ideological, etc. — have been created and have become active only in the 1960s and 1970s. As the internal political processes have changed, through reform and reorganization in the White House, Congress, and the party system, the nature and role of interest groups in politics has changed accordingly. Groups have changed their methods and techniques of influence, relying more heavily, for example, on the provision of technical and complex information to harried and overburdened legislators, and using sophisticated techniques to activate grass-roots communications — a tactic which will be discussed in the next chapter. But perhaps the most signifi- cant change is the general expansion in group numbers and range of activity.

This is not to say that nineteenth-century and pre-World War II twentieth-century groups were solely or largely eco- nomic in basis; there have been symbolic, ideological, and instrumental goal-oriented groups since the beginning of the Republic. Some of the earliest lobbying in America, for example, was done by groups striving for government- ordered prohibition of alcoholic beverages. But it is also clear that the expansion of groups in recent years has particularly been noticeable in these noneconomic areas. We have seen major growth, for example, in the number and significance of public interest groups, with Ralph Nader and Common Cause being the most prominent. In many cases, today — much more than 30 or 40 years ago — legislative or adminis- trative decisions involve clashes between economically- oriented and noneconomically-based groups. The following chapters, as well as the case studies, will suggest examples and will also reflect upon the causes and consequences of these recent trends.

NOTES

1. For a discussion of COPE, see Judith G. Smith, ed., *Political Brokers* (New York: Liveright/National Journal, 1972).
2. David Truman, *The Governmental Process* (New York: Knopf, 1971), p. 65.
3. Robert H. Salisbury, "An Exchange Theory of Interest Groups," *Midwest Journal of Political Science* (February 1969), p. 16.
4. Congressional Quarterly *Weekly Report,* May 3, 1975, p. 940.
5. *Congress and the Nation,* Volume IV, 1973-1976 (Washington: Congressional Quarterly, 1977), p. 97.
6. Andrew S. McFarland, *Public Interest Lobbies* (Washington: American Enterprise Institute, 1976), p. 4.
7. See, for example, Carol S. Greenwald, *Group Power: Lobbying & Public Policy* (New York: Praeger, 1977), p. 39.
8. See Joseph C. Goulden, *The Super Lawyers* (New York: Dell, 1972); and Mark Green, *The Other Government: The Unseen Power of Washington Lawyers* (New York: Press, 1975).
9. Harmon Ziegler and Wayne Peak, *Interest Groups in American*

Society, 2d ed. (Englewood Cliffs, N.J.: Prentice-Hall, 1972), p. 229.

10. Congressional Quarterly *Weekly Report,* Nov. 15, 1975, p. 2457 and *National Journal,* August 7, 1976, pp. 1102-1107.
11. Daniel J. Balz, "The Chamber and the NAM—A Marriage of Convenience," *National Journal,* August 7, 1976, p. 1103.
12. Irving S. Shapiro, quoted in *Ibid.,* p. 1107.
13. Congressional Quarterly *Weekly Report,* November 23, 1974, pp. 3180-3181.
14. Congressional Quarterly *Weekly Report,* June 12, 1976, p. 1512.
15. *National Journal,* August 7, 1976, p. 1107.
16. See Congressional Quarterly's *Guide to Current American Government,* Spring 1975 (Washington: Congressional Quarterly, 1975), p. 108.
17. Much of the data in this section comes from Richard E. Cohen, "Small Business is Getting a Big Reception in Washington," *National Journal,* June 11, 1977, p. 896-899.
18. Jeffrey Berry, *Lobbying for the People* (Princeton: Princeton University Press, 1977), p. 7.
19. *Ibid.,* p. 14.
20. McFarland, *Public Interest Lobbies,* pp. 67-69.
21. *Ibid.,* p. 20.
22. Berry, *Lobbying for the People,* p. 93.
23. See Smith, *Political Brokers,* pp. 1-34.
24. *Ibid.,* p. 49.
25. *Ibid.,* p. 38.
26. For a survey, see Norman J. Ornstein, "Lobbying for Fun and Policy," *Foreign Policy* (Fall, 1977) pp. 156-165.
27. "Arab-American Lobby Counterattacks," *The Washington Post,* May 8, 1978, p. A6.
28. See Stephen J. Wayne, *The Legislative Presidency* (New York: Harper & Row, 1978), pp. 140-168.
29. Karl Schriftgeisser, *The Lobbyists* (Boston: Little, Brown, 1951), p. 3.
30. Greenwald, *Group Power: Lobbying & Public Policy,* p. 55.
31. The unattributed quotations in this chapter are from the author's interviews with lobbyists, members of Congress, and staff people, conducted between 1975 and 1978.
32. See Richard Harris, *Decision* (New York: E.P. Dutton, 1971).
33. Thomas Cronin, *The State of the Presidency* (Boston: Little, Brown, 1975), p. 123.
34. *Ibid.*
35. Independent regulatory commissions are set up by Congress as part of the executive branch. Commissioners are appointed by the president and confirmed by the Senate. Commission actions are independent of Congress and the president.
36. Harris, *Decision.*

3

Interest Group Resources and Strategies

As the previous chapter has suggested, groups vary widely in their motivations, interests, memberships, leaderships, budgets, and scopes of activity. Moreover, groups operate differently. Some for example have huge Washington headquarters. Others operate through the offices of a Washington law firm. Some groups are involved in the gamut of policy questions, foreign and domestic, while others focus narrowly on a single policy issue. Some interests will engage in the full range of political activities, while others may be involved only in research, or reporting to group members about relevant political actions.

These characteristics, which begin to define the whys, wheres, whens, and hows of group political involvement, are affected to a large degree by the *resources* available to a group to promote its interests. The overall resources of a group in turn determine its political resources. And the uses of these political resources are shaped by the needs of political actors and the characteristics of the political arena.

GROUP RESOURCES

Group resources fall in several categories: *physical* resources, particularly money and membership size; *organizational* resources, including membership skills and unity, leadership skills, substantive expertise; *political* resources, such as campaign expertise, political process knowledge, political strategy expertise, political reputation; *motivational* resources, such as ideological commitment; and *intangibles,* such as overall prestige or status. Each group has its own peculiar mix of resources, depending on its membership base and primary function. The combination of a group's goals, focus of activity, motivation, mix of resources, and skill at using them — along with the nature of the government institutions and the motivations and viewpoints of the government decisionmakers — determine the political influence of the group.

Physical Resources

Money is perhaps the most important resource available to a group in influencing public policy, because it can be used to attract many other resources, including substantive, political, and leadership expertise, as well as public relations talent. At the least, if a group is denied access to decisionmakers through the regular channels, it can buy space in newspapers or time on radio and television to make its case.[1] With substantial monetary resources, the American Petroleum Institute maintains impressive offices in downtown Washington staffed with lobbyists, public relations officials, and petroleum engineers to supply information to Congress and the executive branch, to monitor relevant government activity, and to finance magazine and newspaper advertisements giving the viewpoints of the oil industry. Through a set of local political action committees called AMPACs, the American Medical Association distributes millions of dollars in campaign contributions every two years to House and Senate candidates. On the other hand, groups with fewer monetary resources may rely heavily on volunteers, have storefront offices, obtain public attention through press releases, and give no campaign contributions to legislators.

Groups raise money in a variety of ways, as the brief profiles of groups in chapter 2 suggest. Some, ranging from the AFL-CIO to the National Education Association to the American Medical Association, are financed in large part (though not exclusively) through general membership dues. Others, like the Business Roundtable, operate through assessments on member corporations, determined on a sliding scale. Corporations themselves can finance lobbying operations through their general revenues, as legitimate business expenses. Many groups depend on contributions to finance Washington operations. Some, like Common Cause, have yearly membership dues to pay for lobbying activities. Groups with limited lobbying activity can often qualify as tax-exempt, thus making contributions tax-deductible and easier to obtain. A good example is the Environmental Defense Fund. On the other hand, to maintain its aggressive lobbying posture, Common Cause has eschewed tax-exempt status. Both EDF and Common Cause rely heavily on direct mail appeals to attract new member-contributors.

Using Money: Campaign Contributions. Giving campaign contributions is easily the most publicized tactic of groups for both access and influence in the political process. Campaign finance laws now require relatively detailed disclosure of contributions by individuals and groups to political campaigns. In 1976 — the first year of public financing of *presidential* campaigns — groups gave nearly $23 million to candidates for Congress. Through their political committees, business groups gave $7 million (up from $2.5 million in 1974), labor groups gave more than $8 million (up from $6 million in 1974), health groups, including doctors, gave nearly $3 million (an increase from $2 million two years earlier), and agricultural groups gave $1.5 million (an increase from $360,000 in 1974).

Many incumbent legislators who are unopposed for reelection, or who face only token opposition, still receive hefty contributions from groups and individuals. For example, interest groups gave more than $49,000 in 1976 to Representative Joe D. Waggonner Jr., D-La., a key conservative leader on the House Ways and Means Committee, even though he had no opponent. Many organizations, including business and medical groups, give money to both Democrats and Republicans; the AMA alone in 1976 gave money in varying amounts to more than 400 congressional candidates. Noting that the California Medical Political Action Committee gave money in 1974 both to extremely liberal Democrats (like Ron Dellums) and extremely conservative Republicans (like Bar-

ry Goldwater Jr.), Common Cause executive Fred Wertheimer said, "The ideology involved is that there is an ideology
of incumbency. . . . The money is an investment."[2]Republi-
can National Committee Chairman Bill Brock, commenting
on big business' heavy contributions to incumbent Democrats, said that they reflect a desire "to buy access to
Congress."[3]

Although some groups use a "blanket" strategy, groups
generally target their campaign resources where they will do
the most good, emphasizing contributions to members of important committees. Thus, Common Cause figures show that
doctors' groups contributed to the campaigns of three-fourths
of the members of the House Ways and Means Committee
(the panel with jurisdiction over Medicare and national
health insurance), while education groups contributed to a
similar proportion of Education and Labor Committee members. Banking groups in 1976 gave $91,725 to 15 of the 17
members of the House subcommittee with jurisdiction over
banks and financial institutions.

Even groups and lobbyists with limited financial resources can improve access and goodwill with a few well-
placed contributions. One veteran lobbyist commented:

> Congressmen are always having $50 or $100 a plate fund-
> raising dinners or receptions, and I'll contribute to some of
> these, if they're given by people on the committees I work
> with. It's not much, certainly not compared to big business or
> big labor, but you would be surprised at how closely members
> pay attention to even the smallest contributions. I see them as
> basically insurance — insuring that I'll get beyond the recep-
> tionist when I need to see these guys.[4]

Money is used in politics for more than simple direct
campaign contributions. Outside of illegal bribes and payments — which, while infrequent, still manage to result in
several prominent scandals in each decade *(see chapter 4)* —
groups can give legislators lecture fees or honoraria (in 1974,
bankers' groups gave 28 senators $70,000 in honoraria; medi-
cal associations gave $37,000 to 23 senators. Among others,
the Seafarers' Union is notorious for their generous lecture

fees to port-city representatives). Groups also donate "in-kind" contributions to campaigns, such as free opinion surveys or get-out-the-vote assistance; free trips on corporate planes; and Christmas gifts for legislators and staff. For many years, Sears, Roebuck's Washington office has arranged to have a birthday cake sent to every member of Congress on the appropriate day. Large or small, campaign contribution or gift, these monetary outlays are designed to elicit the appreciation of legislators which in turn can be translated into access and assistance.

Membership Size. The sheer size (and in a related fashion, the geographical distribution) of a group is an important physical resource. Referring to the AFL-CIO, a congressional insider said:

> Their sheer size is one of the important reasons for their strength. Labor has a lot of members — a lot of votes — in virtually every congressional district in the country. Nobody up here can ignore that.

A lobbyist for one of the major farm groups noted:

> It's central for the congressmen to think, to understand that there are votes in back of our organization. If the senators from a state perceive me as the guy speaking for the [group] and with rapport with the membership in [the state] then it heightens my influence here in Washington.

Beyond the direct political translation of size into votes, a large group representing many citizens has a built-in legitimacy; it "speaks" for a sizeable part of America, not just for a handful of individuals. A Chamber of Commerce lobbyist observed:

> We used to just lobby in Washington on behalf of business. But lately, we've grown aware of the potential impact of the grass-roots membership we have. The Chamber has business proprietors and executives in every congressional district, and we can use them to open a lot of doors for us that were closed before.

The close connection for representatives between a constituency link and interest group influence has been explored by John Kingdon. He notes, "If one wants to get something from the whole House membership, it is important to have group members in a large number of congressional districts. The interest group that is widely dispersed is in a position to appeal directly to a large share of the House membership from their constituencies."[5]

Organizational Resources

Beyond money and size, the ability of a group to mobilize its membership strength for political action is a highly valuable resource; a small group that is politically active and cohesive can have more political impact than a large, politically apathetic, and unorganized group. Common Cause has a small membership relative to the AFL-CIO or the Chamber of Commerce, but its members are highly visible, politically active citizens in their states and communities who write letters and telegrams, make phone calls and organize political action in support of an issue or on behalf of a candidate if it is a matter of importance to them and to their organization. One official of the group has said on this point:

> The key, I think, is the ability of our members. The constant contact our members have. On one issue, Peter Rodino [chairman of the House Judiciary Committee] was quoted in the newspapers, "All I do is hear from those people in New Jersey." That's what happens. They are in touch with them.

Similarly, the American Israel Public Affairs Committee, a major lobby for Israel, can take advantage of the political activity of American Jews, and the importance to them of the issue of American aid to Israel. In the words of a Democratic congressman, "If I cast a vote against Israel, every Jew in my district will know about it, and will be on my back."

Group representatives are clearly aware of the value to them of their membership activity. A farm group lobbyist noted:

> One of the things that I found is that I can't go up to the Hill if the senators and House members are not hearing from the field. That is, if there's not a real interest among the people that are voting back in their districts and states, then I can

spend any amount of time I want to writing letters and preparing speeches for them and so on, they are just not listening.

Membership cohesion, and a sense by political actors that group lobbying is representative of group membership opinion, is also important. Kingdon notes, "Without at least a modicum of unanimity, a group finds itself unable to take a position and base legislative action on it."[6] Kingdon quotes a House member who refers to a farm bill and the internal dissension within agriculture groups over its major provisions, "If they can't get their own members together, they aren't going to start lobbying."[7]

Leadership Skills. Another important organizational resource is the skill of a group's leadership. The ability to manage the other resources of the group, to allocate them appropriately, to determine priorities, to choose allies, is crucial to a group's success in the political process. The following comments, taken from interviews with congressional staff and other political insiders, indicate the importance attached to leadership:

> A large part of Common Cause's influence is because of David [Cohen, now president] and Fred [Wertheimer, director of field operations]. They know how to approach Congress, and they know how things work around here.

> Shapiro has really energized the Roundtable [Irving S. Shapiro, chairman of the Business Roundtable]. He's learned the political process, and made them the most effective business lobby, by far.

> The NFIB [National Federation of Independent Business] was really ineffective until they got McKevitt [Michael McKevitt, chief lobbyist].

Substantive Expertise. The ability of a group to command facts, figures, and technical information in support of its positions is another key organizational resource. Substantive information, to be used by legislators or bureaucrats to support their positions or to persuade individuals to change their views, is at a premium in the political process. Whether it is labor offering evidence on the noninflationary impact of increasing the minimum wage, oil interest groups outlining the limits of available oil reserves in the United States, Rockwell International detailing the technical capabilities and strategic necessity of the B-1 bomber, or auto companies describing the scientific reasons for opposing specific limits on various chemical auto emissions, a group that can provide persuasive data to support its case has an important advantage.

Political Resources

Groups that are experienced and knowledgeable about political campaigning can offer important services to political candidates, and can also intelligently and efficiently disperse a group's financial resources for campaign contributions. The AFL-CIO's lobbying operation, as noted, works hand in hand with COPE, its political arm. So does the National Association of Manufacturers and the Business-Industry Political Action Committee (BIPAC) founded by the NAM, and the National Education Association (with their political unit, NEA-PAC), and many other groups which reward their friends and increase their access through campaign assistance. COPE and many other political wings of interest groups will rely as heavily on the expertise of their political pros, who can help candidates target voters and organize campaigns, as on the money available for contributions.

Political Process Expertise. Knowledge of the ins and outs of the legislative process — including the important stages of the process, the relevant committees and subcommittees, the key actors, the best moments to act or withdraw, the personal characteristics, strengths, and weaknesses of members and staff — is vital to a group's legislative success. Many groups, of course, hire former members of Congress or staffers; groups will also employ former regulatory agency commissioners or staff members to give them expertise in the workings of the administrative process. One lobbyist noted, "If you have the subject matter expertise, you still have to know where to go, how to get the job done." Another said:

The most important thing that I have is a sort of general political savvy. One has to know what's going on, who to contact, when a case is hopeless, when it isn't, when to fight the fight and when it would be a waste of time or worse. So a general kind of political knowledge and a feel for what's happening in Washington is more important than anything else.

Beyond the specific knowledge of the players and the panels, a group is strengthened by its expertise in parliamentary ploys and strategy. A young lobbyist complained:

We're really at a disadvantage around here [in Congress] because we don't have anyone who knows the rules. More than once, we've thought we had an issue won only to be bamboozled by some parliamentary trick. I wish we had a parliamentary hot shot to counter that.

Political Reputation. A group's or lobbyist's political reputation — the reputation as an honest political broker and honest information source, as well as the general reputation for political influence — is a crucial element in political success. Echoing a theme mentioned by various interest group representatives, a lobbyist commented: "In the final analysis, my reputation is all I really have to work with. As long as the members believe I'm honest and play straight with them, I'll have the chance to make my case." From the opposite perspective, a member of Congress said:

It doesn't take very long to figure out which lobbyists are straightforward, and which ones are trying to snow you. The good ones will give you the weak points as well as the strong points of their case. If anyone ever gives me false or misleading information, that's it — I'll never see him again.

Another lobbyist said, "It's all built on confidence. It really is, it's just amazing, it's credibility and confidence." And a veteran group representative, a long-time member of Congress, noted:

You can't ever afford to lie to a member of Congress because if you lose access to him, you've had it. I've often said the mark of a good lobbyist is someone who will tell the representative the truth, even if the truth hurts him in particular. Because once you've lost that, the ability to go in and talk to people, then you've lost everything you have.

Motivational Resources

If a group is composed of "true believers" who are focused on their important issue or issues and who are committed to the cause, that intensity of feeling can multiply the group's influence far beyond its membership numbers. Legislators and lobbyists frequently refer to the members of the National Rifle Association and the right-to-life movement as having influence enhanced and exaggerated by their ideological fervor. To know that a bloc of people might vote for you or against you at the next election based solely on your position on a single issue is a powerful motivating force.

A corollary to ideological fervor is moral rectitude. Many groups have their basis in a moral conviction about the right or wrong/morality or immorality of a particular policy or policy alternative. Examples include the disarmament groups of the 1950s, the various anti-Vietnam War groups, and the right-to-life movement as well. Moral rectitude serves not only as a motivational force for group cohesion and activity, but it also provides a powerful line of argument to use in persuading public officials.

Intangible Resources

The overall prestige of a group can aid it in pursuit of its goals, both in the political meaning attached to a position it takes, and in terms of the access available to policymakers. For example, the fact that the Business Roundtable is composed of the chief executive officers of the nation's largest corporations gives it a status unmatched by any other business group. Julian Spirer, an aide to Representative Benjamin S. Rosenthal, D-N.Y., noted that the Roundtable is composed of "the senior statesmen of the industrial community . . . you can be sure that there would be very few members of Congress who would *not* meet with the president of a Business Roundtable corporation, even if there were no district connection."[8]

Similarly, a Common Cause executive noted:

> We weren't taken seriously around here for a long time. But after seniority reform and a few other victories, our whole image changed. Now there are very few people in Congress who don't pay attention to us.[9]

The more resources a group has and can use, the more advantages it brings to the competition over access and influence on policy. This whole issue was cogently summarized by a lobbyist with keen perceptions of the nature of the political process:

> Different kinds of assets can be effective, but the individual has to, to some extent, decide what are his assets and then use them to the maximum. That is, if you have a special asset that you can develop arguments, you can do research and develop tight information that is useful and reliable to senators and congressmen. Then you use that to the maximum. If your asset is sitting around the Congressional Hotel, in the Democratic Club, drinking cocktails and just hitting issues lightly but maximizing your contacts with senators and congressmen, then you use that to the maximum. . . . On the other hand, it depends on the type of group that you're working with. The former thing, that is, using more information, being a source of reliable information to congressmen, that tends to work better and be a more effective tactic if you are a small group or if you're working for a group that doesn't put large amounts of money into campaigns, one that has good contacts with a minimum number of senators and congressmen. On the other hand, if you're working for the AFL-CIO where you put money into campaigns and you're also spread in the field among a lot of districts in all the states, or if you're working for a corporation or the American Medical Association, a group that puts significant amounts of money into a large number of campaigns, then you can stand in the lobbies or you can sit in the Congressional Hotel and you can communicate. That is, you have the money behind you or the votes behind you, that in a sense is doing the talking and your job is to make sure that on a little more than superficial level, you're making sure that the maximum number of congressmen and senators know what that money is supposed to be doing. That is, how they are supposed to be acting in order to "earn" that money or support. The tactics have to vary with the kind of organization.[10]

STRATEGIES AND TACTICS

Tactics and strategies refer to the ways in which groups use their resources and assets to influence public policy. Although strategies of groups are obviously related to the resources available to them and to their goals, they are also shaped by the nature of the political process. And, as the political process, especially within Congress, changed in the 1970s, the context of group involvement — and thus the nature of group strategies — changed as well. We will begin this section by briefly discussing the major shifts in rules, structures, and power that have occurred in Congress in the past decade, and relate them to lobbying techniques in more detail.

Change in Congress in the 1970s

From 1968 to 1978, Congress, through waves of reform, ended or revised long-established practices that critics had claimed made it the most ossified of the nation's governmental institutions. The changes were made in the rules and procedures of the Senate and House under the unremitting pressure of middle- and low-ranking members. They produced a Congress that was much different in 1978 than it had been a decade earlier.

The changes, which reached a peak in 1974-75, brought about a basic upheaval in the manner that power is held and exercised in Congress. Through the 1950s and 1960s, almost absolute authority had been vested, through the seniority system, in representatives and senators who had served longest and thus managed to become committee chairmen. Their power, exercised primarily through the committee system, rarely was challenged successfully. The changes wrought in the 1970s overturned these traditional power preserves. By the beginning of the 94th Congress in January 1975, after three sitting committee chairmen in the House had been ousted from their positions by the Democratic (majority party) caucus, the rigid seniority system was in shambles as the primary method by which members rose to power.[11] The system still functioned as a useful device for ordering the hierarchy on committees, but it no longer enabled members to attain committee chairmanships by remaining on the committee longer than anybody else, to retain the chairmanships without fear of challenge or removal, and to exercise a dominant power in the legislative process. In the House in particular, mechanisms were established by which committee work would be spread more evenly among a much larger number of subcommittee chairmen as well as rank-and-file members, and committees would operate under written and continuing procedures that could not be undercut by chairmen.[12]

Power was now spread out to subcommittee chairmen and rank-and-file members; this produced, in the 1970s, a vast expansion of staffs on Capitol Hill, in subcommittees and members' offices. During this period, Congress also reduced the opportunity for aggrandizement of power by becoming a more open institution. The 1970 Legislative Reorganization Act required that votes on amendments on the House floor be recorded. In the past, these votes — called "teller" votes because members would walk up the center aisle and be counted off by tellers — never were recorded, in terms of who voted or did not, or how individuals voted. Only the overall numbers were registered. Representatives thus could cast a ballot on controversial issues without being publicly accountable for their actions.

A second change in the 1970 law was more modest, but was the precursor of major reforms later. The law required that roll-call votes taken in closed committee meetings be made public. This was the first step toward making members accountable for their actions in committee as well as on the floor, and led three years later in the House — five years later in the Senate — to open committee meetings during most bill-drafting sessions (called markups). Moreover, the traditionally secret Senate-House conference committees that iron out differences in bills were opened to the public in 1975.

All these changes altered the art of lobbying in fundamental ways. "It's not like the old days when you could see one or two people and your job was done," a corporate consultant said. "You have to work harder now, see more people." In the days when committee chairman exercised nearly complete control of the flow of legislation, a lobbyist, to make his point, needed only to contact a chairman and a handful of powerful senior members. But with the opening up of the system, younger legislators began to share the power — and there were many more people to be contacted and persuaded to support a lobbyist's point of view.

These changes made life rather more difficult for traditional lobbyists in many ways. Lobbyists not only had to be more active, to communicate their messages to a much broader range of members — and staff — but they also had to adopt more sophisticated lobbying techniques. New techniques were necessary not only to persuade more skeptical and better-trained political decisionmakers, but also to counter the arguments of opposing groups. Moreover, as access to policymakers increased, new groups formed to lobby Congress. Thus the 1970s saw the development and expansion of both Washington-based and grass-roots lobbying efforts from a wider range of groups. We will describe some of these strategies in the next section, with specific examples to follow in the case studies.

Influencing Policy

Group tactics are designed to reach policymakers in two interrelated ways: by obtaining access and by influencing decisions. Interest group behavior can be viewed in terms of these objectives, keeping in mind that access can be either direct (through face-to-face communications) or indirect (through political aides, mass media, or appeals to public opinion), and influence can be particular (a specific vote on a specific bill) or diffuse (general attitudes towards a subject area or the welfare of a group).

Group strategies may be "inside," focusing on members or staff of the political body, "outside," focusing on grass-roots opinion and pressure, or a combination of the two, depending on circumstances and timing. In addition, a group may use different tactics to handle the House of Representatives and the Senate, because of the varying and unique political and institutional characteristics of the two legislative chambers.

"Inside" Strategies. An inside strategy focuses on the interaction between groups and their representatives, and political actors on Capitol Hill and in the executive branch. Inside strategies rely less on the constituency relationship of groups and legislators, and more on the internal legislative and political needs of members of Congress, as well as the web of social friendships and relationships in Washington, to cultivate access and exert influence.

To maximize access and to enhance their "inside" contacts, interest groups frequently will employ former members of Congress, former staff aides, or old "Washington hands" — that is, people who already have close ties with Congress. Washington representatives tend to cultivate their relationships with members and their staffs, by taking them to lunch, stopping by offices to chat, and by providing whatever help and useful information members might need. As the following comments from interviews with a range of lobbyists indicate, inside approaches for access in Congress are taken for a variety of reasons, depending not only on the style and resources of the lobbyists, but also in part on the political realities of Capitol Hill and the psychic, political, legislative, or strategic needs of the members and their staffs:

> Access in the end really means having a relationship and that's what you're aiming toward. Just getting a chance to talk to them for openers is damn important . . . when you don't have a relationship to begin with, you might use another lobbyist who does, to gain entree.

> At certain times, you go see people. If I don't have an agriculture bill, you know, I won't see [two key members of the House Agriculture Committee] for a while, except sometimes, I'll call them up and say, "How are you doing?" or I will see them on the floor in the House and we'll have a cup of coffee downstairs and so on . . . you have to keep up your contacts. . . . I will be in front of the House on something at least once a week or two weeks helping somebody out on something I know; it's so much easier than making goddamn appointments. The House has created such a bureaucracy that it's difficult to make an appointment because everybody creates work for the poor bastards. It's a cycle that feeds on itself and it's so much easier to catch a guy off the floor [when] the debate is probably boring anyway and he doesn't

give a damn about it so he will be willing to come out and talk.

These guys are busy as hell, but they want to know that they are wanted, that they're in demand, that they're important to you. If I don't get in touch with my allies on the Hill for a couple months, they will ask where I've been, why I haven't called.

Groups that emphasize inside strategies do so in part because they realize that members of Congress and their staffs have day-to-day demands, pressures, and social relationships that may have only the most indirect ties to their constituencies. Groups can befriend or assist overworked legislators and in return have their legislative goals represented.

Information is one of the most important resources a group has. Information, as we have noted, may be political, substantive, or strategic; the comments of members of Congress illustrate the value, to them, of lobbyists' information of all these types. One analysis of lobbying noted:

The corporate representative is often effective because he is a specialist, trading in information about an industry that may be crucial to the wording and effect of a given piece of legislation.

"Every industry has its little quirks," explained one liberal Democrat [member of Congress]. . . . Even if you are against them [the industry], you need their lobbyist to help you get your head on straight. The thing that runs through your head all the time is, "Can I defend this vote?"[13]

Another member of Congress added:

I learn a lot from lobbyists because after they have given me all the arguments on their side I invariably ask this question: "What are the three major arguments your opponents use and how do you answer them?" . . .This usually provides me with additional information which would not otherwise come to my attention.[14]

In a broader sense, a veteran lobbyist suggested that "basically these people [members of Congress] are willing to talk, want to talk to almost everybody, because they want to find out what's going on."

Groups can also point out to legislators exactly how an issue or a bill would affect their constituencies if translated into law. For example, a group might tell a legislator that an amendment would mean an additional $180,000 going to the VA hospital in his district, or that approving the authorization for a supersonic transport plant (SST) would mean an additional 250 jobs available at the local aerospace plant. Groups without direct constituency ties to particular members of Congress will often spend a lot of time and resources developing this type of information, to solidify their "inside" contacts.

As a related strategy, interest groups often try to provide regular sources of information to harried members of Congress and overworked staff aides. One Senate aide commented:

> My boss demands a speech and a statement for the *Congressional Record* for every bill we introduce or cosponsor — and we have a *lot* of bills. I just can't do it all myself. The better lobbyists, when they have a proposal they are pushing, bring it to me along with a couple of speeches, a Record insert, and a fact sheet. They know their clout is tripled that way.

When a bill is being debated on the floor or is in a joint House-Senate conference committee, such assistance is particularly valuable. An account of the dramatic 1977 Senate filibuster on gas deregulation described one group's strategy during the Senate marathon all-night session:

> The Natural Gas Committee, organized with a $600,000 annual budget to work solely for deregulation, set up a post just outside the Senate chamber by commandeering a corridor bench and stacking it with manila envelopes full of position papers on pending amendments. . . .
>
> "We keep a person sitting at a window seat with the files," said one lobbyist for the committee, which represents more than 100 companies. "Everybody knows where he is. We also have a group of runners because there isn't even a phone there. . . ."
>
> To cope with the staggering pile of 508 inhibiting amendments . . . the gas industry put a computer to work cranking out "instant economic replay" [showing the consequences of each amendment] to a terminal in the National Gas Commit-

tee's Connecticut Avenue headquarters, with the results quickly taxied to Capitol Hill. Thus, when deregulation-minded aides for Sens. Lloyd M. Bentsen, D-Texas, or James B. Pearson, R-Kan., "come out and ask for information, we're there, we're ready," the lobbyist said. . . . "We also pull together speech material. If someone wants some material on competition in the gas industry, we've got it in the files."[15]

Finally, another important tactic for cultivating and maintaining inside influence in Washington is to use the social scene, to build contacts and to cement both friendships and business relationships. This, of course, was the strategy employed by Tongsun Park, whose South Korean background gave him no constituency-based tie to most members of Congress. But by throwing lavish parties in honor of various politicians, Park developed close relationships with some legislators, and he used those relationships to attempt to enhance their support for the South Korean government. One Senate aide described the social phenomenon in this fashion:

> Don't leave out the parties. They're damned important, especially with the new congressmen. The new man arrives in town with his wife. They're both a little awed. And what happens? All of a sudden, they are invited to a little dinner party given by the Washington vice president for a billion-dollar corporation. They're impressed, but there's more to it than that.
> Let's say the congressman is a liberal. He's suspicious of big business. What does he find? The big shot is a darned nice guy. He doesn't have horns and a tail. He charms the wife and he's deferential to the congressman. They go away feeling a little differently. Maybe it doesn't affect the way he votes, at least not right away. But it's a softening process.[16]

House-Senate Differences. Group strategies frequently differ when it comes to handling the House of Representatives and the Senate. Representatives, because of their number, have fewer committee assignments, smaller personal staffs, and in general fewer time commitments than senators. Group strategies for the House thus tend to focus on contacts with the members, while strategies for the Senate put more emphasis on relationships with staffs. One lobbyist noted:

I have handled bills where I have rarely talked to the senator who was my sponsor, except when it gets ready for the floor or when I try to push him into something that I've got the staff to agree on and he hasn't agreed. That's very unlikely to happen in the House.

The House also has less flexible and more formal rules and procedures. The Senate, with only 100 members, has operated for many decades through a parliamentary device called "unanimous consent" — an action is limited or expanded, scheduled or postponed, expedited or denied by an individual senator requesting it by unanimous consent. His request is denied if any single one of the other 99 senators objects. The unanimous consent device gives the Senate more flexibility in its actions, but it also makes the Senate's actions much less predictable and much more subject to abrupt shifts in direction than those of the House. Some group representatives prefer working with the House, others with the Senate:

I like the House better. It's more congenial. I know people better in the House. I have a thing about rules; I really like to tinker with and to play around with rules and procedures, because I think it's fascinating and I think it gives me an edge in the process. That's something you can do in the House — you can talk about and do things with rules. The Senate, they just do everything with unanimous consent. Rules just aren't an important thing. Also in the Senate, just because of the way the institution works, everybody is spread into too many things, they're too busy, they can't spend time with you. The Senate is completely a staff operation. . . . In the House, it's the members who do things.

The Senate in many ways is easier. It has so many fewer people. You don't have the kind of long drawn out committee sessions that you do in the House. A couple of senators can do something in the Senate that takes a lot more than a couple of members in the House to do.

While lobbyists tend to rely more heavily on staff contacts in the Senate and on member contacts in the House, strategies do vary — often with telling effect. On the spirited 1977 Senate battle over a bill to enact user fees for barges and inland waterways, the opposing forces — railroads, who favored the bill, and the barge industry, which fought it — chose different strategies. The railroads opted to work through senators' staffs, and, joined by environmentalists and economists backed by railroad funds, they "tirelessly carried their message — in personal visits and voluminous literature — to every administrative assistant in the Senate."[17] *The Washington Post* commented, "The staff strategy is a proven winner . . . but it also has a hitch. While one lobbyist is busy selling a senator's aide, he may find out that his adversary has been working equally hard on the senator himself."[18] This in fact is what the barge industry was attempting, through its hired lobbyist, former Senator George Smathers of Florida. The barge industry's strategy was carried out skillfully, but ultimately, to its disappointment, the Senate still approved a version of the bill.

"Outside" Strategies

Although groups can choose to work through purely Washington-based connections, it is clear that group activity in legislators' constituencies provides an easier and ultimately more significant entree. Kingdon's numerous interviews with congressmen in 1968-69 led to the conclusion that "unless an interest group had some connection with their constituencies, the group would have little or no influence on their decisions. Said one, 'It doesn't make any difference to me unless it is from the district.' "[19]

As we have seen, groups with inside strategies do use a district tie or connection when they can. An outside strategy focuses more specifically on the electoral or constituency connection. An outside approach, in which groups emphasize external resources — grass-roots ties or the pressure of public opinion — can be used to publicize an issue or to promote a legislative goal. An outside strategy may be used alone or as part of a comprehensive lobbying campaign. It may be selected pragmatically, as the best way to influence policy decisions, or it may be used out of desperation when an "inside" strategy has failed. Sometimes it is used to counteract an aggressive grass-roots campaign by a group's opponents.

Although, as we have noted, a constituency-oriented approach has inherent advantages in obtaining access and having influence, it also has drawbacks, even where a group has ample external resources. For one thing, the grass-roots membership of a group lacks both the flexibility and political sophistication of the Washington representatives. In part, there is a "sheer mechanical problem of manipulating a scattered and undisciplined membership. Once having embarked upon a course, and having started the lobbying process along that course, it is extremely difficult to shift in midstream."[20] In addition, once a group is activated in a particular direction, it may become quite risky for a lobbyist to effect or join a compromise. Finally, a group membership when unleashed runs the risk of overkill — of creating resentment among members of Congress at "pressure tactics" — that might backfire on the group. One frustrated representative, after receiving hundreds of letters and cards from businessmen on a labor law reform bill in 1978, exploded, "This has gone too far. These people are totally uninformed, and they're simply trying to pressure me. They have no reasonable arguments, and I'm going to vote against them."

Outside strategies may be direct or indirect. A direct approach involves explicit assistance or direction to group members or sympathizers to contact representatives or senators about an issue or bill. Thus members of the Association of General Contractors were given postcards urging defeat of the common site picketing bill, which they distributed with the paychecks of their union employees, then collected and mailed to House members; the U.S. Chamber of Commerce used direct mail appeals (targeted to individual business executives by a sophisticated computer program) to generate opposition to common site picketing and the consumer protection agency. A consumer coalition including Ralph Nader groups, Common Cause, the Consumer Federation of America, and the AFL-CIO generated a unique "nickel" campaign, urging supporters of the consumer protection agency each to send a nickel to wavering members of Congress (representing the cost per American of the agency). The nickel strategy evolved after the coalition's essentially inside strategy had faltered in the face of the grass-roots blitz from business-oriented interests.

One significant outside campaign was generated by the American Bankers Association (ABA) over a 1977 banking regulatory bill. The legislation was proposed after Bert Lance resigned as head of the Office of Management and Budget as a result of the disclosure of questionable banking practices by the National Bank of Georgia, of which he was president before joining the Carter administration. Strongly opposed to the House version of the bill, the group "sent out a nationwide alarm on September 23, churning out 14,000 copies of a special 'Executive Report' from ABA executive vice president Willis W. Alexander." Alexander urged bankers: "If the restrictive provisions of HR 9086 are a matter of concern to you, contact your elected representatives. Tell them what this bill would do to your bank...."[21]

As *The Washington Post* noted, "The letters poured in. . . . The Independent Bankers Association of America also took part in the campaign. Delegations of hometown bankers visited the offices of some congressmen."[22] Bill author Fernand St Germain, D-R.I., complained, "The House has been flooded by mail from literally thousands of banks, and much of this mail has been filled with distortions and highly misleading statements about the effects of the bill. It is a nationwide campaign being orchestrated through the Washington offices of the American Bankers Association under the guise of 'grass-roots' opinion."[23]

Indirect outside strategies depend on mass media campaigns — ads in newspapers and magazines, commercials on television and radio. Nearly every day, *The Washington Post* — a popular outlet for lobbying appeals, because of its universal circulation among Washington politicians — has full- or half-page ads placed by groups, either urging public and congressional support for or opposition to a particular legislative proposal, or promoting a general viewpoint on a broad public policy issue.

On October 11, 1977, for example, the International Organization of Masters, Mates and Pilots, a merchant marine affiliate of the AFL-CIO, placed a full-page ad in the main section of the *Post* urging support for HR 1037 and S 61 — the "Oil Cargo Equity" bills requiring that a certain proportion of foreign oil be carried on American-flag ships. The next day, a full-page ad placed by the Whale Protection Fund, phrased as an open letter to President Carter, demanded protection for the Bowhead Whale; that was the second such ad by the group in two weeks.

A smaller ad in the *Post* on September 26, 1977, was placed by the National Right to Work Committee, not to push a particular bill, but to improve the public (and congressional) image of the group and its issue position. The ad noted, "Union officials call us reactionary. Right wing. Antilabor. We're all those things — if you believe individual rights is a right-wing cause. If being uncompromising advocates of freedom of choice is reactionary."

Mobil Oil Co. is the most prominent user of media campaigns to polish its public image and to advocate positions — to Congress, media leaders, the president and the general public — on a range of energy and business-oriented issues. Mobil regularly purchases space in such prominent places as the Sunday New York *Times'* prestigious and widely-read *The Week in Review* section. One recent ad on the page opposite the editorials of the January 9, 1978, *Washington Star* voiced Mobil's strong opposition to the proposed removal of the foreign tax credit for corporations; the ad listed five "facts about the foreign tax credit" headed "Editors Please Note." Mobil also sent to 5,000 small newspapers several professionally-drawn, clever cartoons which expressed its opinions on oil company divestiture and related subjects (the cartoons themselves did not identify Mobil as the sponsor). The cartoons, in the words of a Mobil spokesman, were designed to convey the corporation's feeling that "the government is too strong and industry is being overregulated."[24] The cartoons were sent to newspaper editors with a note that said, "If you like the cartoons, feel free to use them."

As we noted earlier, groups may employ outside lobbying campaigns in concert with inside strategies. Along with their spirited attempts to directly influence senators and their aides, lobbyists on both sides of S 790, the bill to establish barge fees on inland waterways, made "a concerted effort to win the hearts and minds of the news media, on the theory that what was printed about the waterway toll would influence senators' perception of the issue." Among other things, a barge industry group "hosted 20 reporters on a free, two-day barge tour of the Ohio River Valley."[25]

Any discussion of outside strategies cannot be limited to the variety of ways of drumming up grass-roots pressure and support. Public protest by groups is another — often highly effective — form of outside pressure. Protests are not necessarily last resorts, used by powerless and resource-lean groups as a substitute for traditional inside and outside tactics. Protest can be an effective dramatization of a group's strength and intensity — a way of gaining the attention of political institutions and policymakers that other traditional strategies cannot match. In the early 1960s, protests were used frequently and effectively by civil rights groups, highlighted by the August 1963 March on Washington, where 200,000 people walked through the city to the Washington Monument to hear Martin Luther King say, "I Have a Dream."

Civil rights protests were succeeded, in national politics, by protests and demonstrations against the Vietnam War, which continued, at varying times, through 1972 and included the major November 15, 1969, Moratorium demonstration on the Washington Mall, with nearly half-a-million protestors present, coordinated with simultaneous local demonstrations around the country.

Through the 1960s, political analysts and politicians tended to characterize protest-prone groups as largely left-wing or liberal. But that image clearly changed in the 1970s, as a much broader spectrum of groups adopted protest as a strategy of influence. Pro-war "hardhats" staged noisy protests in New York in 1971, to support President Nixon's Vietnam War policy and to counter the antiwar demonstrations. In 1974, truck operators mounted numerous demonstrations on highways around the country to protest the 55 mile-per-hour speed limit. In 1978 farmers drove hundreds of tractors and other farm machines into Washington (clogging highways and outraging motorists in the process) to protest low farm prices and to demand more federal government support; they also descended on the Department of Agriculture building, demanding an audience with Agriculture Secretary Bergland.

In each of these cases, the plight of groups and their intense feelings have been dramatized, through the protests themselves and through their massive media coverage, to policymakers; the impact of protest on policy is more difficult to judge, though it has certainly aided many groups in achieving their goals.[26]

CONCLUSION

The skill with which a group monitors, analyzes, and participates in the political system is a major factor in determining its influence on the public policy process. Immense resources alone do not guarantee that a group will have a significant influence on policy. But the group's ability to use its unique mix of resources to influence political allies, neutral figures, and opponents is of great importance.

In this chapter, we have discussed a variety of strategies that interest groups employ in their attempts to initiate, amend, or block a policy proposal. In the three case studies in this book — common-site picketing, the Clean Air Act, and the B-1 bomber — we will examine in more detail how groups with different sets of resources use a wide range of strategies to influence policy. As each of these case studies will make clear, groups by themselves do not determine the outcome of policy decisions; political actors — representatives, senators, and the president — play an active and independent role. Groups do have, however, a significant role — one that is strongly affected by the factors we have outlined in this chapter.

NOTES

1. Outside strategies are discussed further at the end of this chapter.
2. *National Journal,* March 19, 1977, p. 416.
3. James P. Gannon, "The GOP and the Fortune 500," *Wall Street Journal,* March 23, 1977.
4. The unattributed quotations in this chapter come from the author's interviews, conducted in 1976 and 1977.
5. John Kingdon, *Congressmen's Voting Decisions* (New York: Harper & Row, 1973), p. 145.
6. *Ibid.,* p. 161.
7. *Ibid.*
8. Congressional Quarterly *Weekly Report,* September 17, 1977, p. 1965.
9. *The Washington Star,* December 16, 1975, p. A-8.
10. *Ibid.*
11. See Norman J. Ornstein, "Congress: Democrats Reform the House of Representatives," in *America in the Seventies,* ed. Allan P. Sindler (Boston: Little, Brown, 1977).
12. See Norman J. Ornstein, "Causes and Consequences of Congressional Change: Subcommittee Reforms in the House of Representatives," in *Congress in Change: Evolution and Reform* (New York: Praeger, 1975).
13. *The Washington Star,* December 16, 1977, p. A-12.
14. *Ibid.*
15. *The Washington Post,* September 29, 1977, p. A-12.
16. James Deakin, *The Lobbyists* (Washington: Public Affairs Press, 1966), pp. 8-9.
17. *The Washington Post,* June 19, 1977, p. A-13.
18. *Ibid.*
19. Kingdon, *Congressmen's Voting Decisions,* p. 143.
20. *Ibid.,* p. 161.
21. *The Washington Post,* November 25, 1977, p. A-2.
22. *Ibid.*
23. *Ibid.*
24. *Ibid.,* July 22, 1977, p. A-27.
25. *Ibid.,* June 19, 1977, p. A-15.
26. Michael Lipsky, "Protest as a Political Resource," *American Political Science Review* (December 1968), pp. 1144-1158.

4

Lobby Regulation

The participation of groups in the American political process has its constitutional basis in the First Amendment's guarantees of "freedom of speech" and the "right of citizens to petition the government for a redress of grievances." Abuse of these basic rights, however — instances of inordinate group influence as well as outright corruption of elected political officials by lobbyists — has led to repeated calls for reform and regulation of lobbying.

Until 1946, the usual congressional response to excessive lobbying and to corruption was limited to periodic investigations of some of the more egregious cases. With the brief exception of regulation by the 44th Congress (1875-1876), no comprehensive lobby regulation legislation passed Congress. Historically, there has been a general reluctance on the part of Congress to enact tough lobby laws because of the legislative and political support lobbyists have often provided for members. Members of Congress — even the great majority who never had illegal connections with lobbyists — have traditionally been chary of policing the activities of their fellow members. This institutional trait combined with the First Amendment's protections has made it difficult to enact strict lobby legislation. The legislation that ultimately passed focused on the disclosure of lobbying rather than its control.

In the reform-oriented atmosphere of post-World War II Washington, the first comprehensive lobby disclosure bill

was enacted into law. The 1946 law, which survived a constitutional challenge in the Supreme Court, was still on the
books in mid-1978, although it has come under increasing
attacks in the 1970s, with proposals advanced for a much
more comprehensive disclosure law. A bill requiring strict
lobby registration and reporting passed the House of Representatives in April 1978.

This chapter surveys early attempts to regulate lobbying
in the nineteenth and early twentieth centuries, focusing on
the principal congressional investigations of lobbying and efforts prior to 1946 to enact lobby regulation laws. We analyse
the 1946 Federal Regulation of Lobbying Act, the Supreme
Court's narrow interpretation of that act in its 1954 *Harriss*
decision and lobby activity and regulation under the 1946 act.
Finally we look at efforts in the 1970s to enact a stronger lobby
law, and the major contemporary controversies surrounding
lobby regulation.

EARLY LOBBYING
AND CALLS FOR REGULATION

Although the word "lobbyist" was not coined until the
late 1820s, it came into frequent use in Washington by the
1830s — as a pejorative term. Indeed, throughout the
nineteenth century, lobbying by interest groups inspired tales
of corruption, bribery, and, especially as seen in today's
perspective, monumental conflicts of interest. Daniel
Webster, for example, while a senator from Massachusetts in
1833-34, made eloquent pleas on the Senate floor to protect
Nicholas Biddle's Bank of the United States against attack
from President Andrew Jackson. On December 21, 1883,
Webster wrote to Biddle: "If it is wished that my relation to
the Bank should be continued, it may be well to send me the
usual retainers."[1] Biddle promptly paid Webster $10,000;
Webster ultimately received a total of $32,000 for his efforts in
the Senate on behalf of the bank.

By the 1850s, as tariff bills came up and were subject to
bitter struggles in Congress, and as industrialization continued, lobbying and group involvement in Washington in-

creased dramatically to the dismay of some observers. In correspondence between two leading politicians who both later became president, James Buchanan wrote to Franklin Pierce in 1852: "The host of contractors, speculators, stockjobbers and lobby members which haunt the halls of Congress, all desirous . . . and . . . [using] every pretext to get their arms into the public treasury are sufficient to alarm every friend of his country. Their progress must be arrested."[2]

As group involvement and lobbying increased, so did the incidents and volume of corruption. A historian has described the situation:

> In those wide-open days Washington was filled with a variety of gambling houses whose proprietors worked closely with the lobbyists. When a representative or a senator was unlucky enough to fall into debt, as he frequently did, the managers of the gambling halls had him where he would do them the most good. By threatening exposure, or by demanding payment, they could force the hapless legislator to vote as they wished. The best known of these subdivisions of Congress was Pendleton's. Here Commodore Vanderbilt [a wealthy industrialist], on his frequent excursions to Washington, was a regular diner. It hardly seems reasonable to assume that it was mere friendship which caused him to present a team of horses to Pendleton after one of his visits which happened to coincide with a vote on the mail contracts bill.[3]

Edward Pendleton's "Palace of Fortune," was located on Pennsylvania Avenue, surrounded by other gambling halls and hotels filled by women lobbyists, a common feature of mid-nineteenth century Washington. Edward W. Martin wrote of women lobbyists in *Behind the Scenes in Washington* (published in 1873):

> In any single "first-class" hotel in Washington, at any time during midsession, at least half a dozen of these lobbyesses are thus at work at once, each one roping in her dozen or ten of wild-cat Congressmen. The lever of lust is used to pry up more legislators to the sticking point than money itself avails to seduce. . . . This lobbying is transacted under the guise of social visits — open sesame to a Congressman any and everywhere in Washington.[4]

The most famous lobbyist during this period was Sam Ward, called "King of the Lobby," whose motto was, "The way to a man's 'Aye' is through his stomach." Ward threw lavish dinner parties for members of Congress on behalf of his many clients, including Hugh McCullough, an Indiana banker (later Lincoln's secretary of the treasury), who paid Ward $12,000 a year "plus dinner expenses" to "court, woo and charm congressmen, especially Democrats, prone to oppose the war" between the states.[5] Ward was also associated with Joe Morrisey, an organizer of lotteries, who wanted passage of a bill to tax lotteries, calculated to put his less wealthy rivals out of business.[6] A great deal of the lobbying and group pressure of the post-Civil War era came from railroad lobbyists. One commentator has noted:

> In the Age of Expansion, the railroad lobbyists were so active and so effective that Senator J. S. Morrill, a man of rare wit, once rose towards the end of a session and, calling attention to the presence in the outer lobby of the president of the Pennsylvania Railroad, moved the appointment of a committee to wait upon him and learn if there was any further legislation he desired before adjournment.[7]

With these types of activities came periodic investigations by Congress. A select committee of Congress released a report in 1855 that showed numerous abuses by lobbyists, including, for example, the payment by Samuel Colt of a $10,000 "contingent fee" to one House member to encourage him to support a bill to extend Colt's patent on revolvers.

Congressional investigations of lobbying intensified during the latter part of the nineteenth century, with the two most prominent inquiries involving the 1875 "Whiskey Ring" scandal concerning federal liquor taxes and the 1872 "Credit Mobilier" scandal surrounding the expansion of the Union Pacific railroad. Soon after the episodes, in 1876, the House of Representatives adopted a resolution requiring all lobbyists to register with the clerk of the House. The resolution was short-lived, however; it was not renewed in the next Congress. Subsequently, many state legislatures passed their own lobby registration laws, with Massachusetts leading the way in 1890.[8]

The first comprehensive congressional investigation of lobbying was undertaken by the Senate in 1913 in response to President Woodrow Wilson's charges that the tariff lobby was trying to undercut the administration's tariff bill through a massive grass-roots lobbying attack. The Senate Judiciary Committee found a good deal of evidence to support Wilson's charge that "money without limit is being spent to sustain this lobby and to create an appearance of a pressure of public opinion antagonistic to some of the chief items of the tariff."[9] The judiciary panel discovered that more than $500,000 had been spent on lobbying on this bill, that about 1.5 million pieces of mail had been sent to members, that deliberately falsified statistics had been submitted to committees, and that members of Congress had been threatened with political reprisals. The committee went on to investigate the lobbying tactics of a wide variety of groups. As a result of the investigation, lobbying disclosure legislation was introduced in 1913, by Senator William Kenyon of Iowa. As a researcher noted some years later, Kenyon's bill "encountered unexpected opposition from farm and labor organizations whose representatives joined with other lobbyists in opposing it and succeeded in preventing it from coming to a final vote."[10] It took 17 more Congresses before a lobby disclosure bill was finally enacted in 1946.

REGULATION LEGISLATION PRIOR TO 1946

In the interim period, Congress' interest in lobby regulation and control ebbed and flowed, with investigation favored over legislation. In 1928, following some pressure from President Calvin Coolidge, the Senate passed a lobby registration bill introduced by Senator Thaddeus Caraway of Arkansas, but the bill died quietly in the House of Representatives. Despite the bill's demise, Senator Caraway was able the next year to set up a special Senate committee to investigate lobbying, on the heels of a minor scandal in the Senate. A business lobbyist, Charles Evanson, was said to have posed as the staff assistant to Senator Hiram Bingham of Connecticut and to have sat in with him on secret sessions of the Finance Committee's deliberations on the important and controversial Smoot-Hawley tariff bill. A broad-ranging investigation of lobbying by the special committee resulted in reports confirming the charges against Senator Bingham and detailing a pattern of questionable practices by a variety of lobbyists, but no disclosure or regulation bill emerged from the probe.

In the Revenue Act of 1934, Congress included a provision affecting, and perhaps discouraging — but not regulating — Washington lobbying. The 1934 act denied tax-exempt status to groups that devoted a "substantial part" of their activities to propaganda or other efforts to influence legislation.[11] No guidelines were set, and the Internal Revenue Service has interpreted this provision (which is still on the books) on an ad hoc basis, sometimes with controversial results. For example, the Sierra Club, which had had tax-exempt status, lost it in 1966 following an aggressive campaign against two power dams on the Colorado River that had been proposed by the Department of the Interior. The Center for Corporate Responsibility, engaged in a major shareholder-based campaign to change General Motors' practices on pollution control, minority hiring, and other areas, had its application for tax-exempt status stalled in the IRS, from early 1970 to May 1972, when it was finally rejected.[12]

In 1935, another public airing of lobbying activities resulted in new legislative initiatives. Federal Trade Commission reports in that year described ongoing Washington activity by public utility holding companies. The reports focused popular attention particularly on the utility lobbies' actions against the Wheeler-Rayburn bill to regulate the public utility industry. Urged on by public opinion, Congress, in the Public Utility Holding Company Act of 1935, added a provision requiring holding company lobbyists to register with the Securities and Exchange Commission (SEC) and to file reports on their lobbyists' duties and compensation. The law covered attempts to influence Congress, the SEC, and the Federal Power Commission, and is still in force (but not very rigorously applied). Following passage of the 1935 act, the Senate took the unusual step of setting up a special committee to investigate lobbying by utility companies against the measure itself. The committee found that roughly 250,000 telegrams and five million letters had been sent to legislators, nearly all generated by utility lobbyists and paid for by the power companies.[13]

A similar issue arose at the same time over the tactics of shipping company lobbies on merchant marine bills and resulted in a parallel registration provision in the Merchant Marine Act of 1936. But apart from these specific actions, no lobby regulation bill was adopted by Congress at that time.

In 1938, the looming international war precipitated another regulation law. The propaganda efforts in the United States of Nazi and Fascist agents resulted in passage by Congress of the Foreign Agents Registration Act, which required every agent of a foreign interest to file a statement of activities with the secretary of state (a function later assumed by the Justice Department).[14]

THE 1946 FEDERAL REGULATION OF LOBBYING ACT

As so often happens with major legislation, the ultimate passage of a broad lobbying disclosure law — after decades of conflict, controversy, and investigatory activity — came quietly and quickly, with little debate or forewarning. The Federal Regulation of Lobbying Act of 1946 was not even passed as a separate bill; rather it was made a part of the landmark Legislative Reorganization Act of 1946 as Title III.

The Legislative Reorganization Act was the product of a Joint Committee on the Organization of Congress, which devoted comparatively little attention to lobbying disclosure or regulation in its extensive hearings in 1945 and 1946, or in its final report, except to express the view that requiring representatives of interest groups to register would aid Congress in its ability to evaluate accurately the nature of public opinion.

Passage of Title III on the floor of the House and Senate also attracted little attention or debate, and the title, its language basically grafted from bills drawn up by representatives and senators a decade earlier, sailed through unamended. Although the lobbying provision was favorably received by the press, it did not fare well among many legal experts. It was criticized within months of its passage in both the *Columbia Law Review* and the *Yale Law Journal* as "ambiguous,"[15] "neither carefully drafted nor fully considered,"[16] "modelled on anachronistic precedent,"[17] and motivated by "political expediency."[18] Many of the specific criticisms of the 1946 act continued to be repeated two decades later.

The 1946 Lobbying Act reflected the ambivalent attitudes of the American public about the role of interest groups and lobbying in the political system. The act did not restrict in any way the activities, strategic or financial, of interest groups. Rather, it based its regulating provisions almost entirely on the principle of public disclosure. The act required any individual who received monetary compensation from any person or group for the purpose of exerting pressure on Congress to register with the clerk of the House of Representatives and the secretary of the Senate. Lobbyists were required to identify their employers and state their general legislative objectives. These "registered lobbyists" — as well as lobbying organizations — also had to file quarterly reports with the House and Senate disclosing their lobbying expenses. The act specified misdemeanor criminal penalties for violation of these disclosure provisions.

Criticism of the 1946 act did not focus on Congress (which showed little interest in refining its product), but soon showed up in the court system. In January 1948, the first "test case" emerged with a National Association of Manufacturers suit challenging the constitutionality of the law. In March 1952, a Washington, D.C., federal court agreed with the NAM, ruling the statute unconstitutional. But eight months later, the Supreme Court reversed the lower court on a technicality, leaving the 1946 law intact. Also in 1948, the federal government brought a variety of indictments against individuals and organizations, including the U.S. Savings and Loan League and ex-Representative Roger Slaughter, a lobbyist for the North American Grain Association, for violations of the 1946 lobbying act. None were found guilty. More importantly, other indictments, brought in June 1948 against several farm lobbyists, led ultimately to the key Supreme Court decision on the lobbying law, in 1954.

THE 1954 SUPREME COURT DECISION

The 1954 Supreme Court decision, *U.S.* v. *Harriss,* concerned a New York cotton broker, Robert M. Harriss, who, without registering with Congress, had allegedly made payments (unreported to the relevant authorities, that is, the clerk of the House and secretary of the Senate) to various other individuals to lobby Congress on legislation.

A lower court had thrown both the indictments and the law out, holding that the 1946 act was unconstitutional because it was too vague and indefinite to meet the requirements of due process. To the lower court, registration and reporting requirements violated the First Amendment, and certain of the penalty provisions violated the constitutional right to petition Congress. The Supreme Court reversed the lower court and, in a 5-3 decision, upheld the constitutionality of the 1946 Act; in the process, however, it greatly narrowed the focus and applicability of the statute.[19] The Court's ruling itself provoked a storm of criticism; a number of law review articles suggested that the ruling only added to the problems inherent in the act.

LOOPHOLES IN THE 1946 LOBBYING ACT

As soon as the 1946 legislation went into effect, loopholes became obvious. The narrow interpretation of the 1954 Court ruling tended to increase opportunities for evading the provisions of the act. Among the loopholes:

● The act, in the eyes of the Supreme Court, covered only groups that solicited or collected money for influencing legislation — exempting from registration groups or individuals that spent their own money for lobbying.

● The act left it up to the group or its representative to determine what proportion of his total expenditures were required to be reported as spending on lobbying. Groups could thus, at their discretion, include or ignore substantial amounts of money spent for "public education" or other such purposes, making lobbying financial disclosure reports unreliable and unsystematic at best.

● The court narrowly interpreted the act's definition of a group or individual's "principal purpose" for collecting or receiving money. To the Court, the law applied only to groups or individuals whose principal purpose was influencing legislation through *direct contacts* with members of Congress. Not only did this allow several large organizations (including, for nearly 30 years, the National Association of Manufacturers)[20] to avoid registration on the grounds that they served many purposes in addition to direct lobbying, but it also exempted groups whose main efforts were geared towards stimulating public pressure on Congress — that is, *grass-roots* lobbying.

● The act was vague about what types of contacts with Congress would be considered lobbying. The law specifically exempted testimony before a congressional committee, but other kinds of contacts were left open to different interpretations by different groups; many groups ignored contacts with congressional staffers, and others drew a fine line between informational or social contacts and lobbying contacts.

● The act covered only lobbying before Congress, not attempts to influence executive agencies, regulatory commissions, or the executive branch as a whole.

● The act did not designate or empower any agency to investigate or require registrations and reports, or to enforce compliance. The Justice Department, which can prosecute violators of the law, has since the first few cases in the late 1940s acted only when it has received a complaint — that is, rarely. In only one case has a conviction been obtained under the law. This occurred in 1956 when Senator Francis Case of South Dakota revealed that he had been offered a campaign contribution in exchange for a favorable vote on a natural gas bill.

Most, if not all, of these criticisms of the 1946 law were offered soon after the *Harriss* decision in 1954, and they have been repeated, with varying intensity and by varying groups and individuals, up until the present.

LOBBY LEGISLATION EFFORTS:
THE 1950s AND 1960s

The history of lobbying legislation following the 1946 act is very similar to the pre-1946 period; it is characterized by special investigating committees, scandals and controversy — but little in the way of new legislation. The Senate recommended minor changes in 1948; the House created a select committee to investigate lobbying in 1949; the Senate held hearings on lobby legislation in 1951 and 1953, and introduced bills in 1954 and 1955 (sponsored by Senator John F. Kennedy of Massachusetts) designed to tighten some of the loopholes in the 1946 act. Following the Case scandal, the Senate created a *new* special committee in 1956 to investigate corrupt practices involving lobbying and campaign contributions. The committee was chaired by Senator John McClellan of Arkansas, who introduced a new lobby registration bill in 1957. The McClellan bill would have closed several of the 1946 act's loopholes, but it died at the end of the 85th Congress.

Massive lobbying for sugar quotas in the 87th Congress (1961-62) provoked the Senate Foreign Relations Committee to undertake a comprehensive investigation of foreign lobbying, with an eye toward revising the 1938 Foreign Agents Registration Act (FARA). Following extensive hearings in 1962 and 1963, Senators J. William Fulbright, D-Ark., and Bourke Hickenlooper, R-Ind., introduced a bill revising the 1938 act, which was eventually enacted into law in 1966. The 1966 amendments to FARA narrowed its scope, cutting down required registrations and changing the law's focus from subversive activities to the influence of foreign political propaganda on the regular decisionmaking process in Congress. Further changes in this law were being contemplated in 1977-78, following the Tongsun Park affair, which involved a South Korean businessman with ties to the Korean government giving large sums of money to members of Congress, in exchange both for promoting rice contracts with South Korea and for general support for President Park Chung Hee's regime.

NEW LEGISLATIVE EFFORTS IN THE 1970s

The Bobby Baker scandal of 1965, in which a top Senate aide was accused of taking bribes from interest groups in return for influencing senators' votes (he later served time in a federal prison on related charges), spurred investigations of lobbying improprieties in the Senate and resulted in proposals for new legislation to strengthen the 1946 Lobbying Act. In 1967, the Senate passed a bill, endorsed by President Lyndon B. Johnson, that broadened lobby registration requirements and contained relatively stringent and complete disclosure guidelines; however, the bill died in the House of Representatives.

The House became more deeply involved in lobby regulation reform in 1970-71, when its Committee on Standards of Official Conduct held hearings on lobbying in which witnesses uniformly denounced the 1946 act as replete with loopholes. The committee drafted a new lobby bill — titled the Legislative Activities Disclosure Act — but it was not well-received by interest groups. The Chamber of Commerce's general counsel said the bill's proposed toughened reporting requirements would impose "an intolerable and unjustified burden . . . on thousands of persons and organizations."[21] The bill was also criticized by the National Association of Manufacturers and the District of Columbia Bar Association. It never reached the floor of the House.

In the meantime, in 1974-75, several state legislatures, led by California, responded to internal and outside pressure and passed lobbying statutes. The California law (adopted through a referendum) imposed tough regulations on lobby disclosures and limited lobbying activities.

Failure in the 94th Congress (1975-76)

Following the Watergate scandals, the Senate returned to the subject in the 94th Congress, as its Government Operations Committee held hearings, put together a bill, and, in March 1976, sent the Lobbying Disclosure Act of 1976 to the full Senate. The Senate passed it in June 1976, by a vote of 82 to 9. Although not indicated by the overwhelming final vote margin in its favor, the bill was not passed without controversy or division. A wide range of interest groups bitterly opposed various of its provisions. The most interesting split occurred within the "public interest" lobbying ranks, as Common Cause, the major force behind lobby reform, defended the sweeping provisions of the bill, while Ralph Nader's Congress Watch and Public Citizen opposed many of the disclosure requirements.

The Senate bill made substantial alterations in the 1946 act. It defined a lobbyist in terms of an organization (to satisfy the constitutional protection of freedom of speech, individuals were not required to register) and specified that an organization have at least one paid officer or employee to qualify as a lobby. Thus, unpaid volunteer groups were exempted. For an organization to be classified as a lobbying organization, and hence, be required to register, it had to do any one of three things:

1. Retain a law firm or person to lobby for the organization for at least $250 in compensation in a quarter year;

2. Engage on its own behalf in 12 or more oral lobbying communications with Congress in a quarter year; or

3. Spend $5,000 or more in a quarter year on direct expenses for a lobbying solicitation — a grass-roots campaign — to persuade others to lobby Congress.

Like the 1946 Act, the Senate revision dealt only with lobbying of Congress; covered only disclosure of lobbying expenses and activities (and not curbs on the activities themselves); and required quarterly reports. But the registrations and reports would contain much more information in the Senate plan than in the 1946 act, including the size and nature of an organization's membership, how it determined its issue positions, and detailed data on grass-roots solicitations. The administrative and enforcement responsibilities would be placed in the General Accounting Office (GAO), an auditing and investigatory agency that is part of the legislative branch.

While the Senate debated its bill in 1976, the House was preparing to take action on two alternatives, drawn up in separate committees. One, from the House Judiciary Committee, defined lobbying in organizational terms, but set standards for qualification of an organization as a lobbyist that were quite different from those of the Senate. An organization qualified as a lobbyist if it either:

1. Spent over $1,250 in a quarter to retain an individual or group to lobby for it; or

2. Employed at least one individual who, in a particular quarter year, spent 20 percent of his or her time engaged in lobbying activities for the organization.

The House Judiciary Committee bill did not cover grass-roots lobbying, but it did deal with lobbying of top-level executive branch officials — two major differences with the Senate bill. Like the Senate, the House Judiciary bill gave enforcement powers to the GAO.

The second House bill was a product of the Committee on Standards of Official Conduct, and it broadened the Judiciary Committee's version in several respects. It included a grass-roots qualification standard and a somewhat tougher registration provision. The full House took up the two bills at the end of September 1976, in the final days of the 94th Congress. After 14 straight hours of debate (in which opponents of the bill tried to stretch out debate in hopes of killing the bill in the end-of-session crunch), the House finally adopted a somewhat revised version of the Judiciary Committee bill in the early morning hours of September 29. However, the extensive differences between the House and Senate bills could not be compromised before time ran out in the session. So once again, a flurry of activity — in which *both* chambers actually passed lobbying reform bills — produced no new lobbying law.

Renewed Efforts in the 95th Congress (1977-78)

In spite of the frustrating conclusion to their efforts in the previous Congress, lobbying reform advocates began again early in the 95th Congress in 1977. After several meetings, a House Judiciary subcommittee reported out a new lobbying bill on July 20. The bill basically resembled its predecessor, though with variations; it required an organization to register and to file quarterly reports if it:

1) Spent $2500 or more in a quarter year to retain an individual or group to lobby for it; or

2) Spent $2500 or more in a quarter to make oral or written lobbying communications and employed one or more individuals who together made lobbying communications on 13 or more days per quarter (meaning roughly once a week).

The subcommittee bill included no provision covering executive branch lobbying. Originally, it included a provision requiring disclosure of grass-roots solicitations, but that provision was taken out by a vote of the full Judiciary Committee when it reported the bill to the House on February 23, 1978.

The Senate, for its part, took little action in 1977, as its Governmental Affairs Committee, caught in a backlog of other work, was able to hold only a single day of hearings on lobbying reform. 1978 produced more activity.

Indeed, the persistent congressional efforts to tighten the 1946 lobby law produced results in 1978, with House passage of legislation imposing strict new registration and reporting requirements on lobby groups. Approval of the bill came on April 26; it was passed by a vote of 259-140 (R 75-67; D 184-73).

In three days of floor debate, the House turned back nearly 20 efforts to weaken the bill. Two major amendments that significantly expanded the bill's disclosure requirements were adopted. The two amendments required disclosure of: 1) grass-roots lobbying efforts and 2) the names of major organizations contributing to lobby groups. The addition of these provisions led major business, civil liberties, church, and environmental groups to charge that the bill interfered with privacy and with citizens' rights to petition public officials.

Two weeks after the House passed its lobbying bill, the Senate Governmental Affairs Committee began work on its own version of the legislation. The first version of the committee's bill was far more rigorous than the House-passed bill. Besides requiring more groups to file reports, the Senate committee's bill contained more comprehensive grass-roots lobbying and contributor disclosure provisions and more extensive coverage of lobbying of executive branch officials.

CONTEMPORARY CONTROVERSIES

Lobby regulation, as is evident, has always been controversial. In the 1970s, the controversy centered on several basic questions:

1. Who should be required to register?
2. Should indirect lobbying be covered in some manner?
3. Should lobbying of the executive branch be included?
4. How comprehensive and complex should reporting requirements be?
5. Should contributors to lobbying organizations be made public?
6. How should enforcement be handled?
7. How much regulation is constitutional — that is, when does lobby legislation run the risk of being invalidated or made meaningless by the Supreme Court?

The first question — who should be required to register — has created the most conflict among groups and within Congress. Both the House and the Senate chose to define lobbyists as organizations, not individuals, to avoid controversy over the constitutional rights to freedom of speech and petition. The conflict focused on the various "threshold" standards determining at what point lobbyists would be required to register. For example, one amendment offered on the House floor in 1976 would have extended the lobbying registration provisions to *any* organization making 12 or more contacts with government officials in a six-month period. In vigorously opposing the amendment, Representative Walter Flowers of Alabama said that this threshold would cover an absurdly wide variety of Americans, including "local Boy Scout troops that write 12 letters in a six-month period."[22] Not surprisingly, groups tend to favor provisions that benefit them and to oppose others. Business lobbies have pushed for a provision that would require registration of unpaid volunteers for registered lobbying organizations — a strategy aimed directly at Ralph Nader, who is not paid for his lobbying.

The second issue focuses on grass-roots lobbying, which, as the case studies in this book will underscore, has become a widespread and potent lobbying tool. The grass-roots controversy reflects two other major issues that underlie the lobby disclosure debate: the question of a group's constituency (does the group in fact represent the people it purports to represent?); and the extent to which communications (letters, telegrams, etc., to Washington) from people in a variety of locations represent the views of broader groups.

The 1946 act, and many recent alternatives, cover only direct contact with legislators — Washington lobbying. Common Cause, among other groups, has insisted that a bill ignoring indirect lobbying would be too narrow and too weak. The 1978 House-passed version of a new lobby bill contained a grass-roots provision.

The third area of controversy involves whether only lobbying of Congress should be regulated or disclosed, or whether coverage should extend to the *executive branch* as well — and, if so, to what *kinds* of executive branch lobbying, and to what types of executive branch officials. Not surprisingly, groups that bid for government contracts or have extensive dealings with regulatory commissions vigorously oppose inclusion of the executive branch, and House and Senate bills have differed in this area.

The most publicized split among groups has occurred over the reporting requirements. It was this issue that divided Nader's Congress Watch and Common Cause, with Nader's representatives arguing that requiring complex and lengthy reports every quarter for every group would drain, discourage, and possibly destroy small public interest-oriented groups that do not lobby extensively and have few resources at their disposal. As a compromise, Common Cause proposed a "two-tier" system of reporting requirements, with comprehensive reporting for most organizations, but with abbreviated reports for less active groups. This provision was included in the major Senate bill sent to the Governmental Affairs Committee for deliberation in 1977-78.

Also in dispute was whether the names of contributors to membership organizations (as well as amounts contributed) should be made public in the same way in which political campaign contributions are disclosed. The 1978 House-passed bill included a provision requiring identification of organizations contributing $3,000 or more in a year to a lobbying organization and the amount given if the contribution was spent in whole or in part for lobbying and the lobbying group spent at least one percent of its budget on lobbying activities. Opponents have objected that the one percent limitation discriminated against small organizations with relatively few contributors, who might be publicized while a heavy contributor to a multimillion dollar group would remain anonymous. In the future, this is sure to be a continuing controversy, as many groups feel that requiring public disclosure of contributors has a "dampening effect" on fund-raising.

An additional area of contention has been the issue of enforcement — especially since the 1946 act was particularly deficient in its failure to pinpoint enforcement responsibility. After casting about for a non-biased and effective institution, some proponents of lobbying reform settled on the General Accounting Office as the administrator and enforcer.[23] GAO has ties by law to Congress, but it is not an intimate part of the legislature. The 1978 House bill required GAO to compile and index information filed under the bill but gave enforcement authority to the Justice Department. In addition, the *nature* of enforcement — the toughness of the penalties, civil and criminal, for violation of the new act — is at issue.

Finally, a key question underlying the whole debate over lobby regulation and disclosure is the constitutionality of a lobby law. Who can constitutionally be required to submit to congressional regulation and how extensive can that regulation be and still safeguard constitutional guarantees? These were major implicit considerations in the process of formulating lobby policy. Proponents of tightening the existing lobby laws are always aware of the enormous impact of the Supreme Court's *Harriss* decision. While the court did uphold the constitutionality of *some* disclosure of lobbyists and their activities, the *Harriss* decision severely constrained (some would say crippled) the 1946 act's provisions. Proponents of change do not want their new legislation to be struck down or narrowed by the courts, and consequently, they have been careful to limit the scope of proposed revisions, requiring only organizations and not individuals to register and focusing only on disclosure requirements and not activities. This position is likely to avoid problems with the Supreme Court over constitutionality, but it could also stimulate the criticism that the proposals do not go much further than the 1946 act — and thus do not go far enough toward restricting the negative effects of massive lobbying by interest groups on government decisionmakers.

CONCLUSION

The drumbeat of congressional support for lobbying disclosure legislation has reflected a more widespread public unease about the nature and impact of lobbying on government — a malaise that has been fueled by a variety of critical comments about "special interests" made by President Carter and other important public officials, and one that extends to public perceptions of the contemporary political process itself. A Harris poll in 1975 found 72 percent of the American public agreeing with the statement, "Congress is still too much under the influence of special interest lobbies."[24]

The push for a new law has accelerated in the 1970s, in part as a manifestation of a broader governmental reform movement, in part in response to tremendous growth in recent years in the amount of lobbying and the number of lobbying groups active in Washington. Even groups with long histories of Washington activity — like the Chamber of Commerce and the NAM — have expanded, modernized, and energized their lobbying efforts.

More lobbying activity on a wider range of issues has reactivated the ambivalent feelings Americans have toward group political behavior and has led to renewed pressures for a revised lobbying law — but a law which reflects that ambivalence.

None of the proposed statutes would seriously curtail lobbying activities; rather, they emphasize *public disclosure* in one form or another, on the theory that lobbying as such is legal and constitutional, but should be publicly identified to discourage any illegal activity or "insidious effects." The public's attitude toward lobbying has its closest parallel in the laws surrounding cigarette smoking and advertising — that smoking is legal, but the government requires a public warning that "it may be hazardous to your health."

Public disclosure of lobbying activities is one way for Congress and the public to evaluate the legitimacy of groups — it can shed light on how groups make decisions internally, how hierarchical their own structures are, how representative the group's leaders are of the group's membership; in general, how much credence to give to a group's claim to represent a constituency. Although this has not surfaced as a major area of controversy in the contemporary debate over lobby regulation, it clearly underlies the issue of regulation and disclosure.

Finally, it should be mentioned that laws regulating lobbying are not confined to the few mentioned in this chapter. One of the most important steps affecting group activity and influence in Washington was passage of campaign finance laws that implemented public financing of presidential campaigns. As we noted in an earlier chapter, the importance of this law to interest groups — and its effect on the process — was evident in the dramatic increase in campaign contributions to candidates for Congress between 1974 and 1976, the first year of the presidential law. Future efforts to implement public financing of *congressional* campaigns (such a bill was filibustered to death in the Senate in 1977) are likely to become major battlegrounds for groups seeking to maintain or expand their influence in the political process; passage of a law allowing public financing of congressional campaigns would bring about major changes in the behavior and strategy of groups in Washington.

NOTES

1. James Deakin, *The Lobbyists* (Washington: Public Affairs Press, 1966), p. 52.

2. Karl Schriftgiesser, *The Lobbyists* (Boston: Little, Brown, 1951), p. 7.
3. *Ibid.*, p. 12.
4. Quoted in Neil MacNeil, *Forge of Democracy* (New York: David McKay, 1963), pp. 211-212.
5. Schriftgiesser, *The Lobbyists,* p. 14.
6. *Ibid.*
7. *Ibid.*, p. 19.
8. Daniel P. Mulhollan, "An Overview of Lobbying Organizations," in *Senators: Offices, Ethics and Pressures,* a compilation of papers prepared for the Commission on the Operation of the Senate. (Washington, D.C.: U.S. Government Printing Office, 1977), pp. 157-192.
9. *Ibid.*
10. Richard Boeckel, "Regulation of Congressional Lobbies," *Editorial Research Reports,* March 7, 1928, pp. 216-217.
11. The Revenue Act of 1939 added a provision disallowing individual tax deductions for contributions to charitable groups which engage in substantial lobbying.
12. Jeffrey M. Berry, *Lobbying for the People* (Princeton, N.J.: Princeton University Press, 1977) pp. 47-55.
13. Mulhollan, "Overview of Lobbying Organizations," pp. 168-170.
14. *Ibid.*
15. See "Federal Lobbying Act of 1946," *Columbia Law Review* (January 1947), pp. 98-109.
16. *Ibid.*
17. See "Improving the Legislative Process: Federal Regulation of Lobbying," *Yale Law Journal* (January 1947), pp. 304-342.
18. *Ibid.*
19. In the process, the Court did not judge the guilt or innocence of Harriss or his colleagues, but sent the individual cases back to the lower court. None were found guilty.
20. The NAM registered under the act only after forced to by a 1975 court suit brought by Common Cause.
21. See details in *The Washington Lobby* (Washington, D.C.; Congressional Quarterly, 1974), p. 28.
22. Congressional Quarterly *Weekly Report,* October 2, 1976, p. 2715.
23. Except, of course, for criminal prosecution of lobbying law violations, which would remain with the Justice Department.
24. U.S. Congress, Senate Committee on Government Operations, 94th Cong., 2d sess., Report on "Lobbying Disclosure Act of 1976," p. 3.

PART II

Case Studies

In Part I, we have examined the nature, composition and behavior of groups involved in the policy process in America. Our analysis, however, has not focused in detail on the *impact* of groups on policymaking, or on the policies themselves. In Part II, we will provide three varied and in-depth case studies of groups and their roles in initiating, facilitating, changing, or blocking public policy alternatives.

Group impact on policy can occur in various ways. A group may initiate a policy idea, or it may identify a policy problem. Groups might, in effect, say to government decisionmakers, "There is a problem out here in society that requires a public policy solution," or, "Here is an idea for a policy directive that will solve a problem and thus improve society." Not all policy ideas come from interest groups, of course; nor are all problems first identified or labeled by groups. Government itself (through the president, the White House staff, the Cabinet, the Civil Service, members of Congress or congressional staffs), the academic community (or "intellectuals"), the press, or events themselves (such as a gasoline shortage, a foreign invasion, or a scandal) can precipitate policy initiatives. But in many instances, the ideas for policy come directly from interest groups.

In a directly related way, groups can serve to *get ideas placed on the policy agenda*. At any given time, there are many more policy ideas floating around than could become concrete and viable proposals actively considered by governmental policymakers. As Nelson Polsby notes, ideas frequently germinate for several years before being taken seriously by policy actors: The number of potential ideas and their proponents vastly outnumber the total that can realistically reach the serious attention of Congress, the president and the executive branch. By acting through "sponsors" on relevant congressional committees or in agencies, and by using whatever clout they possess, groups can have a direct influence on the composition and content of the policy agency. As we shall see in a case study, common-site picketing was one such idea; it was conceived, initiated, and pushed onto the policy table by organized labor. Congress and the White House played basically reactive roles on this issue (though their reactions proved ultimately to be decisive in killing the bill).

At other times interest groups primarily *react to policy initiatives* coming from Congress or the executive. As earlier chapters indicate, groups devote a good portion of their Washington activities to monitoring of government agencies and congressional committees, watching for actions that would affect the groups or their members. When such actions are contemplated or set in motion, the groups themselves move to get their positions on the record, and to facilitate, amend, or block the initiatives. This was basically the situation with the B-1 bomber, which emerged from the Pentagon as a proposed element of strategic policy; antiwar and other groups reacted, and provoked a counterreaction from the plane's contractors and their allies. The battle was then fought in the committee rooms and chambers of the House and Senate, and ultimately decided in the Oval Office. As our case study makes clear, however, the role of groups in this issue was not entirely a reactive one. The issue did emerge on the policy agenda under the auspices of the executive branch — but it was the anti-B-1 coalition of groups that made the bomber a salient issue on the presidential campaign agenda in 1976.

Many issues are hybrids, falling between these two avenues. The clean air issue, for example, clearly was first placed on the policy agenda in the late 1960s by the newly emerging environmental movement, with its groups stimulating Earth Day and passage of the National Environmental Policy Act (NEPA) in 1969 and the Clean Air Act in 1970. But by the mid-1970s, the specific issues of air pollution control had become governmental ones, stimulated not directly by groups, but by the provisions of the 1970 act. The auto industry and other affected groups reacted, provoking counter-pressure from the environmentalists.

Along with their stimulative or reactive roles in influencing policy, interest groups can play either a *dominant* or a *subordinate* role through the decisionmaking stage of the policy process. On common site picketing, groups are clearly dominant throughout the process; legislative and executive actors are more pawns than players in a chess game between labor and business. The groups, in other words, are not so much consultants to the governmental decisionmakers on this issue as they are the dominant forces in the decisions, with Congress and the executive branch being merely the fields of battle.

Although groups are important in our other two case studies (in part deliberately so; we chose issues where group involvement was great), they are at base quite different; members of Congress played much more aggressive and dominant roles throughout the policy battles on clean air and the B-1 bomber, using interest groups for information, support, and strategic assistance, rather than the other way around.

Finally, group involvement in policy issues can be one-sided or involve intense clashes of opposing interests. Our case studies show powerful sets of interests pitted against one another — the auto industry and auto workers vs. environmentalists on clean air; labor vs. business and the building industry on common-site picketing; defense contractors and laborers vs. anti-defense spending groups on the B-1. It should be noted that none of the three issues started this way. Common-site picketing appeared at first to be relatively uncontroversial, with the AFL-CIO as its patron and little interest or involvement from business. Similarly, the initial Clean Air Act, pushed by environmentalists, and the B-1 bomber, supported by the Pentagon and defense contractors, did not arouse major controversy in their early years. Many issues, of course, especially smaller and more narrow ones, never develop major opposing group pressures.

5

Common-Site Picketing:
Major Defeat for Labor

On March 23, 1977, in a stunning defeat for the labor lobby, the House of Representatives narrowly defeated a bill to legalize common-site picketing* in the construction industry. It was the first important piece of labor legislation to come before the 95th Congress (1977-78). Sponsors of the measure conceded that the 205-217 vote (R 14-129; D 191-88) left them virtually no chance of resurrecting the bill any time soon. It was a major setback for organized labor — particularly the construction trades — which had sought the controversial picketing rights for more than 20 years. The bill, which would have allowed unions with a grievance against a single contractor to picket and potentially close down an entire building site, would have overturned a 1951 Supreme Court ruling that such practices constituted an illegal secondary boycott.

Labor came close to success on the issue in the 1975 session of the 94th Congress, when both the House and Senate passed picketing legislation that President Ford initially said he could support. But an intense campaign by opposition groups — mainly construction contractors, business associations, and other conservative interests — persuaded Ford to reconsider, and he vetoed the bill January 2, 1976. Because of the relatively narrow margins of support for the bill in both

---

*Also referred to as common situs or situs picketing.

chambers, supporters of the legislation decided to let the veto stand uncontested.

Unions had anticipated another tough fight in 1977, but clearly thought the Democratic presidential victory in November 1976 removed a key obstacle. Though he did not work actively to round up votes for the common-site bill, the new president, Jimmy Carter, said he would sign the legislation. But the same coalition that formed in 1975 emerged again to oppose the bill, concentrating its efforts on the House, where passage looked more likely. Mass mailings — such as a postcard campaign enlisting construction union members to express their fears that common-site picketing would cost them their jobs — chipped away at support in the House. In the end, even major concessions by the Democratic leadership that would have exempted much of the construction industry from common-site picketing could not save the bill. It never came up in the Senate.

Prior to House floor debate on the legislation, Speaker of the House Thomas P. O'Neill Jr., D-Mass., criticized organized labor for not working hard enough for the bill's passage. While opposition lobbyists were flooding members with mail from their districts, he maintained, labor groups let things slide until the last minute. "When you get careless, the train goes off the track," said O'Neill.[1] Fearing a loss, the Democratic leadership had suggested pulling the bill off the schedule for floor action, but labor leaders insisted their vote count showed a slim majority of the House ready to support their side. However, on the morning of March 23, 1977 — the day of the crucial vote — Majority Whip John Brademas, D-Ind., had counted only 190 solid Democratic votes favoring the bill.

The legislation produced a classic lobbying battle: organized labor *v.* big business. The key proponents of the legislation were the Building and Construction Trades Department of the AFL-CIO and its 17 separate national craft unions, ranging from the 4,000-member granite cutters to the 957,000-member electrical workers. They were backed by the AFL-CIO as a whole and by independent unions such as the Teamsters, which included 100,000 construction workers.

Opposing the bill were the Associated General Contractors of America (AGC), Associated Builders and Contractors, Inc., the National Right to Work Committee, the Chamber of Commerce of the United States, the National Association of Manufacturers (NAM), the Business Roundtable, and several individual corporations. An ad hoc organization — the National Action Committee on Secondary Boycotts — was established in mid-1975 under the auspices of AGC to coordinate the efforts of 40 interest groups opposed to the picketing bill.

Two factors in particular were responsible for the successful lobbying effort against the common-site bill. The first was its sheer intensity. The second was what the business lobbyists proudly referred to as the "rifle" as opposed to the "shotgun" strategy in which they had carefully targeted those members of Congress they thought could be swayed to alter the outcome (the "swing" votes).

The intensity of the lobbying was apparent from the outset. House Labor-Management Relations Subcommittee Chairman Frank Thompson Jr., D-N.J., the bill's floor manager both in 1975 and 1977, referred to the lobbying as "massive" and blamed it for defeat of the legislation. Just before the House began debating the bill in 1977, Speaker O'Neill said he had "never seen an organization function like the Associated General Contractors, the home builders and the other groups" opposed to common-site picketing.[2]

Although the business opponents of the picketing bill were credited with a well-orchestrated lobbying effort, labor's own lobbyists conceded that some laxity on their part also contributed to the bill's defeat. Victor Kamber, head of the AFL-CIO task force on labor law reform, explained the failure to generate adequate pressure by saying, "We took for granted that the Congress understood our position, and knew that our people around the country cared. I do not believe on situs that the opposition won. We lost."

BACKGROUND

"The guy who gave it that name, situs picketing [or common site picketing], must have been an enemy of labor,"

125

complained a spokesman for the Building and Construction Trades Department of the AFL-CIO. "All we want is the right accorded any other worker to advertise our grievances at the place where we work, at a construction site."

But it is not that simple. The issue arises from the unique character and place of the building and construction industry in the United States. The $150-billion-plus annual construction industry accounts for almost nine percent of the nation's Gross National Product. It is one of the largest users of raw materials and manufactured items. One of every seven Americans makes a living, directly or indirectly, from construction.

Ordinarily, the developer of a large project, an office building, for example, contracts with a general contractor to build the project. In turn, the general contractor signs up subcontractors to handle specific jobs like plumbing, electrical work, carpentry, and so forth. There may be a dozen or more smaller firms working with the general contractor, and the employees in each may be organized by a different union. The question then becomes: Can the employees of one subcontractor, a plumbing firm, for example, protest their employer's policies by throwing up a picket line at the construction site? Under the 1935 Wagner Act, guaranteeing workers the right to organize and strike, the answer would seem to be "yes." But under subsequent legislation and court rulings, the answer is "no" for construction jobs.

The struggle that was to climax in 1977 began 20 years earlier when Congress in 1947 passed the Taft-Hartley Act (PL 80-101) over President Truman's veto. The new law made it an unfair labor practice to strike or walk off the job if the goal was to pressure employers other than the immediate one. Garment workers striking for higher wages, for example, could not legally persuade department store workers to strike in sympathy. Such a move would amount to pressure on the department store owner not to buy the garment workers' product, when in fact the grievance was only between garment workers and their employer. To carry the strike to another employer would constitute an illegal secondary boycott.

Debate on applying the law to the construction industry began almost immediately: Could a craft union strike one subcontractor on a building project if the resulting picket line barred other unions, affected other employers and shut down the entire job? A lawsuit was initiated to answer this question. In 1951, the Supreme Court ruled that a union involved in a dispute with one subcontractor at a construction site could not picket the entire site. By affecting other employers at the site with whom there was no dispute, the union was engaging in an illegal secondary boycott.[3]

In the years following the Supreme Court decision, Presidents Eisenhower, Kennedy, and Johnson, and all the secretaries of labor supported enactment of labor-backed legislation to allow unions with a grievance against a single contractor to picket and potentially close down an entire building site. Throughout the 1950s and 1960s, committees in both chambers held periodic hearings on common-site bills, but no legislation was enacted. There were several reasons for the lack of action on common-site legislation. First, there were disagreements within the labor movement over what to list as priority legislative aims. Craft unions wanted to press for common-site picketing bills, but the AFL-CIO focused its attention on trying to repeal Section 14-b of the Taft-Hartley Act, which permitted states to enact "right to work" laws barring closed union shops. Under these laws, a worker cannot be forced to join a union as a condition of employment. Repeal of 14-b was an issue of broad union concern; common-site picketing affected only construction trades. Another explanation for inaction on common site was that, in the late 1960s and early 1970s, the business-minded Nixon administration did not lend strong support to labor legislation. National attention was distracted by the increasingly unpopular war in Vietnam, and there simply was no opportune moment to press forward.

With the election of an overwhelmingly Democratic Congress in November 1974, however, labor saw 1975 as the ideal year to try again. Many of the Democrats were beholden to labor for campaign contributions (organized labor spent more than $5.75 million in the 1974 congressional elections). Furthermore, President Ford both publicly and privately promised to sign a common-site picketing bill, if it incorporated certain safeguards he wanted and if he also received legislation creating a collective bargaining committee for the badly fragmented construction industry. The House passed the common-site bill containing Ford's safeguards by a vote of 230-178 (R 26-107; D 204-71) on July 25. On October 7, by a vote of 302-95 (R 66-67; D 236-28), the House passed legislation establishing a collective bargaining committee for the construction industry that closely followed proposals drawn up by Secretary of Labor John T. Dunlop.

Although the legislation's opponents, mostly conservative Republicans, mounted a strong attack in the Senate, its supporters overcame two filibusters, combined the two bills into one and passed the legislation, 52-45 (R 11-25; D 41-20), November 19. With minimal differences between the Senate and House versions of the bill, and with President Ford's promise to sign it, labor thought that victory was in hand.

House conferees appointed to work out a compromise between the two versions of the bill filed their report on December 8. They had agreed to combine both the common-site picketing and collective bargaining measures into one bill as the Senate had done. The House adopted the compromise version of the bill December 11 on a 229-189 vote (R 24-118; D 205-71). After opponents agreed not to attempt a filibuster, the Senate adopted the conference bill December 15 on a 52-43 vote (R 11-24; D 41-19), thus clearing the bill for the president's signature.

Presidential politics became the most influential factor in Ford's decision to change his mind and veto the bill. Republican presidential challenger Ronald Reagan announced his opposition to the measure, and there were broad hints that many Republican businessmen would shift their 1976 campaign support to Reagan if Ford signed the bill.

Ford announced his veto decision December 22. "Unfortunately, my earlier optimism that this bill provided a resolution which would have the support of all parties was unfounded," he said in a statement. "As a result, I cannot in good conscience sign this measure, given the lack of agreement among the various parties to the historical dispute over the impact of this bill on the construction industry."

Congressional supporters of the bill decided to let the veto stand uncontested, since neither the House nor the Senate had adopted the conference bill with anywhere near the two-thirds majority needed to override.

Ford's veto was a bitter defeat for the bill's supporters. On January 8, 1976, all nine labor members of the president's advisory Collective Bargaining Committee in Construction (the precursor of the proposed new standing Collective Bargaining Committee) resigned in protest. Six days later, Labor Secretary Dunlop, frustrated and disappointed, also quit.

But the battle was not yet over. With the election of a Democratic president and an overwhelmingly Democratic Congress in November 1976, labor decided to try again in 1977 — only to go down to defeat in the House on March 23.

THE GROUPS INVOLVED

Pitted against each other in the 1975 and 1977 battles on common-site picketing were two traditional enemies — business and organized labor. They were well-established, well-financed, and broad-based groups that activated the considerable resources at their disposal to lobby on one piece of legislation, common-site picketing. Both factions used varying methods of persuasion, including mobilization of grass-roots opinion to put constituent pressure on members of Congress, as well as direct contacts with the members themselves, both through professional lobbyists and "fly-ins" to Washington of the groups' representatives at the local level.

Though well-established and with proven ability to lobby successfully, both business and labor had to modify their techniques in the 1970s to adapt to a changing Congress. It was no longer sufficient to maintain alliances with committee chairmen and a handful of senior members and party leaders to achieve one's legislative goal. Organizational reforms had weakened the hierarchy of power, requiring lobbyists to spread out their efforts. Moreover, the new members of Congress were more independent of their party and committee leaders and more skeptical of voting the way the leadership told them to. They wanted the facts.

Both sides of the common-site picketing battle designed their lobbying efforts to take these changes into account. The AFL-CIO and its opponents in the business community both emphasized the economic impact of the legislation, deluging members of Congress with information packages and downplaying emotional, or "vote-party-line" appeals. The lobbying effort concentrated less on the senior members of Congress (most of whose votes were "in the bag" one way or another) and relied less on cronyism than on gaining the ear of freshmen, whose positions were often undetermined. In particular, it was the anti-common-site lobby's concentration on these members (the "swing votes") that was largely responsible for defeat of the bill in 1977.

Taking a cue from the tactics of the "citizens' lobbies" (Nader, Common Cause and other such groups), organized labor and business interests involved in the bill tried to broaden their support by appealing to the general public. "The fate of this legislation will have a marked impact on *every American*," stated a brochure published by the National Action Committee on Secondary Boycotts in urging the bill's defeat. "Who Wants Secondary Boycotts in Construction??? Not the American Public — Not Even Union Construction Workers!!!" "Our Big Issue is Jobs," pronounced an AFL-CIO Building and Construction Trades Department flyer endorsing congressional candidates (and Carter) in the 1976 elections. "We Need a Friend in Congress" — "Committed to the needs of America's working people."

In addition to grass-roots lobbying and direct contacts on Capitol Hill, both sides made campaign contributions — with mixed results. Although labor worked hard to elect a Democratic Congress and president in 1976, the character of that Congress was less inclined than in the past to do labor's bidding. Nor was the president as enthusiastic and energetic a supporter of the picketing bill as his Democratic predecessors had been.

One other factor was particularly important to the lobbying effort on common site, and that was the existence of a coalition formed to work exclusively on that piece of legislation. Like the Clean Air coalition and the anti-B-1 group, the National Action Committee on Secondary Boycotts (the brainchild of the Associated General Contractors) drew into its ranks numerous groups interested in defeating the bill. In so doing, the coalition could draw upon the varied resources and expertise of well-established groups while broadening its base of appeal. By focusing on this one issue, the action committee kept common-site picketing alive and could keep its member groups abreast of the latest legislative developments. For many of the participating groups — such as the Chamber of Commerce and the Business Roundtable — common site was only one of many issues they were interested in, and thus they were not as able to devote their full attention to it as could the hard-core workers in the action committee. The existence of a coalition was one important asset in the anti-common-site lobby that was lacking in the labor effort. The AFL-CIO as a whole had on its legislative agenda a wide range of priorities considered more important to workers in general than common site. Moreover, there were divisions within the union about whether to support common-site picketing. In 1977, only the Building and Construction Trades Department was working hard on the bill, and the effort eventually proved inadequate.

Back in 1975, however, the success of the opposition to common-site picketing was unanticipated. It appeared that organized labor would continue to be a more persuasive influence on Capitol Hill than business interests, which had to face a Democratic Congress and retool their lobbying strategy to meet the many changes on Capitol Hill.

The AFL-CIO

In the early 1970s, organized labor, notably the AFL-CIO, came closer than any other major national group to meeting the varied demands of modern lobbying. Through a national network of union locals, leaders could mobilize workers to write letters to their congressmen, buttonhole the lawmakers when on home district visits, offer election day help, buy ads in local newspapers and earmark money through union dues for multi-million dollar campaign war chests administered by labor leaders. *(For a further description of the AFL-CIO, see pp. 24-26.)*

In Washington, the AFL-CIO maintained a professional, knowledgeable, and highly respected lobbying force backed up by research departments in specific subject areas — economics, social security, labor law, etc. — which could produce fact sheets and position papers to bolster labor's arguments. As in most successful lobbying operations, the AFL-CIO legislative office has had a strong personal link with Capitol Hill in its director, Andrew J. Biemiller, who served two terms in the House before joining the AFL-CIO in 1953. Biemiller has continued to maintain personal contacts in Congress.

For many years, the leading man-on-the scene for labor, the man who spent much of his time at the Capitol, in the hallways and reception rooms outside the House and Senate chambers, has been Kenneth Young, a career labor employee who joined the Biemiller staff in 1965. Among conservatives as well as liberals, Young has been considered one of Washington's most effective and highly respected lobbyists.

A former Senate Labor Committee aide, for years a target of union lobbying, offered this assessment of Young: "He's very soft-spoken, soft-sell; he knows his facts. If you've got a question, he's got an answer for it. He doesn't threaten; he doesn't cajole; he doesn't plead. But he won't take no for an answer."[4]

If there is one trademark of AFL-CIO and union lobbyists, it is their physical presence at the Capitol. Members of Congress sympathetic to labor goals never need to guess what the AFL-CIO lobbyists want them to do. There are almost always one or more of them around to make sure members know. Labor opponents express a grudging respect for this patience and willingness to stay around for hours on end. "They're alert, and they're always there," said Andrew Hare, a lobbyist for the anti-organized-labor Right-to-Work Committee. "There's so damn many of them there's always bound to be somebody on the scene. And they've got the resources to provide information on any subject."[5]

Young points out that the AFL-CIO legislative department uses the same tools of persuasion available to any lobbyist. "I can get a member's ear because I'm AFL-CIO," he said. "But that doesn't mean I get his vote. I'd better know what I'm talking about or I can't think of a single member — whether he's supposed to be in our pocket or not — that won't tell me to go to hell."

Organized labor has traditionally had a number of loyal friends in Congress. Frank Thompson, D-N.J., has been one of labor's key allies, as chairman of the Labor-Management Relations Subcommittee of the House Education and Labor Committee. Common-site picketing fell under his subcommittee's jurisdiction. Thompson has been the perennial nemesis of those who oppose labor's interests in Congress. "Thompson sponsors a bill," complained Hare of the Right-to-Work Committee in 1975, and "Thompson's subcommittee calls hearings on it. Legislation opposed by labor is ignored by the committee." Concluded Rep. John M. Ashbrook, R-Ohio, a conservative member of the committee: "It's not fair to say labor runs the committee, but it has the first leg up in influence."

In some ways, the Senate Labor and Public Welfare Committee (reorganized and renamed the Human Resources Committee in 1977) has been a more stable ally for the AFL-CIO than the House Education and Labor Committee, which in the 1970s had developed a reputation for introducing unacceptably liberal bills. The chairman of the Senate committee, Harrison A. Williams Jr., D-N.J., has been as much a labor loyalist as Reps. Thompson and Carl D. Perkins, D-Ky. (chairman of the full House Education and Labor Committee), and Republicans on the Senate committee have been much more sympathetic to labor goals than their counterparts on the House panel. Williams' labor connections are easy to document. Unions provided much of the financial help with his 1970 re-election campaign, and from January 1 through September 30, 1976, he received $125,525 from labor groups — the largest amount received by any Senate candidate. (At the same time, Williams received $69,723 from business, professional and agricultural groups, ranking ninth in Senate recipients of funds from those organizations.)[6]

The Business Roundtable

By 1975, corporate executives, working through the Business Roundtable, had begun to wield new persuasive power in Congress through direct personal involvement in lobbying.[7] Indeed, the comparatively young Roundtable, formally organized in 1974, emerged as a potent pressure group largely because of its unique mobilization of the talent and prestige of the nation's top corporate heads. The defeat of the common-site picketing bill and labor's difficulties in pushing for other labor-related legislation were attributed mainly to aggressive lobbying by the Roundtable and other business groups. *(For further details on the Roundtable, see pp. 38-39.)*

The Roundtable brings together 190 chief executive officers of major corporations, including General Motors, General Electric, Dupont, International Business Machines (IBM), and American Telephone and Telegraph (AT&T). Despite the inherent influence possessed by these Roundtable members — who collectively direct billions of dollars of the gross national product and millions of American employees — the Roundtable has succeeded in keeping a low profile. The group has not sought publicity and seldom takes officially announced positions on issues. It has not gone in for major advertising campaigns or mass mailings. Instead, the Roundtable has worked to influence legislation primarily through direct contact between its members or their corporate representatives on the one hand and Congress and the executive branch on the other.

Membership in the Roundtable requires a heavy commitment of many business executives' time, even if they rarely get to Capitol Hill. The real work of the Roundtable is done by its policy committee. This group, composed of 43 members in 1977, meets once every two months in New York City. Attendance at these meetings has been high, given the time constraints on these business leaders. At this bimonthly meeting, the members determine what their positions and legislative priorities will be. The raw material before the executives as they work through issues and arrive at a consensus is the product of more than a dozen task forces, each one chaired by a member of the policy committee.

The full contingent of 190 Roundtable members gets together only once a year. Hence, membership on the backbone policy committee is rotated annually in the interests of full participation. John Post, a former New York and Houston lawyer and businessman who was the Roundtable's executive director in Washington in 1977, and his top legislative associate, Walter Hasty, direct a small staff in a modest Washington office.

According to Post, the Roundtable's budget is about $2 million a year. That sum supports the Washington and New York offices and pays for publications, outside research and legal work. The costs of attendance by the chief executive officers at Roundtable meetings are borne by the executives and their corporations, not by the Roundtable. Each member corporation pays an annual assessment, based on the company's annual revenues and its stockholders' equities; amounts in 1978 ranged from as little as $2,600 to as much as $40,000.

One labor union spokesman noted that the Roundtable, along with other business groups in the extensive anti-common-site coalition, "hurt us badly" with the defeat of the common-site picketing proposal early in 1977. The business community's new aggressiveness forced the unions to retool their own lobbying efforts. The Roundtable has at times, however, worked *with* labor unions, notably in the intensive fight in 1977 over standards for automobile exhaust emissions and requirements for stationary pollution sources such as smokestacks contained in the Clean Air Act. On the hotly lobbied auto emissions issue, the linkage between threatened production slowdowns and feared job losses had the chief executives of the major auto companies knocking on congressional doors side-by-side with former United Auto Workers head Leonard Woodcock. *(See chapter on Clean Air Act lobbying, p. 155.)*

The U.S. Chamber of Commerce

In contrast to the Business Roundtable, the organization most consistently identified with business, the U.S. Chamber of Commerce, is huge.[8] More than 400 employees operate out of the chamber's headquarters across from the White House and around the corner from the AFL-CIO. *(For further description of the chamber, see pp. 36-37.)*

The chamber believes that "the voice of business" can be heard best in Washington by making noise in lawmakers' districts. So-called grass-roots or indirect lobbying has been the principal tool of the national chamber in dealing with Congress, and by 1975, that technique was playing a growing role in all business lobbying efforts.

General manager of the legislative action department in 1977 was R. Hilton (Dixie) Davis, a one-time newspaper editor in Tarboro, N.C., and a former FBI agent, who went to work for the chamber in 1954. He had seven assistants, three of whom, besides Davis, were registered lobbyists. There are approximately 30 standing committees, special committees, task forces and panels that generally initiate chamber policy positions. The groups have been composed largely of professionals and corporate executives, although members sometimes are drawn from university faculties.

Although much of the chamber's annual budget of approximately $13 million in 1977-78 (covering all operations except *Nation's Business* magazine) is devoted to legislative action, the chamber itself has not registered as a lobby. Nor has it filed any financial reports with the clerk of the House or the secretary of the Senate. The assistant general counsel for the chamber said that it has not felt obliged to register under existing laws. The chamber has defined lobbying strictly as direct contact with members of Congress.

"Most of our effort is designed to inform our members," Davis said. "We try to keep them informed and to keep them motivated to register their views." Grass-roots lobbying is by far the best way the chamber can get through to senators and representatives, Davis observed. "No one in this building votes for them [the lawmakers] but their constituents do."

Davis' principal objective has been to get chamber members to write their senators or representatives on any given issue, and he has four techniques for doing this:

• What he calls the "lowest key" method is the use of the legislative action operation's weekly newsletter, "Congressional Action," which is distributed to all organizational members requesting the service.

• Much more sophisticated are "action calls," a direct mail campaign to a selected audience "when issues start to reach the critical stage." An action call memorandum provides the information letter-writers would need to send detailed messages to their lawmakers.

• The next step in intensity is the distribution of a memorandum from Davis, similar in format to the "action call" but briefer and printed on a different letterhead intended to make it look even more urgent. These memos are mailed to a very small group of members, primarily those whose lawmakers' votes are critical to the outcome of the issue at hand.

• When time is extremely short and the issue deemed sufficiently vital, Davis will send out mailgrams. He said he tries to keep them to a minimum because "the cost builds up."

The national chamber has done relatively little telephone campaigning. Occasionally, the Washington office may try to contact a few influential chamber members by phone, but more often any telephone operation has been delegated to the six regional offices.

In line with this policy, the chamber has emphasized letter-writing on the part of its members, telling them to send a telegram or to telephone only when time is very short. The chamber does not try to get businessmen to visit their representatives and senators in Washington, as some other corporate and trade groups, such as the Business Roundtable, do.

"We rarely send action calls across the board," Davis said. ". . .Every member [of the chamber] isn't contacted on every issue." He said that a chamber member likely would be contacted only once or twice a year, and often might not be contacted at all except through the newsletter.

One reason the chamber has been able to be selective is the computerization of its membership lists, which are broken down by congressional districts and states. Davis and his aides need only determine which legislators hold the swing votes and the computer will churn out address labels for chamber members in those districts.

Other lobbying activities undertaken by the national chamber have included the preparation of a variety of publications and audio-visual aids. The national chamber has encouraged local and state chambers to form their own congressional action committees, and supplies them with such materials as a monthly videotaped discussion of pending legislation.

Davis also has tried to maintain a rapport with other business lobbyists in Washington. He has hosted a breakfast meeting of corporate lobbyists at chamber headquarters the first and third Thursdays of each month when Congress is in session, and a similar meeting on the first and third Wednesdays for trade association lobbyists. A member of Congress usually is invited to speak, and the status of legislation is discussed.

Few on Capitol Hill question the potential effectiveness of indirect lobbying, but the specific performance of the chamber's operation receives mixed reviews. "The chamber generates a lot of mail," Rep. John B. Anderson, R-Ill., chairman of the House Republican Conference, said in an interview. "But it's often obvious that the letters are not entirely spontaneous. . . . The lobbyists by the door are always from labor."

Right to Work Committee

Founded in 1955 to combat union attempts to repeal Section 14-b of the Taft-Hartley Act, which permits states to enact nonunion — or right-to-work — laws, the National Right to Work Committee by 1977 had quadrupled in size to a membership of 1.3 million.[9]

The volume of mail to and from the committee's headquarters in the Virginia suburbs of Washington has been so great that the Postal Service has assigned the committee its own zip code. On an average day the committee receives 4,000 to 5,000 letters. But this pales by comparison with the amount of mail the committee sends out — upwards of 46,-000 pieces each working day. The group sends 12-15 million letters a year to all parts of the country.

As the numbers suggest, the Right to Work Committee is a believer in grass-roots lobbying — using the mails to win followers and exhort them, in turn, to bring pressure on members of Congress. While it usually operated independently, the committee's campaign against common-site picketing in 1975-77 was in harmony with the other grass-roots business lobbying against the bill. Mailings from the Right to Work Committee are carefully targeted and analyzed. As Andrew Hare, the committee's chief lobbyist, put it, with that volume of mail "you can't simply dump it on the street." The organization has analyzed the response rate by almost every conceivable index: congressional district, economic status, ethnic group and, improbable as it may sound, altitude. Hare noted with some humor that people who live at higher altitudes respond to the committee better than those at lower altitudes. Rather than pick issues on which to do battle, however, Hare said the committee generally reacts to labor initiatives considered serious threats to individual freedoms.

Although a member of the business coalition against common-site picketing, the committee's president, Reed Larson, saw defeat of the bill as a special project for the Right to Work Committee, viewing the legislation as another encroachment of compulsory unionism on individual freedoms. In the fall of 1975, the committee launched a $750,000 direct mail and newspaper advertising campaign against the bill. Millions of letters went out to Right to Work Committee members and others on selected mailing lists. Each contained two postcards, one addressed to a senator urging a "no" vote on the bill and one addressed to President Ford urging a veto should the bill pass. The committee also placed full-page ads in 50 newspapers in 17 states where the votes of 34 senators from these states were seen as critical to the outcome of the fight.

"The purpose of the legislation is no secret," Larson said in a press release. "Union officials want to be able to shut down any construction project where nonunion workmen are employed. They want to turn the construction industry into a nationwide closed shop — meaning that only union members will be able to work. Anyone who would rather not join a union, or who is denied entry into a union, will have to find another trade."

The AGC and the National Action Committee

Although several influential business associations had long opposed common-site picketing legislation, it was the Associated General Contractors (AGC) that orchestrated business efforts in a successful lobbying campaign. The impetus behind the formation of the coalition came from its opposition: organized labor and its supporters in Congress.

On May 16, 1975, Rep. Thompson announced a schedule of hearings before his Labor-Management Relations Subcommittee on the common-site picketing bill, promising quick action. The next day, Richard Creighton, an assistant executive director of the AGC received a call from one of the association's directors asking him for ideas on ways to defeat the bill.[10] Creighton said later that he figured that builders and builders trades groups such as AGC and the Associated Builders and Contractors (ABC) could not win without some help. And he had seen how effective public interest groups had been in rallying support from many different organizations. Consequently, he invited the legislative representatives of 27 groups to attend a meeting on "secondary boycott legislation" on May 22, 1975. Included were:

American Concrete Pipe Association
American Farm Bureau Federation
American Institute of Architects
American Retail Federation
American Road Builders Association
American Trucking Association
Associated Builders and Contractors
Associated Equipment Distributors

Council of Construction Employes
Labor Policy Association, Inc.
Mechanical Contractors Association of America
National Asphalt Paving Association
National Association of Home Builders
National Association of Manufacturers
National Association of Plumbing-Heating-Cooling Contractors
National Crushed Stone Association
National Electrical Contractors Association
National Ready Mixed Concrete Association
National Labor-Management Foundation
National Right to Work Committee
National Small Business Association
Painting and Decorating Contractors of America
Sheet Metal and Air Conditioning Contractors
Shipbuilders Council of America
U.S. Chamber of Commerce
International Association of Wall and Ceiling Contractors
Heavy Specialized Carriers Conference

"At first," Creighton said in an interview later, "there were a lot of doubting Thomases. They said labor introduces that bill every year. Why worry? We were still slowly getting our act together when our ears were pinned back in the House." The Thompson subcommittee had finished its hearings promptly, and on July 18, the bill cleared the full committee. The legislation was set for a House vote July 25.

By that time, Creighton's colleagues were beginning to agree they had a problem. The group took on a formal name: the National Action Committee on Secondary Boycotts. It met regularly, usually in the auditorium of the AGC building in Washington. Not all participated with equal vigor, some lacking manpower, money, or interest. But the mere existence of a group provided the means to coordinate a broad-based effort.

Putting together a coalition is not easy, as Creighton discovered. Gradually he developed a theory about why coalitions fail and then set out to counter these problems in advance. He described the three major problem areas in this way.

● The "I'd love to help you, but" response. These groups say they lack either time, money, staff, or compelling interest. For them, Creighton said, you make it easy to do just a little bit — enough to stay involved and be part of a team.

● The "big ego fellows" who think their ideas are the answer to all problems. To counter this, the national action committee was limited to staff workers, not chief executive officers. There was no spokesman, and no member was more important than any other.

● The "compromisers." Creighton said the committee had to be alert to offers of minor compromises in the legislation that would lure away members and therefore weaken the group. To counter this possibility, Creighton said, the work of the committee focused on the single basic point of secondary boycotts and stayed away from details of other titles or provisions of the bill.

But it takes time to identify these problems and to put together an effective lobbying group; and in 1975, the momentum was on labor's side. Nonetheless, the anti-common-site group went to work. Led by AGC lobbyist Warren Richardson, teams were organized to try to get the construction business viewpoint out to all members of the House. Richardson's strategy in team lobbying was to ask three or four representatives from different industries (hence presenting a balanced view), armed with facts and information kits, to visit a certain number of House members to present their case. "We never used high pressure tactics," Richardson said. "No threats. The entire effort was based on information. We felt that if they understood the issue, they would vote against the bill."

1974-75: GEARING UP THE EFFORT

In 1974, President Ford and other Republicans warned that heavy Democratic gains in the November elections would result in a Congress under the domination of organized labor. Elect enough Democrats, they insisted, and George Meany (president of the AFL-CIO) might just as well be

Speaker of the House. Organized labor contributed heavily to the 1974 congressional campaigns, and Democrats, riding the crest of Watergate, swept the elections despite the warnings. Yet the labor-controlled 94th Congress never emerged.

There were some early hints, largely ignored, of fading labor influence on Capitol Hill. A basic philosophical difference began to emerge between organized labor and their traditional Democratic allies in Congress. The newly elected Democrats — younger and more independent than their predecessors — were more concerned about inflation than about labor-backed spending bills. "The freshman Democrat today is likely to be an upper-income type," said the AFL-CIO's Young, "and that causes some problems with economic issues. It's not that they don't vote what they perceive to be working-class concerns, but I think a lot of them are more concerned with inflation than with unemployment. They aren't emotionally involved in unemployment. It's a political issue, and they came down on the side that unemployment is bad, but inflation is more important to their constituents."[11]

Few would argue, however, that organized labor had won its share of battles in Congress over the years. The irony was that labor could deliver votes when working with other liberal groups on issues like the civil rights and Great Society legislation of the 1960s. But the union lobbyists were often frustrated when they turned to legislation directly concerning unions.

The unions lost in 1948 when Congress overrode President Truman's veto of the Taft-Hartley Act. They lost in 1959, when they could not prevent passage of the restrictions in the Landrum-Griffin Labor-Management Reporting Act. They lost in 1966, when the Senate failed to pass legislation repealing Section 14-b of Taft-Hartley, which permits states to enact "right-to-work" laws sanctioning a nonunion shop. And they lost in 1975 and again in 1977 in their effort to enact the common-site picketing bill.

The reason labor often failed to win on its own issues, members of Congress and lobbyists agreed, was that these bills were perceived as special interests. Labor was serving itself, not the general public interest as was seen in its support of social legislation. "We do our best when we're part of a coalition," said Young, "and you don't have a coalition on a pure labor issue."

The common-site picketing bill was just such an issue — and labor was caught somewhat off-guard. As the full House Education and Labor Committee prepared to approve the legislation (which it did on July 18, 1975), the National Action Committee on Secondary Boycotts organized a one-day "fly-in" of executives from more than 700 firms from around the country. Each was given a "Ban the Boycott" button and then dispatched in large groups to talk to representatives about the issue.

A similar strategy was employed by labor. On July 22, trade unionists were brought to Washington for their own lobbying blitz. Each was given a large brown envelope with red block letters: EQUAL TREATMENT. Inside were names of those who had cosponsored the bill, a fact sheet, a statement in support of the bill by George Meany, instructions, and a report card to be filled out after every visit. Each House member was to be listed as "for us," "against us," or "other." Lobby teams were assigned on the basis of union membership or hometown ties, so each representative would be contacted by someone in his own district.

Although the common-site picketing bill passed the House by a vote of 230-178 (R 26-107; D 204-71) on July 25, 1975, there was an important message in the vote: without some dramatic changes, labor would not have the two-thirds majority necessary to override a possible presidential veto of the measure.

With the vote over in the House, attention focused on the Senate, where the heavily prolabor Labor and Public Welfare Committee approved the picketing bill on October 29. Opponents of the legislation decided to mount a filibuster against the bill on the Senate floor. "I went to [Paul] Laxalt [R-Nev., the most conservative and junior minority member of the committee]," said AGC lobbyist Warren Richardson. "He was the only one on the committee on our side. He was somewhat apprehensive. This was not only his first term but his first year in the Senate. He was very nervous, but finally he said yes.'[12] Richardson promised Laxalt he would not be alone. Strong backup support would come from two veterans of filibustering, Senators James B. Allen, D-Ala., and Jesse A. Helms, R-N.C. And the National Action Committee on Secondary Boycotts would arm them all with pages of documents, speeches, and reports to keep the conversation going indefinitely on the Senate floor. Meanwhile, at AGC headquarters, members of the action committee were given various topics relating to the legislation to work on to deliver to the senators leading the filibuster.

After several days of debate, labor supporters broke the filibuster on November 18 with a 62-37 (R 15-22; D 47-15) vote (in the Senate, a three-fifths majority, 60, is needed to invoke cloture, or limit debate, on a bill). The bill then passed, 52-45 (R 11-25; D 41-20) — again not by the two-thirds majority required to override a veto.

The Associated Press reported November 19 that of the 62 senators who voted for cloture November 18, 26 of those who were up for election in 1974 had received campaign contributions from organized labor totaling more than $1.4 million. An aide to a senator who had been undecided on the issue but ultimately voted to cut off debate said labor "had kept the pressure on" the senator, mostly through labor people in his state. Labor had not tried to threaten the senator, the aide said, but had emphasized that it considered the common-site picketing bill to be high priority labor legislation.[13]

There were only minor differences in the versions of the bill as passed by the House and Senate. These were ironed out in a House-Senate conference committee, and both chambers passed the compromise version by votes of 229-189 (R 24-118; D 205-71) in the House and 52-43 (R 11-24; D 41-19) in the Senate in mid-December 1975. Debate on the final version of the bill centered on the question of whether the president was committed to sign the bill. Before the earlier July 25 House vote on the bill, Ford had told some Republican members of Congress he would not sign the legislation unless it was accompanied by a measure establishing a collective bargaining committee for the construction industry.

That the final version of the bill contained this provision seemed to indicate that Ford would sign the legislation. However, on December 11, House Minority Leader John J. Rhodes, R-Ariz., said, "The president is not morally, legally or any other way obligated to sign this bill." Thompson called Rhodes' opinion "sheer unadulterated sophistry."[14]

With the decision up to Ford, the bill's opponents turned their pressure on the White House, mounting an intensive postcard and letter-writing campaign estimated at 700,000 to 750,000 pieces of mail, while only 26,000 persons wrote in to support the bill. At the same time, Ford's potential opponent for the 1976 Republican presidential nomination, Ronald Reagan, came out strongly against the measure.

Chamber of Commerce President Richard L. Lesher sent Ford a personal letter emphasizing the concern of the business community. Key members of the Business Roundtable went to the White House for a meeting with Ford to underscore their position. At the same time, the AGC activated its "legislative network," a group of contacts in every state, linked by telephone. "We called five or six in the network," Richardson said, "until we found someone who would raise the issue at the White House. . . . He told Ford flat out he would not get money from the business community" for his presidential campaign if he signed the bill.[15]

On October 21, Richard Obenshain, co-chairman of the Republican National Committee, wrote to a White House adviser that signing the bill would offend some of Ford's strongest supporters without any offsetting gain: labor leaders would not be likely to choose Ford over a Democrat in 1976. The president apparently heeded the warning and vetoed the bill.

1976-77: A SECOND TRY

Labor's second attempt to win a common-site picketing bill began with the 1976 elections. As in the past, organized labor was the largest single source of campaign funds in the congressional campaigns. The unions contributed a total of $8.2 million, but business groups, spurred by a rapid growth of political action committees were not far behind, donating more than $7 million to congressional election campaigns.[16] Among the most active of labor organizations was the Building and Construction Trades Department of the AFL-CIO. Nearly 100 candidates for Congress were targeted for the building trades campaign effort. In addition to money, they provided phone bank help (where voters are telephoned and reminded to vote), buses to carry voters to the polls, and three general mailings to all building tradesmen in the particular district. For incumbent House members who had voted for common-site picketing in 1975, the pamphlets announced: "[Candidate X] has earned our support." For challengers who supported the bill from afar, the pamphlets read: "Endorsed as a Friend by Building Trades Labor, We Need [Candidate X] in Congress." Similar pamphlets were sent out endorsing candidates for the Senate.

When the returns were in, it appeared that the strategy had been successful. Labor had a Democratic president, Democrats picked up two seats in the House (for a total of 292 to 143 Republicans), and the Senate stayed at 62 Democrats and 38 Republicans. "We concluded," said Victor Kamber of the Building and Construction Trades Department, "that no member of Congress lost because of his vote on situs picketing. Four who voted for the bill lost for other reasons. Of 68 new members, 35 had gotten brochures [mailed to building tradesmen in their districts] and 50 to 55 had gotten contributions. There was no reason to believe we had any problems. . . . We won."[17]

It was this attitude — we won, therefore we have nothing to worry about — that led to labor's eventual defeat. Labor lobbyists, in their weekly strategy sessions, immediately began looking beyond the House to the Senate and the White House, figuring they would win easily in the House, face a filibuster in the Senate, and ultimately triumph at the White House (Carter had said he would sign a common-site bill).

Early in 1977, the building trades officers targeted 30 senators for mass mailings. Nearly two million letters and brochures went out to union members. Included were preprinted postcards addressed to both senators and to Carter asking for their support.

Little prolabor common-site lobbying work was done in the House, however. Everyone seemed to think someone else was taking care of what little they felt needed to be done. House Democratic leaders endorsed the bill but twisted no arms to bring reluctant troops into line. AFL-CIO and other labor lobbyists left the task to the six or seven building trades legislative representatives. Common-site picketing affected only the building trades, and organized labor, buoyed by victories in the November 1976 elections, had begun working on a long list of labor law reforms.

Throughout 1976, meanwhile, the National Action Committee on Secondary Boycotts had been somewhat dormant on common-site picketing, meeting monthly instead of weekly. For most of the member associations of the coalition, common-site picketing was only one of a number of issues concerning them in the 1976 elections. For the National Right to Work Committee, however, it was the most important issue. "We just did not let the thing die," said Hare. "We were constantly reminding our members how their congressman voted or where their local candidates stood on the issue." The committee canvassed every candidate for Congress offered by every party in every congressional district. Each was asked to take a position on common-site picketing. Special mailings went into districts where the committee felt it could have an impact.

Like labor, the business groups figured common-site picketing would pass in the House; they would make their stand in the Senate behind a filibuster. But they decided not to surrender in the House without a fight. Based on its pre-election canvasses, the Right to Work Committee produced a list of 198 House members who had indicated opposition to a common-site bill in the new Congress. Twenty more votes would give them an absolute majority of the 435-member House. Through the wide use of computers, the Right to Work Committee's mailing list, like many others, is broken down by congressional district. Thus, the group was able to focus attention on the members it wanted to influence. Special mailings went into target districts. In all, the committee sent out about two million pieces of mail, urging supporters to contact their congressman and to urge friends to do the same.

Meanwhile, the Chamber of Commerce, in its weekly Congressional Action newsletters which went to state and local chambers and trade associations, warned of the impending vote on the measure. The newsletters were followed by more explicit lobbying instructions in "Action Calls" to individuals in various congressional districts. Again, with the help of computers, different action calls went to different districts, depending on whether the congressman voted *for* the bill in 1975 ("Make a persuasive case for him [or her] to switch"), *against* it ("Make a persuasive case against Common Situs"), or was a new member of Congress ("Help him [or her] see why a NO vote is the ONLY vote").

The chamber also used the visual arts. Member groups could get a 10-minute anti-common-site slide show. A weekly radio program, "What's the Issue," prepared by the chamber and distributed to some 250 stations via Mutual Broadcasting, devoted several programs to the picketing bill before the House vote March 23.

Other business groups did their share, trying to persuade members through newsletters and magazines. The precise targeting of common-site opponents centered on the freshmen members of Congress. A National Association of Manufacturers lobbyist said that NAM had targeted 91 congressional districts for their campaign, of which 68 were represented by freshmen. The attention paid to the freshmen was based on the business groups' assessment that many of the new members were "truly open-minded, not committed on the issue," as Argyll Campbell of the Chamber of Commerce explained. A spokesman for the contractors association broke the numbers down more specifically, saying that "after the last election, it was apparent that we were pretty strong on the Hill; 25 freshmen were committed to us on this issue, and only four to labor." By Monday, March 21, Campbell estimated the freshmen were one-third for, one-third against, and one-third undecided, with the business groups confident they could still win the votes of some of the uncommitted third.[18]

On Capitol Hill, in addition to the individual efforts of member groups (by 1977, more than 100 business associations and corporations were involved in the effort), the National Action Committee on Secondary Boycotts again swung into action. Beginning in February, weekly meetings were held to plan strategy. "We divided up into teams for Hill heat," or personal lobbying of members, said one lobbyist. Hundreds of newspaper editorials opposing common-site picketing in 1975 were reprinted in a booklet handed out to members of Congress, and then each of the newspapers was contacted and urged to oppose the bill again. Included in the packet of information left in congressional offices was a copy of an economic impact statement (concluding that the bill would cause economic dislocation in every part of the country). This was the only large expense, $17,000, incurred by the coalition. (Creighton estimated that the coalition spent only $30,000 on its entire campaign; but that figure in no way reflects the total amount spent on all phases of the lobbying effort by all the various groups involved.)

Meanwhile, labor had begun to be aware of the intense business lobbying effort against the common-site picketing bill. About a month before the House vote, Daniel J. Mundy, legislation director for the building trades, brought up the issue at the weekly legislative meeting at AFL-CIO headquarters. "I'm not crying wolf," he later recalled saying. "But we're in trouble." On the eve of the vote, Mundy's report was gloomy. "Our hard count showed us not winning," he said. "Our soft count showed that we should be able to push it through — with a bit of hard work." In the lexicon of lobbyists, "hard counts" list those who support a position unequivocally; "soft counts" list those who say "maybe" or who say nothing at all.

Indeed, the freshman-targeted lobbying effort of the business community apparently paid dividends. A majority of the freshmen voting, 37 of 68, voted against the common-site bill, including 13 freshmen who were supported in the 1976 campaigns by the AFL-CIO. *(Box, p. 151)* Spokespersons from the offices of several freshmen supported by labor confirmed that the flow of mail and the personal lobbying

HOW THEY VOTED IN 1977

The March 23, 1977, 205-217 House vote to defeat the common-site picketing bill (HR 4250) showed some interesting and unusual alliances. Predictably enough, a coalition of Republicans and southern Democrats provided the main source of opposition; along with 129 Republicans, 65 southern Democrats and 23 northern Democrats voted against the bill. The supporters, as well, were regionally concentrated. Ten of the 14 Republicans voting for the bill came from the East, while 132 of the 191 Democratic supporters came from the East or Midwest.

But support for the bill had eroded considerably since the House cleared a very similar measure (HR 5900) in December 1975. Only one member, Majority Leader Jim Wright, D-Texas, joined supporters of HR 4250 after having voted against the final version of HR 5900, which former President Ford subsequently vetoed. In contrast, 15 supporters of the earlier bill voted against HR 4250. This group included:

Democrats (9): Breaux (La.), Edgar (Pa.), Ford (Tenn.), Hamilton (Ind.), McCormack (Wash.), Natcher (Ky.), Ryan (Calif.), Santini (Nev.), Ullman (Ore.).

Republicans (6): Fish (N.Y.), Goldwater (Calif.), Hillis (Ind.), Lagomarsino (Calif.), Pritchard (Wash.), Quie (Minn.).

Of the 68 newly elected members of the 95th Congress, 37 voted against the picketing measure. This group, which consisted of 19 Republicans and 18 Democrats, included 13 Democrats who received endorsements from the AFL-CIO's Committee on Political Education (COPE) during 1976 campaigns.

In many cases new members replaced representatives who had voted the opposite way on the common-site picketing issue in 1975. Sixteen new members voted against the bill in 1977; they replaced representatives who had supported the legislation in 1975. There were six switches the other way, with new members supporting the bill in contrast to their predecessors who had opposed it.

had been the most intensive yet seen by the new members and that it had played a role in determining their votes.

One labor lobbyist said that "many of the freshmen did not understand the issue, they took the scare stuff of the opposition and believed it." But if the freshmen were "ill-informed," many observers would blame an inadequate lobbying effort by labor for the bill's defeat. "I don't mean to be critical of anyone . . . they've worked awfully hard these last few days, but they may have started a few days late," said Rep. Frank Thompson, who again managed the bill in the House.[19]

"We didn't do our homework," said another labor lobbyist, listing reasons for the defeat: Democratic leaders failed to do their share; the timing was bad; common-site picketing, not easily understood in the best of times, became the first difficult vote of a new Congress and a new president; confusion reigned among prolabor groups, and, as a result, a number of congressmen were never lobbied directly; and, finally, all failed to recognize the intensity of the opposition. "We had relaxed," he said. "We thought we did the job in November. But now we know our friends have to be reminded."

CONCLUSION

The common-site picketing battle was an example of an issue that was originated and pushed by an outside lobby, a labor union, rather than by members of Congress themselves or the executive branch. Capitol Hill was the primary scene of the clash, and there was less pressure on the White House or active involvement by the executive branch than in the case of the B-1 or Clean Air Act battles (however, in 1975, it was partly due to business pressures that Ford vetoed the common-site bill).

The strategies and tactics of the pro- and anti-common-site groups were similar in many respects: the use of computers to generate grass-roots pressure in crucial districts; provision of "hard facts" to members of Congress; analyses of vote breakdowns and trends; face-to-face contact between members of Congress and group lobbyists; and last-minute lobbying "blitzes" and "fly-ins" of group representatives from the member's home district. These were the similarities; but there were also differences which, in the end, paid off for the opponents of the common-site bill. For example, knowing that it was practically a foregone conclusion that the House Education and Labor Committee would support the union and the common-site bill, the National Action Committee concentrated its efforts in 1975 on reversing the action when the bill came to the floor of the House. When labor won there, the opposition forces immediately turned to the Senate, planning to use the filibuster strategy to break the back of the legislation. At the same time, hedging their bets in the event that the tactic failed, the anti-common-site business interests put pressure on Ford to veto the bill, threatening to withdraw their financial support for his re-election campaign if he signed the legislation.

Two years later, labor thought a common-site bill was a shoo-in — at least in the House. Business interests also figured that labor would win in the House and, accordingly, they planned to concentrate their lobbying effort on the Senate. Nonetheless, while labor assumed a rather complacent attitude in expecting the House vote to go its way, the anti-common-site lobby did not surrender the House entirely. Armed with vote tallies showing a substantial number of members who were undecided about or opposed to the bill, the National Action Committee and the Right to Work Committee, as well as other groups, swung into action with their computerized mailing lists and professional lobbyists. On March 23, 1977, they could reap the rewards of their efforts.

NOTES

1. "House Rejects Labor-Backed Picketing Bill," Congressional Quarterly *Weekly Report*, March 26, 1977, p. 521.
2. *Ibid.*, p. 522.
3. *National Labor Relations Board* v. *Denver Building and Construction Trades Council* (341 U.S. 674), 1951.
4. "The AFL-CIO: How Much Clout in Congress?" Congressional Quarterly *Weekly Report*, July 19, 1975, p. 1534.
5. *Ibid.*, p. 1537.

6. Campaign contribution figures from "Interest Group Contributions to Congressional Campaigns," Congressional Quarterly *Weekly Report,* Nov. 6, 1976, p. 3137.

7. For a description of Roundtable operations, see "Business Roundtable: New Lobbying Force," Congressional Quarterly *Weekly Report,* Sept. 17, 1977, pp. 1964-68.

8. For a description of chamber operations, see "U.S. Chamber: It Speaks Through Members," Congressional Quarterly *Weekly Report,* Nov. 15, 1975, pp. 2457-63.

9. On the Right to Work Committee (as well as the labor lobby), see "Labor Lowers its Sights, Redoubles its Efforts," Congressional Quarterly *Weekly Report,* July 30, 1977, p. 1606.

10. Much of the following is derived from the author's interviews.

11. "The AFL-CIO: How Much Clout in Congress?", p. 1532.

12. Interview with the author.

13. Congressional Quarterly, *1975 Almanac* (Washington: Congressional Quarterly Inc., 1976), p. 483.

14. *Ibid.,* p. 490.

15. Interview with the author.

16. On campaign contributions, see "Interest Group Donations to Congressional Campaigns Almost Doubled in 1976," Congressional Quarterly *Weekly Report,* Feb. 19, 1977, p. 321.

17. Interview with the author.

18. Congressional Quarterly, *1977 Almanac* (Washington: Congressional Quarterly Inc., 1978), p. 124.

19. *Ibid.*

6

Clean Air Legislation:
Traditional Foes Align

One of the most intense and long-lived lobbying battles fought on Capitol Hill in the mid-1970s involved the nation's most complex and far-reaching environmental law — the Clean Air Act. Between its enactment in 1970 and passage of major amendments in 1977, the law was the focal point of a myriad of groups working either to strengthen or weaken various of its provisions. Affecting virtually all industrial and transportation activities, the production and use of energy and real estate development, the fundamental purpose of the 1970 act was to protect public health by preventing further contamination of the air.

One of the major provisions of the 1970 act required reductions in noxious automobile emissions — carbon monoxide (CO), hydrocarbons (HC) and oxides of nitrogen (NOx) — and set deadlines to achieve them. In the original act, the standards for CO and HC tailpipe exhaust emissions were to be achieved by the 1975 model year; for NOx, by 1976. However, Congress also added a provision that allowed the administrator of the Environmental Protection Agency (EPA) to allow a one-year extension of the emission deadlines. (Created in 1970, the EPA consolidated all major programs to combat pollution into a single agency.) Pressured by the insistence of the major auto companies that the 1975 and 1976 deadlines could not be met, EPA administrator William D. Ruckelshaus in 1973 extended the CO and HC deadline for one year and called on Congress to relax the NOx standards.

But pressures continued to mount. Having granted the EPA authority for only one extension, it was up to Congress to act. In 1974, Congress responded by amending the 1970 bill to extend to 1977, from 1976, the deadline for achieving CO and HC standards, and to 1978, from 1977, the NOx standards. Again, the bill gave the EPA authority to grant yet another one-year extension. And again, the EPA administrator (then Russell E. Train) March 5, 1975, stretched the deadline to 1978 model year automobiles for all three pollutants.

Meanwhile, the authorization for funding the Clean Air Act was due to expire midway through 1975. Congress filled the gap for the rest of the year through a continuing funding resolution; another appropriations bill included money to administer the act through fiscal 1976.

The issue came to a head in 1976, when comprehensive amendments to the 1970 Clean Air Act, first introduced in 1975, reached the floor of both chambers. But the bill was killed on the Senate floor by a last-minute filibuster — not over the auto emissions provisions of the bill, but over another section that would have established a new system for regulating growth in areas of the country with relatively pure air ("nondegradation"). Congress, however, extended the operations of the Clean Air Act by appropriating funds through September 1977.[1]

Without further changes in the 1970 act, as amended in 1974, the auto manufacturers were faced with achieving the emissions deadlines in 1978 model cars — or they would face fines of up to $10,000 per car (according to the law) for producing "illegal" automobiles. Industry spokesmen insisted that the standards could not be met and threatened to shut down assembly lines rather than produce "illegal" cars.

Congress was thus up against two deadlines — one legislative and one economic. Authorization for the act was due to expire in September 1977, and the auto industry had to begin producing model 1978 cars that fall; moreover, Congress was scheduled to take its annual summer recess in August.

Comparison of Auto Emissions Timetables

The following table compares the national standards and schedules for automobile exhaust pollutants considered by the 95th Congress. The standards are stated in grams per mile of hydrocarbons (HC), carbon monoxide (CO) and nitrogen oxide (NOx).

Model Year	1970 Act (PL 91-604)			Senate Bill			House Bill			Final Bill		
	HC	CO	NOx	HC	CO	NOx	HC	CO	NOx	HC	CO	NOx
77	1.5	15.0	2.0	1.5	15.0	2.0	1.5	15.0	2.0	1.5	15.0	2.0
78	.41	3.4	.4	1.5	15.0	2.0	1.5	15.0	2.0	1.5	15.0	2.0
79	.41	3.4	.4	1.5	15.0	2.0	1.5	15.0	2.0	1.5	15.0	2.0
80	.41	3.4	.4	.41	3.4	1.0	.41	9.0	2.0	.41	7.0	2.0
81	.41	3.4	.4	.41	3.4	1.0	.41	9.0	2.0	.41	3.4	1.0
82 and beyond	.41	3.4	.4	.41	3.4	1.0	.41	9.0	1.0	.41	3.4	1.0

The House and Senate had passed differing versions of the bill, with the Senate setting more stringent emissions standards and deadlines; a compromise had to be reached. Under pressure by both the White House and the automobile industry, House and Senate conferees negotiated on the legislation for eight days before reaching agreement on a compromise bill at 2:30 a.m. on August 3. President Carter signed the bill — the Clean Air Act Amendments of 1977 (PL 95-95) — into law August 7, with a promise to enforce it, particularly the controversial provisions to control automobile exhausts.[2]

When the struggle was over, most observers, including lobbyists involved in the fight, agreed that the slate tallied victories and losses for all sides. The automobile industry and the auto workers' union had succeeded in obtaining a delay in imposition of the standards, while environmentalists and the Carter administration had obtained legislation that in the long run bound auto manufacturers to producing cars that emitted significantly lower levels of noxious exhausts.

The complex issues of the Clean Air Act Amendments of 1977 acted as a magnet for lobbyists and produced one of the most intense lobbying efforts of 1977. That the bill would directly or indirectly affect almost every sector of the economy was demonstrated by the sheer number and diversity of the groups involved in lobbying on the bill and by their varied reasons for doing so. The United Auto Workers (UAW), foreign and domestic car manufacturers, auto wholesalers groups, the American Federation of Labor-Congress of Industrial Organization (AFL-CIO), the American Automobile Association, service station groups, the Highway Users Federation, the American Trucking Association, the National Automobile Dealers Association, and the National Rural Letter-carriers Association were among those interested in weakening the auto emissions standards provisions of the bill. The U.S. Chamber of Commerce, the National Association of Manufacturers, the Business Roundtable, and major electric power companies (represented by the National Association of Electric Companies) argued that the bill's provisions would impede industrial expansion and slow economic growth. And because pollution control devices on cars require lead-free gasoline (more costly to produce), the American Petroleum Institute and National Congress of Petroleum Retailers, as well as gasoline retailers groups, joined in the fight to weaken the auto emissions standards.

Despite the presence of the Business Roundtable, the Chamber of Commerce, the automobile majors, and other big business interests in fighting for weakening amendments, business was not altogether united against the stronger version supported by majorities in the House and Senate committees that drew up the legislation and by the Carter administration.

Paul G. Rogers, D-Fla., chairman of the House Commerce Subcommittee on Health and the Environment and floor manager for the bill in the House, issued a list of 58 business associations, corporations and public interest groups supporting his committee's bill. On that list were the American Retail Federation, the Building Owners and Managers Association, the Independent Gasoline Marketers, the International Council of Shopping Centers, J. C. Penney, Montgomery Ward, and Sears, Roebuck and Co. Retailers, shopping center interests and realtors were concerned that relaxation of the emissions limits for automobiles would shift the burden of cleaning the nation's air to local developers and would curb local growth. Other groups, such as auto parts manufacturers, were concerned over comparatively obscure, but to them vital, provisions such as those concerning the warranties on clean air auto equipment and who would be allowed to do warranty repair work.[3]

Finally, lobbying to uphold the standards of environmental purity against all economic considerations was the National Clean Air Coalition, which included in its membership the 85-year-old Sierra Club, the National Audubon Society, Common Cause, Ralph Nader's Public Interest Research Group, the American Lung Association, numerous local citizens' clean air groups, the League of Women Voters, Friends of the Earth, Environmental Action, and the Oil, Chemical and Atomic Workers Union. The Governors Conference, United Mine Workers, American Medical Association and various public health groups, National League of Cities/U.S. Conference of Mayors, and the Automotive Parts and Accessories Association also lobbied on behalf of the stronger version of the bill.

Because of the complexity of the 400-page bill, this chapter focuses on the lobbying on only one major provision of the legislation: the auto emissions standards established by the act.

BACKGROUND

The precursor to the 1977 Clean Air Act legislation — the Clean Air Act of 1970 — was one result of a growing interest in controlling pollution of the nation's natural resources — air, water and land. Indeed, by the late 1960s, the concern about the environment expressed for years by scientists and conservationists had spread to the general public. From the industrialized megalopolis along the eastern seaboard from Boston to Washington, D.C., to the oil-blackened beaches of Santa Barbara, California, individual citizens were being affected by and alarmed about the environmental emergency. Popular interest in ecology (a word that suddenly entered the political lexicon) was highlighted on April 22, 1970, with the celebration of "Earth Day." Millions of Americans attended environmental teach-ins and participated in antipollution protests and various cleanup projects, all under the green and white banner of the new ecology flag. Congress adjourned for the day while members addressed rallies throughout the nation.

The race to clean up America had begun, and the mood was one of urgency and commonality of interest — after all, who could be against the environment? And, as usually happens when an idea begins gathering support, people were coming together to share information and experiences. Groups, some formal, some informal, were formed to publicize various aspects of the issue. Existing groups were drawn in, expanding their interests to take on a new problem. The dire warnings of the experts, coupled with results of the latest public opinion polls, were not lost on the White House or Congress. Both political parties embraced the environment as a potentially explosive issue which no longer could be accorded back-seat treatment. By 1970, conservation — once the concern of garden clubs, bird watchers, and wilderness lovers — had become a rallying point for a disparate group of adherents cutting across state, party, ideological, and age lines. "Conservation is really one cause that no politician can take a stand against," said an aide to Senator Gaylord Nelson, D-Wis., a prominent conservation spokesman in the Senate. "We get practically unlimited support from groups that disagree with Senator Nelson on every other issue except protection of the environment."[4]

For the Democrats, environment joined Vietnam and the economy as primary issues. Nelson and Senator Edmund S. Muskie, D-Maine, then (in 1970) considered the frontrunner for his party's 1972 presidential nomination, formed a nucleus of Democratic Party opposition to the Nixon administration, centered around the environment crisis. Nixon countered Muskie and Nelson on January 1, 1970, by signing into law an environmental quality bill that created a three-man Council on Environmental Quality and by announcing that the 1970s "absolutely must be the years when America pays its debt to the past by reclaiming the purity of its air, its waters and our living environment. It is literally now or never."[5]

Emphasis on the Environment

With the sudden emphasis on the environment, the older conservation movement began to change, becoming larger, more sophisticated, wealthier, and more militant. The growth in membership was illustrated by the Sierra Club, founded in 1892 and one of the oldest and most prominent of conservation groups. Based in San Francisco, the club's membership increased from 15,000 to 85,000 in the 1960s. By 1977, it had 180,000 members.

A number of new organizations also appeared. An internal struggle within the Sierra Club in the spring of 1969 culminated in the ouster of the club's executive director, David Brower, who had advocated militant activities many club officials found unacceptable. Brower and some friends quickly organized a new group called Friends of the Earth (FOE) in mid-September 1969, along with a politically oriented subsidiary, the League of Conservation Voters.

"We'll be politically active — intervening in campaigns of office-holders and office-seekers . . . all the way from local fights to the presidency," Brower said. "Conservation needs this kind of muscle . . . and it hasn't had it before."[6] By 1977, FOE had about 25,000 members, who paid $25 in annual dues, and a Washington lobbying staff of six.

More militant than FOE were other new groups such as Ecology Action, Ecology Center, and Zero Population Growth. Staffed by young activists, many of them college students who had participated in civil rights and anti-Vietnam War protests, the new organizations had a marked influence on the older, established conservation groups such as the Sierra Club and the equally large National Audubon Society.

Another new lobbying group growing out of Earth Day in 1970 was Environmental Action. By 1977, the organization had more than 15,000 members, a sophisticated, magazine-style "newsletter," and a reputation for aggressive lobbying. "We wanted to be a bit more radical than others," said lobbyist Phillip Michael. Building on a base of "Earth Day" activists, Environmental Action was able to play an important role in generating support for strong antipollution legislation.

For conservationists, the new emphasis on the environment was accompanied by added problems and new directions. To present the conservationist case, the emotional appeal for aesthetic beauty no longer sufficed; technical knowledge and scientific evidence were needed. Many of the new offspring of environmental publications, for instance, no longer contained color photographs of the Everglades, Big Sur, the Colorado River, or Grand Canyon. Instead, their pages were replete with columns of complicated formulae, charts and graphs, and highly technical articles pointing out the physical dangers and economic losses of pollution.

In addition to the growing number of environmental groups, their political activism and emphasis on technical expertise, the environmental lawsuit was beginning to play an important role not only in blocking individual encroachments on the environment but also in provoking the legislative and executive branches of government into action.

Among those actions in 1970 were creation of an independent Environmental Protection Agency (the EPA) and passage of a Water Quality Improvement Act establishing liability for cleanup costs of oil spills — as well as enactment of the Clean Air Act (PL 91-604), which built on a law enacted in 1963. The $1.1 billion, three-year program sailed through the House 374-1 and the Senate 73-0. The bill was signed into law by President Nixon December 31, despite his disapproval of congressional deadlines on auto emissions controls. (Both the Nixon administration and the automobile industry had wanted Congress to allow the EPA administrator to set those deadlines.)

Energy vs. Environment?

At the same time that Congress was passing unprecedented environmental legislation, the energy shortage was emerging as a counter problem. By the middle of the decade, the drive to stop pollution, which came to resemble a national crusade in the aftermath of "Earth Day" 1970, was running head-on into not only energy shortages but rising inflation, spreading unemployment, and deepening recession as well. Cleaning up the environment and getting the economy back on its feet began to be regarded by many as mutually exclusive. Industry officials — and sometimes labor spokesmen as well — found many conflicts between the move toward stiffer federal environmental controls on the one hand, and the demand for increased energy production and economic growth on the other.

The Republican administrations and Democratic-controlled Congresses of 1973-76 lent an increasingly sympathetic ear to arguments against new environmental regulations and in favor of relaxing some already in force. After he became president in August 1974, Gerald R. Ford offered few initiatives in the area and was similarly disposed to side with industry in clashes over environmental issues. "I pursue the goal of clean air and pure water, but I must also pursue the objective of maximum jobs and continued economic progress," Ford said in 1975, arguing that expensive pollution controls fueled both inflation and unemployment. "Unemployment is as real and sickening a blight as any pollutant that threatens the nation."

Environmentalists, in response, contended that pollution control expenditures represented only a small percentage of overall industry outlays, and that the expenditures actually increased employment in the nation as a whole. Acknowledging that the environmental movement sometimes had been insensitive to the needs and views of working people, some of its leaders sought to forge an alliance with labor unions and community groups on the premise that they had many common interests. Nevertheless, environmental groups and labor interests clashed on many issues, as evidenced by the United Auto Workers alliance with the automobile industry in 1976 and 1977 in its successful opposition to the auto pollution cleanup timetable supported by the environmentalists.

When the arguments against environmental protection proposals were based primarily on energy considerations, environmentalists responded that there was no reason to make pollution control efforts a "scapegoat" of the energy crisis. They argued in favor of strict energy conservation measures and increased attention to developing measures that would cut down on the pollution effects of using coal as a plentiful source of energy, while opposing or urging caution in the development of nuclear energy facilities and other large-scale energy projects with potential for creating environmental disasters.

Environmental activists often found themselves in the mid-1970s fighting a holding action to preserve the hard-won gains of earlier years. This defensive position, and their growing awareness of the complexity of environmental problems, made environmentalists more receptive to compromise on some issues. Environmental lobbyists became more adept at dealing with Congress, and public interest lawyers continued to play a major role in enforcement of environmental laws through court suits.

1974 Changes in the Clean Air Act

Responding to the national energy crisis and the government's decision to strive for reduced dependence on foreign energy sources (the oil-producing Arab nations had imposed an embargo on oil shipments to the United States on October 18, 1973), Congress made the first substantial changes in the Clean Air Act in 1974. Among other things, the 1974 bill — partly acknowledging the fact that automobile pollution control devices increased gasoline consumption — delayed final auto emission standards a second time. At the same time, the Clean Air Act program was extended for one more year, thus enabling Congress to put off a complete review of the act until 1975 and to sidestep a series of controversial Clean Air amendments proposed by the Nixon administration in March. But the holding pattern in fact continued through 1975 and 1976.

THE GROUPS INVOLVED

Three major groups were involved in the 1977 legislative battle over the auto emissions standards of the Clean Air Act. On the one hand, an unusual alliance of labor and business — the United Auto Workers, the "big four" auto manufacturers, and an association of 21,000 auto dealers — teamed up to dilute the auto pollution standards. They faced a coalition of environmental groups formed to lobby together solely to protect the standards established by the original 1970 act. The third contender in the battle was the Carter administration, which found itself on the losing side on the key auto emissions deadline issue when it passed the House but was more successful in the Senate and with the final compromise bill.

The Clean Air Coalition

In 1973 and 1974, when Congress began considering the first changes in the 1970 Clean Air Act, no one environmental group was lobbying solely on that legislative issue. In September 1973, however, a young man named Rafe Pomerance who was anxious to see a coordinated lobbying effort come into being to try to hold the 1970 act together, organized a meeting with several others interested in protecting the act.[7] Pomerance had been working with the Urban Environment Conference, an urban problems study group established in 1971. On September 27, 1973, Pomerance and representatives of the Sierra Club, United Steelworkers, League of Women Voters, and the American Public Health Association, among others, released a statement that read:

> "Now that the deadlines for meeting the air quality standards are approaching and the attainment of the goals set forth by Congress are in reach, many in industry and government are calling for a major weakening of the act, citing reasons such as . . . excessive economic costs, unavailable control technology, and the energy crisis."

"We must," said Pomerance at the time, "bring the issue before the American people and make them aware of what's going on and what we think about it." A memorandum set out the coalition's program and strategy: "The coalition will work to focus the attention of the nation on the need to implement and enforce the provisions of the Clean Air Act. This will be done by working with local, state, and national organizations in order that continuing public support for clean air can be expressed most effectively. . . ."

By November 1973, the coalition was in operation, working out of a desk at Urban Environment Conference offices. By then, other groups had joined in, including Ralph Nader's Public Interest Research Group *(see p. 48)*, the American Lung Association, and the National Wildlife Federation. In the first days of the coalition's existence, dozens of letters were sent to groups and individuals who might be interested in the Clean Air Act. "The Federal Clean Air Act is in danger, and with it, prospects for clean air in this decade. . . . The coalition will lobby to defend the strong provisions of the act. It will serve as a two-way clearing house for information on the clean air issue and the current legislative situation. It will coordinate the efforts of member organizations to make the most effective use of our collective resources."

The first letter was followed by memos and, finally, directions: "What to do right now." People were urged to contact members of the House and Senate committees working on the legislation, contact their own senators and representatives, and pass the word to others to do the same.

Although the coalition operated on low budgets of between $20,000 and $30,000 a year, gathered mostly in contributions from member groups (Pomerance's salary was paid by Friends of the Earth), it could draw on personnel and equipment from interested, well-established organizations. Through the coalition, Pomerance could reach thousands of people known to be concerned about environmental issues because they paid dues to some permanently established groups. Whenever there was a need to stimulate grass-roots pressure, member groups were contacted and they, in turn, alerted their members through magazines, newsletters, and action calls. The membership figures give an idea of the potential clout of such tactics:

> Environmental Action, 15,000 members.
>
> Common Cause, 250,000 members.
>
> League of Women Voters, 140,000 members.
>
> Friends of the Earth, 20,000 to 25,000 members.
>
> Sierra Club, 180,000 members.
>
> National Audubon Society, 375,000 members.
>
> Oil, Chemical and Atomic Workers, 177,000 members.

Citizen activity requires some well organized prodding. The coalition developed a field organization, starting with a list of about 150 active environmentalists around the country who could be called on to act swiftly. Each would be asked to contact a dozen or so fellow activists who, in turn, would contact others — until a sizable turnout was produced.

In addition to generating grass-roots pressure, the coalition mimeographed almost daily bulletins during the clean air debate in 1976 and 1977, distributing them to congressional staff assistants. The bulletins contained medical research on illness and deaths attributable to foul air and automotive research data to buttress the argument that Congress must not ease up on clean air goals.

"Lobbying," said Pomerance, "is a reflection of organized power, not unorganized power, and that's the weakness of it. Those with the greatest economic resources can win. . . . But there are [215] million people who breathe auto emissions and are concerned about air. How do these people get representation when there is no easily available means for them to be organized?"

The Automobile Companies

General Motors is one of the wealthiest corporations in the country, the world's largest automobile manufacturer and the second biggest single employer in the United States (after American Telephone and Telegraph) — and yet, GM had no lobbying office in Washington until 1969. Seven years later, GM's lobbying effort on the Clean Air Act was carried on by only one man, William C. Chapman, an automotive engineer and retired Navy officer.

The Ford Motor Company had one lobbyist in Washington in the early 1950s. The lobbying staff expanded to two in 1958: Wayne H. Smithey, a former aide on the Senate Judiciary Committee, and Robert W. Smith, who formerly worked for the chairman of the subcommittee that handled the Clean Air Act in the House. The third largest auto company, Chrysler, had no lobbyist in Washington until 1970, when Phillip Buckminster, a corporate vice president, was sent from Detroit.

"It took them," one industry spokesman said, "a long time to wake up to the facts of life." Indeed, by the mid-1970s, the Washington lobbying scene had undergone a substantial transformation. In the 1950s and 1960s, it had been easier for one or two people to do the lobbying chores for a giant corporation. "If you could persuade a [committee] chairman or a ranking minority member, that's about all you had to do," explained Smithey. "And in the House, the Rules Committee was more powerful, so you could always try to control the flow of legislation through contacts with that committee."[8] A few phone calls and a couple of taxi rides could do the job. Capitol Hill was ruled by legislative barons, most of them quite senior, quite conservative, and generally friendly with industry.

By the mid-1970s, however, it was clear that lobbying tactics would have to change in response to changes in congressional procedures and the weakening of both the seniority system and the power of committee chairmen. Congressional committees began opening the doors of their working sessions, called "markups," to public view. For lobbyists, this meant spending long hours in hearing room chairs. "Open markups give us somewhat more insight, I guess," said William Chapman of GM. "But they're also a vulgar waste of time. You sit there for eight hours and maybe 10 minutes of it is worthwhile. It detracts from our ability to be effective elsewhere because you're nailed to the damn thing for weeks on end. Under the old system, a couple of staff guys sympathetic to you would tell you what went on. So you'd get it secondhand, but in minutes instead of hours."[9]

Pomerance, Chapman's adversary on the clean air legislation, agreed that attending open markup sessions was a drain on lobbyists' time. But he said that he found the sessions useful. "The best thing about markups, the reason I attend them religiously, is that you pick up the nuances of each member's thinking. You don't get that from their public statements and public postures. You see who's articulate, who's respected, who isn't, how the dynamics work. When you know how they really think, it's much easier to affect their thinking. We used to operate in the blind."[10]

Besides internal changes in rules and procedures in Congress, corporate lobbying on Capitol Hill had to respond to the appearance of new public interest groups — Nader, Common Cause, the environmentalists — which were active with postcards, letters, telephone calls, and direct lobbying. With the increasing power of these groups, business leaders began to realize that their own lobbying efforts would have to be altered to reflect changing times. Criticism had been voiced, both within the industry and within Congress, that business was failing to present its own case effectively. "The automobile industry has drug its feet in the past and has not shown the kind of leadership they ought to," commented Senator Lloyd M. Bentsen, D-Texas.[11]

Other Automobile Groups

Even though slow to learn the changing ways of Washington, the automobile industry was not without help in the clean air battle. In one of the smallest national trade associations, the Motor Vehicle Manufacturers Association (MVMA), the industry had a constant friend on the scene. The MVMA was formed in 1972 out of the Automobile Manufacturers Association; the change from "automobile" to "motor vehicles" reflected more accurately the membership of the organization, which includes truck and bus manufacturers. There are 11 members; each pays dues based on size. The annual budget is about $10 million for a Washington staff of 28.

Like most trade associations, the MVMA looks out for its members' interests, monitoring legislation, filing reports and analyses and occasionally testifying on behalf of the entire industry at congressional hearings. With so small a constituency, however, the MVMA is careful not to offer opinions until a consensus has formed among members. During the years 1970-1977, the MVMA acted primarily as an information coordinator for the big four auto lobbying effort on the clean air legislation.

Another helpful friend to the automakers was one of the larger trade associations, the men and women who sell the cars — The National Automobile Dealers Association (NADA). It was formed in 1917 to fight auto excise taxes, and by the mid-1970s, it had 21,000 members and a Washington legislative staff of eight, working under executive vice president Frank McCarthy, a former House Rules Committee aide. In the clean air fight, men and women from the nation's auto dealerships were to become as well organized as the environmentalists. Automobile dealers, after all, are found in every congressional district; many are important members of the business community, and soon they began to offer advice on politics as well as auto sales. In mid-1976, NADA sent separate letters to each of its 21,000 dealer members, urging personal contacts with vacationing House members. The tactic was repeated in 1977. "Dealers are very effective lobbyists," said David Hunt, a NADA Washington lawyer. "They are important members of the local community. They serve on hospital boards, lead charity drives. Many are active in local politics and know their congressman by his first name. They tend to be outgoing, friendly, They're salesmen. So it's not surprising that they do a good job."[12]

In addition to auto dealers, other groups interested in altering the Clean Air Act began to see the wisdom of working together with the auto industry and UAW. This coalition, said Richard F. Turney, "formed out of necessity. There was no conscious putting together." Turney, a lobbyist in the law firm of Courtney and McCamant, represented the Automotive Service Industry Association (ASIA), a trade organization of 7,000 firms that manufacture and distribute automotive parts. They were interested in only one section of the proposed amendments to the act, a provision that would require the major automakers to provide five-year, or 50,000-mile, warranties on all new cars. Turney argued that the provision would wipe out the after-market parts industry. Commenting on the impact of working together, Turney said, "In 1976, I fought alone. In 1977 . . . many of our interests were similar. They brought some votes to me I wouldn't have had and I brought some votes to them they certainly wouldn't have had."[13]

The United Auto Workers

Many observers of the 1975-77 clean air battle agree that the automobile industry could not have won its emission standards delay without the help of the UAW. But, having suffered repeated defeats at the hands of environmentalists in previous years, the auto industry by 1975 could draw on the arguments of jobs and energy to support its case. The industry claimed that pollution-control devices increased the price of new cars, causing a drop in auto sales and, consequently, laying thousands of workers off their jobs. The industry also argued that antipollution devices increased gasoline consumption, contributing to the energy shortage.

These arguments attracted the attention of UAW President Leonard Woodcock, who has been described as "the labor personality most admired by many congressional Democrats."[14] "The auto companies," said Leon Billings, staff chief of the Muskie subcommittee, "never got to first base in persuading Congress to relax auto-emission standards

171

until they got the support of the UAW on the issue of jobs. The UAW has credibility up here that the auto companies don't."[15]

Woodcock had supported industry in its request for a five-year delay on final emission standards. But labor and management differed on other provisions of the legislation that were aimed at forcing industry to develop the technology for cleaner and more efficient cars. Traditional enemies, the UAW and the industry management were inching closer together, however; and in 1977, they would form a coalition to counter the clean air coalition.

The seeds of the industry-labor detente were sown in January 1973, when Muskie invited Woodcock to have lunch with him and Leon Billings. Industry spokesmen were saying they could not meet the emission standards, said Muskie. Were they telling the truth? "I hadn't any notion of whether they were telling the truth or not," Woodcock said in an interview later. "So we sought out someone with professional standing to go in and take a look at the problem. . . . We spent the whole period of 1973 examining it."[16]

Jarred by the Arab oil embargo and its threat of reduced gasoline supplies and higher gasoline prices, Woodcock and Professor David R. Ragone from the University of Michigan put together a five-part program in the spring of 1974 that would have given industry its five-year pause in emission standards, but only if automakers put more money into research, demonstration models for the most rigid standards, and the search for greater fuel economy. The proposal was significant for what it was saying to the American people — that the powerful UAW, in the forefront among unions on most environmental issues, felt industry deserved a break if it would only show strong good faith in moving toward the ultimate goals of the Clean Air Act. "We went to the [Nixon] administration with the five-point program" Woodcock said. "I started with George Shultz, who was then at Treasury.[17] I've known George for years, so anytime I want to do business with the administration, I usually go through him. . . . Of course, the only thing they were responsive to was the pause." The same was true of the Ford administration.

The problem changed with the election of Carter. The new president had often consulted the labor leader during the 1976 campaign; but on the issue of the Clean Air Act, Carter and Woodcock would not be on the same side. Carter supported stiffer auto emission standards than those favored by the UAW leader.

The intensity of the union's commitment to weaker emission control standards than those in the Clean Air Act as it came to the floor of the House was underlined in a letter from Woodcock to the White House February 3, 1977. In it, Woodcock listed the emission standards the UAW was backing and emphasized that the UAW standards were not negotiable. Woodcock personally underscored his commitment to the UAW position during discussions over naming him envoy to the People's Republic of China. Woodcock told a reporter May 25, "I sent word to the White House that if this position was a problem for them, then to forget about my being an envoy. . . . There was no question of my changing my position."[18]

Howard Paster, the UAW legislative liaison man in Washington, said he contacted "large numbers of people on the [House] Commerce Committee" when the bill was before it. As the House was debating the bill during the week of May 23, the UAW brought to Washington ten union officials from around the country to spend two days lobbying on Capitol Hill.

The Administration

In addition to the environmentalists and the UAW-industry coalition, there was a third contender in the 1977 clean air battle: the Carter administration (the Ford administration had generally supported the auto industry's position in 1976). President Carter had spoken out emphatically for a strong clean air bill. His administration concentrated its lobbying on the emissions section, the bill's most vulnerable point.

When the legislation came up in 1977, the man to step in and direct the White House lobbying effort on behalf of a strong clean air bill was Charles S. Warren, who had been chief legislative aide to Senator Jacob K. Javits, R-N.Y., and was hired by the Carter administration as congressional liaison for the Environmental Protection Agency. Although Warren was not due to move from Capitol Hill to the White House until June 1, 1977, he was pressed into service ahead of time to help Carter work on the clean air legislation.

Warren's operation differed little from the work of other lobbyists, although he had the substantial advantage of the prestige and backing of the White House. There were strategy sessions, phone calls to Capitol Hill offices to make preliminary vote counts, talks with reporters about news stories, and decisions on timing, such as when to release letters of support for a strong bill from White House consumer adviser Esther Peterson and a later one from the president himself. Personal meetings with members of Congress were arranged whenever it was considered necessary or useful. Before the May 26, 1977, House vote on the bill, Warren and White House staff members tried to set up as many meetings as possible between House members and the president. But Carter was away part of the time. There is no easy way to lobby all 435 members of the House. As Warren said, "They are an unwieldy group."

Some critics of the White House lobbying effort questioned the impact of personal phone calls from President Carter. They noted that the president had called three Commerce Committee members to urge their support of a strong auto emissions provision. But when the committee voted on the provision, the three opted in favor of the weaker emissions standards and a delay in imposing them.

1975-76: DEADLOCK ON CLEAN AIR

Congressional consideration of an extension of and modifications in the 1970 Clean Air Act stretched from 1975 to 1977 and represented the first comprehensive revision of the legislation. By 1975, affected industries — auto, steel, electric utilities, and many others — were calling for further modifications in the act to take account of energy shortages and related economic problems such as unemployment and inflation. Environmentalists resisted those appeals and insisted that new evidence about the effects of air pollution on human health made strict enforcement of the law more important than ever.

In an energy bill sent to Congress in January 1975, the Ford administration proposed a series of Clean Air Act amendments that were in line with many of the industry objectives. Among other things, the administration's amendments would have delayed imposition of final auto emission standards for five years (until 1982).

After about a year of hearings and drafting sessions chaired by Senator Edmund S. Muskie, D-Maine, of the Senate Public Works Environmental Pollution Subcommittee, the full panel reported its version of the Clean Air Act amendments on March 29, 1976. The committee bill provided for slightly relaxed, but still tough, auto emission standards and deadlines, and the Senate passed it August 5, 78-13, after rejecting all attempts to weaken or strengthen it.

Meanwhile, on the House side, the Subcommittee on Health and the Environment began drafting its own clean air bill in the spring of 1975. The full Interstate and Foreign Commerce Committee reported it a year later, on May 15, 1976. The committee bill postponed final auto emission standards, then targeted for 1978 model cars, until 1980 for CO and HC and 1981 for NOx (the NOx standards could be waived for four years). The Senate bill, on the other hand, imposed the standards in 1979 and 1980, respectively.

The House began general debate on its bill in early August 1976; but it was then set aside for over a month and finally was passed 324-68 (R 93-38; D 231-30) on September 15. In passing the bill, the House adopted an auto-industry-backed amendment co-sponsored by John D. Dingell, D-Mich. — who represents the district in which the Ford Motor Company headquarters is located — and James T. Broyhill, R-N.C., that delayed the emission standards until 1982. The amendment was adopted by a vote of 224-169 (R 107-27; D 117-142).

House-Senate conference negotiations to compromise the varying emissions deadlines and other differences in the two bills began September 22 and ended near midnight September 29. The sessions were often tense, with members interrupted constantly for floor votes and repeated suggestions from some to abandon the bill in favor of a simple one-year extension of auto controls, so that differences could be ironed out in the next Congress.

The sessions were held in small Capitol conference rooms that could not accommodate the crowds of lobbyists who wanted to watch. Much of the work actually was accomplished in separate House and Senate caucuses, which were not open to the press or public. The auto emissions provision finally agreed on by the conferees was closer to the Senate's tighter schedule.

But the compromise bill never came to the House floor: it was killed October 1 by a last-minute Senate filibuster led by Jake Garn, R-Utah, over provisions barring pollution of generally clean areas such as national parks. In the end, however, the bill was killed as much by the Ford administration and the auto industry as it was by the filibuster. Industry and White House spokesmen had backed away from the bill at the last minute, making all attempts at breaking the filibuster hopeless. The four major automobile manufacturers issued statements opposing the compromise bill on grounds that the 1979-80 deadlines were economically and scientifically impossible to meet. The bill's defeat left them with the timetable in the existing law, imposing strict emission limits for all three tailpipe pollutants on model 1978 cars.

Industry spokesmen were confident that with the help of the UAW they could convince Congress to grant them an extension early in 1977. Senator Muskie vowed he would not help that effort.

"The industry has dragged its feet for 13 years, every step of the way, and now when they see the chance, in the closing hours of Congress, to block a bill . . . they are taking it," Muskie declared. "If they think they can come back in the early months of next year and get a quick fix from the Senate to make them legal, they better take a lot of long, careful thoughts about it."[19]

The auto companies already had begun the process of certifying the engines for model 1978 cars based on their expectation that Congress would relax the emission requirements. "They can close the plants, put someone in jail — maybe me — but we're going to make [1978] cars to 1977 standards," said General Motors president E.M. Estes.[20]

1977: PASSAGE OF THE BILL

With the defeat of a clean air bill in 1976, pressure intensified on the new 95th Congress to come up with some kind of anti-air pollution measure. The manufacturers insisted that the existing tailpipe emission standards could not be met. As the 1978 model cars were readied for production in 1977, industry leaders threatened to shut down their assembly lines rather than produce "illegal" cars subject to fines of up to $10,000 each under the existing requirements.

The two principal sponsors of the legislation, Senator Muskie and Representative Rogers, began working on the Clean Air Act amendments early in 1977. Full-scale hearings, though shorter than in 1975-76, were held by Muskie's Environment and Public Works Subcommittee on Environmental Pollution and by Rogers's Interstate and Foreign Commerce Subcommittee on Health and the Environment.

The House acted first. The Commerce Committee reported its version of the bill May 12. The bill included the Carter administration's recommended schedule for auto emissions announced April 18 that called for meeting the statutory provisions established in the 1970 bill but at a slower pace. Backed by Rogers, the committee wrote them into its bill despite protests from Dingell and Broyhill who supported industry and UAW demands for more relaxed standards and longer delays.

The bill came to the House floor May 24. On May 26, Dingell and Broyhill introduced their amendment containing the UAW-industry-supported auto emissions package. During each roll call, the corridors leading to the House floor were chaotic, jammed with lobbyists. House members had to pick their way through a small forest of upturned and

PROVISIONS OF THE 1977 ACT

In its major provisions, the Clean Air Act Amendments of 1977 did the following:

● Delayed existing standards for automobile emissions for two years, from 1977, to 1978 and 1979, but tightened standards for the 1980 models and again for 1981.

● Set new standards to protect clean-air areas, including national parks, but authorized variances and some development near such areas.

● Extended the deadline for cities to meet national air quality standards until 1982, and in some cases until 1987. The previous deadline was 1977.

● Gave most industrial polluters up to three more years to comply before facing heavy fines.

● Directed the Environmental Protection Agency (EPA) to review criteria for ambient air quality standards before 1981 and required subsequent reviews every five years thereafter.

● Provided for continuing research into the effects of various substances and activities on the stratospheric ozone layer, and authorized EPA to regulate such substances.

● Established a National Commission on Air Quality.

● Required more than a dozen studies concerning air pollution.

downturned thumbs, the traditional lobbying signal. The Dingell-Broyhill weaker emissions amendment finally passed, 255-139 (R 105-21; D 150-118).

Meanwhile, the Senate Public Works Committee unanimously reported its bill May 4, with a timetable for auto emission standards that was in part faster than the Carter administration's proposal. But Senate floor debate on the bill did not take place for over a month. When it did, the auto industry, which had had its way in the House, was rebuffed. By a vote of 56-38 (R 15-22; D 41-16), the Senate June 9 passed a compromise auto emissions provision, offered by Minority Leader Howard H. Baker Jr., R-Tenn., and supported by Muskie and the administration, that delayed the timetable somewhat but followed the stricter emissions requirements in the bill reported by the Public Works Committee. An amendment similar to the Dingell-Broyhill provision adopted by the House was offered by the two senators from the auto industry's home state, Democrat Donald W. Riegle Jr. and Republican Robert P. Griffin, but it went down to defeat.

Lobbying by the car manufacturers, the UAW and business interests, and environmentalists was just as intense in the Senate as it had been two weeks earlier in the House. Gary Hart, D-Colo., one of the leaders in the fight to maintain strict antipollution regulations, described the reception room off the Senate floor as "wall-to-wall lobbyists." Charles H. Percy, R-Ill., said he would be glad when the car emissions vote was over, "so the automobile executives can get back to running their companies and the union leaders can get back to their unions."

There appeared to be several reasons for the auto industry and UAW's relative failure to defeat the bill drawn up by the Senate Public Works Committee. One was the dominance in the Senate debate of Muskie, floor leader for the bill and principal author of the 1970 act. Muskie had a unified committee behind him, and his influence was strengthened because he was also chairman of the Budget Committee. The Carter administration also appeared to be more effective in supporting the Senate bill, and the private environmental interests were better prepared to lobby for the Senate bill than they had been when the measure went to the House floor.

The House-Senate conference to work out a compromise between the two versions of the bill was slow to get started. But once it began, and as pressure for an agreement increased (Congress was scheduled to recess August 5), the conference moved steadily toward a decision. The auto emissions provision was the most hotly debated issue of the conference and the last to be settled. It did not come up until July 29, and most bargaining took place during the night sessions of August 1 and 2, when agreement was reached to extend the existing standards for two years, through the 1979 models, but to tighten them in 1980 and 1981.

As had happened in 1976, the conference took place under difficult circumstances, only one of which was pressure to set new automobile standards. Both chambers were busy with other bills needing action before the recess. The most difficult session was the final marathon the night of August 2-3. The large committee room in the Rayburn House Office Building was filled with lobbyists, reporters, and visitors, most of whom stayed until after 2 a.m. It was hot, and tempers flashed before the long conference ended. Both chambers approved the compromise bill by voice votes August 4.

THE 1977 LOBBY EFFORT

Lobbying on the Clean Air Act in 1977 was just as intense as it had been in 1976 — perhaps even more intense. Probably the key figure in the effort to enact somewhat weaker auto emissions standards and a longer timetable for compliance was UAW's Woodcock. Early in 1977, Woodcock met individually with the four auto company presidents, presenting the case for a bill developed by experts consulting for the union.[21] On February 4, Woodcock and the company executives met in a group with Carter on the auto emissions subject. The automakers had not yet decided whether to ally with Woodcock, perhaps because they were waiting for Carter to announce the administration's position. After the meeting, Woodcock sent identical letters to Carter and Muskie: "Adoption of revised automobile emission standards is an urgent requirement."

Meanwhile, Riegle (who had just been elected to the Senate from Michigan after five terms in the House) and Dingell (representing Michigan's 16th District in Detroit) — working separately — were concerned over the crisis situation that seemed to be developing. "They had a pressing problem that had to be solved," Riegle said later of the industry position.

Meeting with Woodcock and UAW experts in the days before the new 95th Congress convened, Dingell and Riegle agreed on a common position on the auto emissions provision, which would be cosponsored by Broyhill in the House and Griffin in the Senate. When on March 1, Woodcock,

Dingell, Broyhill, Riegle and Griffin unveiled their plan at a Capitol Hill press conference, it still was not clear where industry stood. Testifying earlier in the Senate, representatives of each automaker had said they favored even weaker standards. However, according to UAW lobbyist Howard Paster in a later comment: "Dingell and Riegle accepted [the UAW proposal] . . . as being sound and chose to introduce the legislation. The companies had no place else to go." Also joining in the informal coalition were other groups, including automobile dealers and parts manufacturers, whose lobbyists were in almost daily contact with one another. There was an unstated agreement that no one of them was likely to be successful working alone; although their interests varied somewhat, there was a "trade-off factor," and mutual help could produce results.

The industry-union alliance that formed around the Clean Air Act early in 1977 never was as cohesive as its foe, the National Clean Air Coalition, but it was instantly more powerful. Pomerance had only himself and a smaller core of active environmentalists whose power stemmed from rallying the grass roots. The rival coalition had Woodcock, highly respected and well-known chief of 1.5 million union workers; Henry Ford II, president of the company that bore his name and employed 444,000 persons; Thomas A. Murphy, president of GM with 748,000 employees; John D. Riccardo, president of Chrysler with 245,000 workers; and Roy D. Chapin, president of American Motors with 29,500 employees.

Aware of a strong anti-industry bias on Capitol Hill, however, the industry-union alliance did not rely solely on bigness. Tactics similar to those used by the citizens' lobbies were also brought into play. The UAW, working out of its headquarters, "Solidarity House" in Detroit, spread the word through 40 separate Community Action Program (CAP) councils in various parts of the country, which, in turn, were able to contact every single union member. A typical memorandum from CAP director Henry L. Lacayo read: "The attached materials have been prepared by our national department and sent in considerable quantities to your regional director. Please do all you possibly can to see that our cam-

paign for enactment of UAW's emissions standards is successful. . . . We need to help to arrange visits with U.S. Senators and House members while they are home for the Easter
recess and especially help with the letter-writing efforts. . . ."

At the same time, thousands of brochures were printed
and distributed to union members. The message was simple
and basic: "Congress must be told QUICKLY that your job
is at stake. . . . Write-call-contact-tell Congress you are supporting [the UAW bill] because your future depends on protecting air quality without disrupting jobs." In addition to
the general admonitions, there were specific calls to action.
In April, Lacayo circulated a memo from UAW lobbyist Paster asking that "special attention" be directed at members of
the House Commerce Committee, which was about to consider the UAW-Dingell emissions amendment.

Meanwhile, the auto companies worked through their
own dealers and suppliers as well as through the trade associations representing those groups in Washington. In a March
1977 personalized letter to suppliers signed by Chrysler's
parts purchasing agent, the company asked blanket approval
to use suppliers' names on mailgrams to Washington as the
House and Senate bills came up for a vote.

Throughout the spring and summer of 1977, the mail
continued to pour in on both sides of the issue. Presidents of
all four automakers tried to visit every senator personally. So
did Woodcock. Pomerance concentrated on meeting with
members' staff aides, seeking meetings with senators and
House members only when he felt personal contact would
make a difference. Special Sierra Club grants financed trips
to Washington by out-of-state environmentalists to present
the case for a strong clean air bill.

CONCLUSION

With final enactment of the Clean Air bill in 1977 —
after what House floor manager Rogers called "the heaviest
lobbying I've seen in 23 years in Congress" — the legislation
had all the marks of a perfect compromise. Neither side was
completely happy, but neither side was unhappy enough to
try to kill the bill at the last minute. The auto industry had

something it wanted — delay in the imposition of standards. The environmentalists had something they wanted — a law binding industry to standards that significantly reduced air pollution.

It had been a long battle. Back in 1970, it was largely outside pressure, at the grass-roots level and by existing and newly formed environmental interest groups, that had pressured Congress and the administration into passing the original law. However, members of Congress themselves played an important role in shaping the bill and guiding it through the legislative labyrinth on Capitol Hill.

As other factors entered the picture, among them the energy crisis and threats of high unemployment, outside economic groups seized the initiative from the environmentalists and persuaded a now more sympathetic Congress to reconsider the original emissions standards and deadlines. Forced on the defensive, the environmentalists, Muskie and other members of Congress favoring stringent emissions standards, as well as the Carter administration, engaged in a holding action and agreed, finally, to a compromise. Though their goals were opposed, the tactics of the groups involved were very similar: formation of coalitions, stimulation of grass-roots pressures, direct contact and consultation with key members of Congress.

In 1976, one clean air lobbyist had criticized Muskie for accepting a compromise on the auto emissions standards, arguing that "pressing for the whole thing is the only way you get anything done in this town. I'd rather lose the whole thing than get these incremental bits."

Responded Muskie's aide, Billings, "If the so-called environmentalists, instead of attacking friends like Muskie, had done what they should have been doing, working on strengthening their positions with [swing votes of members who were undecided or were perceived as persuadable]. . ., we wouldn't have had that loss. That's the tragedy of people like that and the things they do."

"There are a couple of rules for good lobbyists, and an important one is 'Never make enemies,' " said Richard Lahn, a former fulltime Sierra Club lobbyist and an organizer of the Clean Air coalition. "You have to agree to disagree. No matter who you are and who your adversary is, if you work around here long enough, today's adversary will some-day be on your side of some issue. . . . Some people come to Washington just to fight on one issue. They can afford to burn their bridges. After they're finished, they just take off. A good lobbyist keeps in mind there'll be other issues, other battles, other times."[22]

NOTES

1. For a legislative history of the Clean Air Act and subsequent amendments, see Congressional Quarterly, *Congress and the Nation, Vol. III, 1969-72* (Washington, D.C.: Congressional Quarterly, 1973), pp. 747, 756-65; *Congress and the Nation, Vol. IV, 1973-76* (Washington, D.C.: Congressional Quarterly, 1977), pp. 292-93, 302-306. For details on 1976 action, see Congressional Quarterly, *1976 Almanac* (Washington, D.C.: Congressional Quarterly, 1977), pp. 128-143.
2. Further details on legislative action in 1977 may be found in Congressional Quarterly, *1977 Almanac* (Washington, D.C.: Congressional Quarterly, 1978), pp. 627-646.
3. *Ibid.*, p. 636.
4. Congressional Quarterly, *Man's Control of the Environment* (Washington, D.C.: Congressional Quarterly, 1970), p. 2.
5. In a January 1, 1970, statement signing into law a new environmental quality bill.
6. Congressional Quarterly, *Man's Control of the Environment*, p. 4.
7. Much of this section is derived from the author's interviews with Pomerance and others and from material supplied by the National Clean Air Coalition.
8. Interview with the author.
9. Bernard Asbell, "The Outlawing of Next Year's Cars," *The New York Times Magazine*, November 21, 1976, p. 128.
10. *Ibid.*
11. *Ibid.*, p. 127.
12. Interview with the author. In 1975, NADA set up an Auto and Truck Dealers Election Action Committee headed by William E. Hancock Jr., a Buick dealer in Columbia, S.C., to contribute funds directly to political candidates.
13. Interview with the author.
14. Asbell, "Next Year's Cars," p. 128.
15. *Ibid.*, p. 131.
16. Much of what follows is from interviews with the author.

17. Shultz, an expert in industrial relations often called in as a negotiator in labor-management disputes, was secretary of labor in 1969 and President Nixon's first director of the Office of Management and Budget in 1970. He became treasury secretary in 1972.
18. Congressional Quarterly, *1977 Almanac*, p. 636.
19. Statement made on the Senate floor October 1, 1976; see Congressional Quarterly, *1976 Almanac*, p. 128.
20. *Ibid.*
21. Much of what follows is from author's interviews.
22. Asbell, "Next Year's Cars," p. 131.

7

The B-1 Bomber:
Organizing at the Grass Roots

"This has been one of the most difficult decisions that I have made since I have been in office," said President Carter at a June 30, 1977, news conference. "During the last few months, I have done my best to assess all the factors involving production of the B-1 bomber. My decision is that we should not continue with deployment of the B-1, and I am directing that we discontinue plans for production of this weapons system. . . . In the meantime, we should begin deployment of cruise missiles using air-launched platforms, such as our B-52s, modernized as necessary. Our triad concept of attaining three basic delivery systems will be continued with submarine-launched ballistic missiles, intercontinental ballistic missiles and a bomber fleet, including cruise missiles as one of its elements. We will continue thereby to have an effective and flexible strategic force whose capability is fully sufficient for our national defense."

With these words, the president appeared to put an end to a ten-year debate over the cost, the necessity, and, at base, the fundamental premise on which U.S. defense policy was predicated. In making his announcement cancelling the $24.8 billion program to build a fleet of 244 B-1s, the president said that instead of continued production of the planes, he favored equipping existing B-52 bombers with air-launched cruise missiles (ALCMs) — small drone (robot) airplanes that could carry a nuclear warhead 1,500 miles or more to within ten yards of a target. At the same time, he called for continued research on the B-1 so that the United States would retain the option of producing the plane if events warranted. *(B-1 characteristics, box, p. 191)*

But the B-1 production program — one of the most hotly debated and intensively lobbied defense projects of the 1970s — did not die easily. Hours after Carter announced his decision to cancel the program, the House passed legislation appropriating $1.5 billion for procurement of five of the planes. The funds were contained in legislation (HR 7933) appropriating $110.6 billion for Pentagon programs for fiscal 1978. Two days earlier, on June 28, the House had rejected 178-243 (R 25-116; D 153-127) an amendment to the bill by Joseph P. Addabbo, D-N.Y., that would have removed the production money for the B-1.

Eighteen days after Carter's announcement, the Senate voted 59-36 (R 11-24; D 48-12) to drop the B-1 production funds contained in the Defense Department appropriations bill. But House conferees refused to concur in the Senate's action, causing the B-1 money to remain an "item in disagreement" when the House took up the conference report on the appropriations bill. The House-Senate compromise bill was filed August 4; on September 8, by a margin of only three votes (202-199: R 33-103; D 169-96), the House backed Carter's decision to cancel production of the bomber. The vote came on a motion by Addabbo to remove the $1.5 billion in B-1 funds from the appropriations bill. The House then adopted the bill. The Senate, which had already voted to remove the B-1 funds, adopted the bill by voice vote September 9, thus clearing the measure for the president.

But B-1 supporters did not surrender their fight. They took to the floor again during the week of October 17, when another bill, making supplemental appropriations for fiscal 1978 (HR 9375) was being debated, offering an amendment to restore the B-1 production money in that bill. The attempt was unsuccessful. Impassioned last-minute appeals by House Democratic leaders and a determined administration lobbying effort led the House to reject the amendment by a 10-vote margin (194-204: R 114-21; D 80-183) on October 20.

Thwarted in their effort, the plane's supporters considered trying to overturn that vote by offering a motion to send the bill back to the Appropriations Committee with instructions that the B-1 funds be added. But when the House took up the bill October 25 for final passage, a nose-count convinced the pro-B-1 forces that they would not be able to overcome the heavy pressure by President Carter and Speaker of the House Thomas P. O'Neill Jr., D-Mass., that helped defeat them on the earlier vote. So they decided not to try again.

Having lost any prospect for immediate production of the plane, B-1 proponents concentrated on preserving the funds already appropriated for fiscal 1977 for production of three B-1s. Carter July 19 had requested rescission of $462 million of this amount — funds that had not yet been spent when the Pentagon halted work on the planes.

According to Rockwell International, the main contractor for the B-1, two of the planes still could be completed with the fiscal 1977 money. This would preserve intact through late 1979 Rockwell's own work force and the network of subcontractors involved in the project. During the period, it would be relatively easy to resume full-scale production of B-1. But if the production line were disbanded because of cancellation of the 1977 planes, it would become practically impossible ever to resume B-1 production.

On September 28, 1977, the House Appropriations Committee killed the president's rescission request by a 34-21 vote. The Senate, which had long been more skeptical of the B-1 than the House, then added the fiscal 1977 rescission provision to the fiscal 1978 supplemental appropriations bill (HR 9375). The House then proceeded to reject the rescission request by a 25-vote margin (166-191: R 16-103; D 150-88), December 6, thus delaying final action on the bill until 1978.

Again the Senate reaffirmed its position favoring cancellation of the fiscal 1977 appropriation of $462 million by a 57-38 vote (R 13-24; D 44-14) February 1, 1978. This time, the House went along, voting February 22 by a surprisingly large margin (234-182: R 30-106; D 204-76) to rescind the fiscal 1977 production funds.

Seven months after he had announced his decision, the president had prevailed, but it had been a long, hard struggle.

BACKGROUND

New defense programs and weapons systems are initiated every year, most without dissent or controversy. Why, then, did the B-1 become such a heated issue and the focal point of such an intense lobbying campaign in the mid-1970s? The answer to that question lies in the nature of the plane itself — both its strengths and weaknesses — as well as the timing of the project and the nature of the groups involved.

An issue does not become a subject of intense lobbying and legislative struggle without the involvement of groups. Interest in the B-1 project was initiated in Congress and later captured the attention of outside pressure groups. The B-1 debate on Capitol Hill began in 1969, when an informal, bipartisan group of anti-Vietnam War senators and representatives called Members of Congress for Peace through Law (MCPL) issued its first military spending report, a 40-page document prepared by nine members and cosponsored by 50 MCPL members. (In 1976, 35 senators and 139 representatives were members of MCPL.) The MCPL report focused on this newly-proposed major weapons system and was highly critical of the cost-effectiveness of the new bomber. The report represented the first organized group effort to demonstrate what some considered to be the military and economic flaws in the thinking behind the B-1.

Founded in 1967, MCPL is one of several informal groupings of members of Congress. By definition these groups operate outside the formal structure of Congress, and their impact on regular congressional procedures is frequently hard to discern. Foreign-policy oriented, MCPL's purpose is to serve as an information clearinghouse to keep members abreast of legislation as well as to promote research through contact with outside experts. The organization arranges formal discussion meetings and provides liaison with citizens' groups. Generally, MCPL members are drawn to join the

CHARACTERISTICS OF THE B-1

The extended and intense B-1 public policy debate focused on a needle-nosed airplane engineered to fly fast and low to elude radar detection, designed as a successor to a line of bomber planes (the B-52s) that began in World War II. As a wholly new bomber replacement line, the B-1 became the most expensive bomber investment to date, rising in price from about $41 million for each plane in 1970, to more than $100 million by 1977.

The airplane, which got its distinctive name because the Defense Department thought that aircraft numbers had become high enough, grew out of the demise of an earlier alternative, the B-70, whose strategic credibility as a high-altitude plane was destroyed in 1960 when the U-2, a high altitude reconnaissance plane piloted by Francis Gary Powers was shot down by a Soviet missile.

After the U-2 incident, flying fast and high was no longer considered the strategic answer; a bomber that could fly fast and low was the official alternative. The B-1 appeared on the scene to meet this criterion, designed to fly at an altitude low enough to avoid detection by radar in time for an effective retaliatory strike.

The B-1 was on the drawing boards for several years. In June 1970, North American Rockwell (renamed Rockwell International in 1973) was awarded the contract to build three prototypes. The new plane was to have four engines, each with a thrust of 30,000 pounds, and the ability to fly at supersonic levels at high altitudes and near the speed of sound at treetop level. Two-thirds the size of the B-52, long considered one of the Air Force's greatest aeronautical achievements, the B-1 operates with a four-man crew and possesses an easy maneuverability that is characteristic only of fighter planes. Carrying 24 short-range attack missiles, it has a maximum range of about 6,000 miles (which would necessitate in-flight refueling on a round trip to the Soviet Union). The B-1 has wings that can sweep forward for fast take-off and back for high speed.

group through a common interest in foreign policy issues. Although there is a broad consensus among the membership on matters such as arms control, closer scrutiny of military spending, and strengthening the United Nations, MCPL has remained a heterogeneous and fluid grouping. While MCPL does not vote as a bloc, nor does the membership take official positions in the name of the organization, MCPL pulled together many like-minded members of Congress who wanted a visible, specific target to focus the debate on what they saw as excessive military spending.[1] Throughout the B-1 debate, the MCPL organization served to orchestrate within Congress the efforts of members opposed to the B-1; it also acted as a liaison between those members and outside groups opposed to the bomber by providing a channel for exchanging information and plotting legislative strategy.

Between 1969 and 1972, individual MCPL members continued to criticize the B-1, but Congress acceded to administration requests for funding the project with little debate or opposition. In those early years, the B-1 was a peripheral issue; the attention of Congress, the administration and the general public was caught up in other defense controversies — whether to go ahead with the antiballistic missile system (ABM), revelations of cost overruns on the huge C5-A military transport plane and the question of terminating U.S. involvement in the Indochina war.

Although these issues overshadowed the B-1 at that time, they represented a new trend toward questioning defense spending in general and costly military projects in particular, as well as the issue of a so-called "peace dividend" resulting from an end to large military expenditures on the Vietnam War. Also, critical attention was increasingly drawn to the ways government defense contracts were awarded to favored corporations whose key executives had recently worked in the Pentagon.

Indeed, weapons cost overruns, the ravages of the Vietnam War, poor morale in the ranks, and Army spying on civilians all captured the headlines in the period 1969-72. Never in the nation's history — with the possible exception of the period between the First and Second World Wars — had the prestige of the men in uniform slipped so low. Both the public and press, tired of the Vietnam War and of the inflation triggered in part by expanding defense budgets, took aim at the Pentagon. It was a far cry from the "Cold War" days when the military could do no wrong.

The mood was set for a critical scrutiny of expensive weapons systems like the B-1. As appropriations for the bomber jumped annually, supporters of defense-spending cutbacks — among them Senators George McGovern, D-S.D., and William Proxmire, D-Wis., and later John C. Culver, D-Iowa, and Representatives Les Aspin, D-Wis., John F. Seiberling, D-Ohio, and Joseph P. Addabbo, D-N.Y. — all MCPL members, began to zero in on the B-1. Increasingly, as other defense issues became defused, the B-1 project stood out as promising to be the most costly single weapon yet built. To both supporters and opponents, the sleek new bomber was a showcase — to supporters, it was a technological leap forward, an economic boost and a strategic necessity, while to opponents, it represented an example of misplaced priorities and economic unsoundness and was of doubtful strategic value.

But strictly internal congressional attempts to erase a major weapons system that was strongly supported by the Nixon administration (and later, by Ford), the Pentagon and the prestigious House and Senate Armed Services Committees did not get very far in a Congress that had until recently tended to defer judgment to the defense experts and the senior committee chairmen. Pressures outside Congress needed to be applied as well.

Such help was forthcoming. By 1973, appropriated funds for the B-1 had reached $448.5 million — and groups outside Congress, which had previously been preoccupied with Vietnam, began to take note. In October 1973, the American Friends Service Committee (AFSC), the Quaker-founded pacifist group, organized a meeting of like-minded organizations at which it was decided to mount a national campaign against the B-1. Working from a small office near Capitol Hill and with interested members of Congress such as Proxmire, Seiberling, McGovern and Addabbo, the group launched an intense lobbying effort both at the grass-roots level and on Capitol Hill that succeeded at the end of 1976 in delaying the full go-ahead to production and placing the decision squarely in the hands of a new Democratic president — one who had stated at the Democratic National Convention in June 1976: "The B-1 is an example of a proposed system which should not be funded and would be wasteful of taxpayers' dollars."

THE GROUPS INVOLVED

The B-1 was at the center of an intense — and in many respects, unique — lobbying effort. Totally committed to the plane were the Air Force; the 1,544,850-strong United International Union of Automobile, Aerospace and Agricultural Implement Workers of America (UAW); and the prime contractor, a multi-million dollar corporation, Rockwell International — and other contractors and subcontractors, a large contingent of members of Congress, including high-ranking members of the House and Senate Armed Services and Appropriations Committees — and the Ford administration. The AFL-CIO leadership also stated its support for the B-1.

Fervently opposed to the B-1 was a coalition of some 36 religious, environmental, consumer, citizens', peace and labor groups that coordinated their efforts under the banner of "The National Campaign to Stop the B-1 Bomber." They were joined in their effort by an initially rather small group of members of Congress and their aides who had consistently opposed the B-1 since it was first proposed.

The anti-B-1 lobby was an ephemeral group, forming briefly around a particular issue, then dissolving and moving on. The coalition was composed of a wide variety of groups who opposed the B-1 for a wide variety of reasons — economic, ideological, environmental, and strategic. In contrast, the major B-1 supporters were well-established and well-funded entities that lobbied for the airplane on a common ground of economic and strategic considerations.

Because of the different character of the pro- and anti-B-1 forces, their resources varied as well. The small-staffed national campaign was formed to organize the numerous groups opposed to the bomber and to coordinate their lobby effort. Operating on a shoe-string budget (about $50,000), it drew on the resources of the existing groups — using their facilities to prepare brochures and newsletters to activate the groups' memberships at the grass-roots level and to lobby members of Congress in Washington. The campaign was broad-based and tried to increase its strength by being widespread, highly visible, vociferous, and persistent. It was essentially an "outside" campaign, pressuring Congress through public channels, although lobbyists for the groups worked directly with interested members of Congress and their staffs on Capitol Hill.

On the other hand, at least initially, the strategy of Rockwell, the Pentagon and the UAW was an "inside" one, relatively low-key, focusing on direct contact with influential senior members of Congress. This was to change, however, as the debate wore on and Rockwell, with subcontractors in 47 states, launched its own grass-roots campaign, asking its 140,000 shareholders and 123,000 employees and local businessmen to pressure their representatives to favor production of the airplane.

Forming the Anti-B-1 Coalition

One major strand in the anti-B-1 campaign began in Germantown, Ohio, in October 1973. The American Friends Service Committee (AFSC) held a convocation of peace organizations there, including members of Clergy and Laity Concerned (CALC), a like-minded organization. Representatives at the meeting decided to mount a national campaign against the B-1 by attempting to build on the old anti-Vietnam War coalition. They sought to identify the kinds of influences and pressures within the economy that they believed led to systems like the B-1. The devastation caused by B-52s in Vietnam was also vividly in their minds.[2]

The new campaign, however, was to differ from the Vietnam protest movement, downplaying mass demonstrations and emphasizing instead an intense and persistent educational campaign at the grass-roots level. Terry Provance of

AFSC and Rick Boardman of CALC set about establishing local anti-B-1 groups throughout the country, drawing on their organizations' own regional and local units. The joint project was billed "Stop the B-1 Bomber/National Peace Conversion Campaign," and by 1977, the network included more than 1,000 local organizers, some 50 campaign offices throughout the nation, 50 full-time staffers, and "Ban the Bomber" groups in 150 cities. The network organized vigils outside Internal Revenue Services offices every April 15 on "tax day" and mounted nationwide demonstrations on special occasions, such as days when Rockwell had special presentations of the B-1 to Pentagon officials, and two days after Carter's inauguration.

More effective than demonstrations, however, was the drumming up of grass-roots support for the effort through the distribution of leaflets, mass mailings to the membership and like-minded citizens, organization of letter-writing campaigns and pressure for meetings with individual members of Congress to try to force them to take a stand on the issue.

For two years, AFSC and CALC worked largely on their own to build up support for the cause. By 1975, however, they realized they had to establish a presence in Washington to engage in some tough lobbying on Capitol Hill. Early that year Provance went to Washington and met with McGovern, Proxmire and other congressional opponents of the B-1. He also talked with representatives of other outside groups that had indicated in one way or another their opposition to the B-1 — among them, Common Cause, the National Taxpayers Union, Environmental Action, the Federation of American Scientists, Womens' International League for Peace and Freedom, SANE (Citizens Committee for a Sane Nuclear Policy), and others — to enlist their support and to offer to help coordinate the effort to down the bomber. Deeply interested in the issue, several groups quickly agreed to join the campaign, and the interested members of Congress welcomed assistance from a coordinated outside pressure group. An anonymous donor gave $4,000 to get things started and SANE donated a desk in its Washington office. Robert P. Brammer, a 1971 philosophy graduate of Earlham College who had been working as a researcher for the Democratic majority in the Iowa legislature, was hired as the first full-time staffer for the National Campaign to Stop the B-1 Bomber.

Brammer was a novice to Washington politics, and his small staff, also young and inexperienced, was mostly made up of volunteers (there were four other paid staffers). Together they organized an effective, wide-ranging lobbying drive. Though not blessed with abundant funds, Brammer and his staff nevertheless managed to orchestrate a substantial grass-roots effort. In each state, there was a nucleus of reliable anti-bomber activists who could be alerted at times of crucial votes. They, in turn, would reach their local sympathizers or go out to recruit them to write letters or send telegrams or make telephone calls to Congress and, later, to the White House. They did not underscore their antiwar background or liberal credentials. Rather, they emphasized pragmatic concerns; the bomber was presented as economically unsound, environmentally harmful, and militarily irrelevant.

"We took an issue people knew little about and turned it into a controversy," said Provance. Concluded Brammer: "If people get organized, they can even fight the Pentagon."

Brammer and Provance came to Washington to gather the support of enough people to generate a perception in Washington that public opinion opposed the B-1. At first, the anti-B-1 campaign was educational. The coalition was convinced that if people just knew the "facts" about the B-1 they would be opposed to it. Newsletters went out to the thousands of members of the various coalition groups. Data sheets and press releases went to newspaper reporters and editorial writers. Both newsletters and data went to members of Congress. Governors and mayors were contacted. The appeal was broadly cast, but narrowly focused. It attempted to coordinate a wide range of political activists who would be likely to be interested in the issue.

One of the coalition's first major projects was preparation of a nine-section "timeline" campaign packet of B-1 information and tips on how to pressure Congress. As with much of the coalition's work, the packet was a joint enterprise, prepared and financed by several coalition members. It was sent out to about 400 political activists around the country in February 1976. The last section of the "timeline" dealt with campaign resources. For two dollars, for example, a field worker could order 1,000 "92 billion dollar" bills a bit larger than a dollar bill, colored green and full of anti-B-1 information. The $92 billion figure was the coalition's estimate at that time of the total B-1 cost for production and operations over a 30-year period. Also available were other brochures, pamphlets, and slide shows presenting a variety of arguments against the B-1. "Our bread and butter was getting people to write letters," Brammer said later. "Our strongest tool was letters to the editors, an indirect kind of influence. They made congressmen aware of the opposition and put pressure on them to take a 'yes' or 'no' stand."

B-1 Opposition: Resource Sharing

The national campaign liked to play up the "David and Goliath" image of a small-staffed, low budget citizens' group fighting a large corporation, a labor union, and the Pentagon — with wealth and influence at their disposal — an image which may well have been an asset. In fact, however, the coalition itself had a vast array of resources to call upon, simply by being a coalition. "Throughout the campaign, we emphasized skill sharing, using what groups do best," said Brammer. Another asset was that the issue could be pitched in a variety of ways, according to the particular interests of each group. Thus, Environmental Action became interested in — and thereby played up — what it saw as the adverse environmental impact of the B-1 as a supersonic and "fuel hungry" plane. The National Taxpayers Union focused on the economic impact of the bomber — what it would cost in tax dollars. The Womens' International League for Peace and Freedom stressed the "guns and butter" questions concerning the new bomber. The American Federation of State, County and Municipal Employees placed ads in newspapers and magazines pointing out what the cost of one B-1 could do to meet domestic needs — how many hospitals could be built, policemen paid, and so forth. The American Federation of Scientists lobbied against the B-1 primarily because it felt the costs of the bomber were unwarranted by "any contributions to our security which it might make."

The national campaign's budget was financed primarily through contributions by individuals. What the groups provided was equipment and expertise. Many of them had worked together on other issues and knew how to coordinate their efforts to achieve the greatest results. Groups like Environmental Action and Common Cause provided copying machines, mimeograph equipment, and use of WATS lines — and hints about lobbying, as well as the lobbyists themselves. The AFSC and its full-time Peace Education organization produced a vast array of educational material, a sophisticated slide show to be shown to local organizations and slick anti-B-1 posters. The National Taxpayers Union provided the campaign with district-by-district and statewide data on its analysis of the tax impact of the B-1, which Brammer then sent to members of Congress and political activists to use as fuel for their anti-B-1 arguments. The Council on Economic Priorities in New York (which was described by its executive director in 1976 as "a sort of hybrid, perched between the world of public interest advocacy groups and the more traditional Wall Street firms"[3]) also provided considerable economic data to support the anti-B-1 case.

Within Congress, there were several legislative aides to members of Congress opposed to the B-1 who were knowledgeable on military matters and could offer the anti-B-1 forces technological arguments to rebut the plane's supporters. The National Association of Social Workers sent out alerts to its grass-roots membership at times of key votes. SANE participated in direct lobbying on the bill and sent numerous letters to its membership. The labor unions (among them, the Oil, Chemical, and Atomic Workers union, the Textile Workers union, and the International Longshoremen's and Warehousemen's union) participated in further "behind the scenes" and low-key lobbying of their membership (as did the UAW on the other side).

The most important function of the national campaign office was to coordinate all these efforts and to keep the groups informed about the issue, what each of them was doing, and when votes were likely to come up in Congress. This was done through informal daily contact and monthly meetings with the groups' representatives in Washington, newsletters, press releases and phone calls.

Some groups in the coalition were more active than others. "We had to provide many of the groups with sample letters and do their work for them — but they'd sign anything and this was a big advantage," said Brammer.[4] There was also an advantage, in terms of prestige and "legitimacy," in claiming to be a national group, in having a masthead listing many diverse organizations. A few groups were added at the last moment — and press releases were sent out announcing the fact — so it would look as if the coalition were still very much alive and growing, a "get-on-the-bandwagon" appeal.

"Communication was the key to our success," said Brammer. "Eventually, we were able to tell you at any hour of any day what the vote breakdown would be. We knew where every congressman was — who was in town, who wasn't. And we could provide this information to other groups and congressional offices. That's an advantage of working on just one issue. Other groups and congressional offices had too many other things to do to be able to keep close tabs on the issue. . . . There were times when we didn't accomplish anything; but just the mere fact that we existed was important and kept the pressure up. The presence of anti-B-1 lobbyists on Capitol Hill kept up our visibility — 'Oh, you're here again,' they'd say." Brammer also noted that most legislative aides were sympathetic to the effort, even if they did not agree with it. "Most of them would be honest and frank with us and would try to get their representatives to take a stand, or they'd just tell us it wasn't worth our while to work on that office."

A closer look at four of the groups involved provides some insight into why such a seemingly small operation could be so effective.[5]

National Taxpayers Union. A nonprofit public interest lobbying organization founded in 1969 and supported by the contributions of its 40,000 members (the annual budget is about $400,000), the NTU has directed its lobbying efforts toward eliminating wasteful government expenditures. Included on its executive committee in 1977 were Robert Kenhart, publisher of the conservative *Human Events* magazine and Ernest Fitzgerald, a former Defense Department official who was fired in 1969 for disclosing Pentagon cost overruns (particularly on the C5-A). NTU opposed the B-1 as "a weapons system of dubious value, failing the tests of cost, effectiveness and necessity" — "less a genuine military project than a public works program."

NTU efforts focused primarily on direct lobbying of members of Congress through letters and personal contact. According to an NTU spokesman, the B-1 issue was not played up among the organization's membership, since NTU members were divided on the issue.

"It was a real asset to have a somewhat 'conservative' organization like NTU on our masthead," said Brammer. "They really helped us in our lobby effort on Capitol Hill — NTU is well respected there."

Federation of American Scientists. FAS, which bills itself as "the voice of science on Capitol Hill," was founded in 1946. It represents 7,000 dues-paying scientists (who pay a minimum of $20 annually) and lobbies for the proper use of science in society and the proper treatment of scientists. Its major lobbying tool is a monthly newsletter, FAS *Public Interest Report*, written by the FAS director, Jeremy J. Stone, with the assistance of various FAS and non-FAS experts.

On May 17, 1976, as the Senate was debating an amendment to delay production expenditures for the bomber, the FAS (which listed 35 Nobel Prize winners on its board of sponsors) issued a statement of opposition to the bomber: "The tens of billions of dollars required to build and operate the B-1 bomber are not warranted by any contribution to our security which it might make." The statement was not endorsed solely by the FAS. It was also signed by prominent members of the so-called "defense community," Republicans and Democrats who had served in important defense positions in and out of government.

On May 18 and 19 NBC News carried photographs of FAS's building and director and comments by Clark Clifford, former Secretary of Defense, who had signed the statement. The newscast suggested that the release had turned the debate around. Commented reporter Marilyn Berger on the newscast: "The prestigious opposition seems to be having an effect. For the first time this year, it's a big question whether the B-1 will ever fly. . . ."

The FAS statement "was very important," said one congressional staff aide who opposed the B-1, "because it postured us as sound and responsible and not just knee-jerk leftists." Indeed, newspapers, began to devote more attention to the B-1, juxtaposing statements by leading pro- and anti-B-1 spokesmen on their "op-ed" pages.

The Women's International League for Peace and Freedom. Founded in 1915, and with sections in 23 countries (there are 120 branches in the United States), the league was very active in the anti-B-1 campaign. Unlike NTU, the group undertook a well-organized grass-roots lobby effort in the campaign, sending out periodic legislative bulletins and action alerts. The group also participated in joint press conferences and direct lobbying on Capitol Hill. Representatives of the league appeared before the Democratic National Convention Platform Committee in June 1976 to urge Carter to oppose the B-1, and they were among those spearheading the tax day protests in 1976 and 1977. League members passed out leaflets with details of the funds earmarked for the B-1 project — money they claimed could be put to better use. The leaflets were designed to be signed on the back and mailed to the president as a show of discontent.

Common Cause. The biggest citizens' lobby, with 250,-000 members, Common Cause entered the B-1 battle for still another reason: its opposition to government waste. "There may be a case to be made for a bomber," Common Cause legislative activities director R. Michael Cole said, "but we wanted to be sure all the facts were in before deciding whether Congress should go ahead with this particular project."[6]

Common Cause joined B-1 foes just as the national coalition was getting organized, and Brammer gave Cole a great deal of credit for advising the fledgling group on how to rally support at the grass-roots level. In line with its emphasis on ethics and accountability in government, Common Cause was particularly interested in the relationship between Rockwell and the Pentagon. On March 19, 1976, the group sent a letter to Secretary of Defense Donald H. Rumsfeld protesting what it considered to be the soft treatment accorded Malcolm Currie, director of defense research and engineering, who apparently had violated Pentagon rules in accepting a Rockwell-paid trip to the Bahamas some months before. Currie acknowledged taking the vacation trip as a Rockwell guest but denied that he had done anything wrong.

Rumsfeld reprimanded Currie and fined him four weeks' pay. Common Cause Chairman John W. Gardner suggested that the punishment was not severe enough. "We believe that one further step is necessary if the Pentagon's position on conflicts of interest is to be maintained," Gardner wrote Rumsfeld. "Mr. Currie should be removed immediately from further involvement in or responsibility for decisions on any project concerning Rockwell International." There was no official response. However, when a Defense Department committee met later in 1976 to decide whether to go ahead with production of the B-1, Currie was not on the panel.

B-1 Supporters' Strategy

That the B-1 was not immediately scrapped after Carter's June 30, 1977, decision was evidence of the strong and sustained support for the bomber among the business community, a major labor union and influential members of Congress. Indeed, in the early years of B-1 development, it appeared that a go-ahead to production would be a foregone conclusion — and consequently, there seemed to be no need to lobby vigorously on behalf of the bomber.

Until 1976, most of Rockwell's lobbying was conducted behind the scenes, in Pentagon and congressional offices. When it became apparent that the B-1 was in jeopardy, however, the company realized that there was a need to wage a more public battle for national opinion to counter the anti-B-1 coalition's grass-roots strategy.

Few major American corporations have been accustomed to taking their messages to Congress through the grass roots. Through their prestige, financial resources, and ability to hire and utilize professional Washington lobbyists with experience and political savvy, corporations have usually had little trouble getting the ear of members of Congress. Moreover, the major corporations are continually developing new contacts among government policymakers, with their executives moving in and out of government jobs, as new presidents urge them to serve their country and as they pull former government officials into their ranks.

Rockwell, like many other large corporations, also had formal ties with Defense Department policymakers. Willard F. Rockwell Jr., chairman of the board, for example, was in 1976 one of 29 members of the Defense Department Industry Advisory Committee which regularly discusses contracting policy and national security needs. Also on the committee were representatives of 11 B-1 subcontractors.

Again as in other corporations, Rockwell executives had an opportunity for numerous social contacts with key government and elected officials, both in "hospitality suites" at various meetings and conventions and in visits to Rockwell hunting lodges and vacation retreats. Among Rockwell guests between 1972 and 1976 were Malcolm Currie, Admiral Thomas H. Moorer, chairman of the Joint Chiefs of Staff, and at least 21 other Air Force officers.

The "defense hospitality" issue came under scrutiny in two days of public hearings February 2-3, 1976, held by the Joint Committee on Defense Production, chaired by Proxmire.[7] Members of the committee queried officials of the Pentagon and of the Rockwell and Northrop companies to determine the scope of corporate hospitality given defense officials — as well as to several members of Congress serving on committees dealing with defense or space legislation — and to weigh its impact on U.S. defense spending decisions. (In fiscal 1975, Rockwell's $732 million in sales to the Defense Department made it the 10th largest contractor to the Pentagon; however, Rockwell's commercial sales outweighed government business by nearly two-to-one.)

During the hearings, Rockwell President Robert Anderson defended the company's efforts to maintain close ties with federal officials. Most contacts, he said, were made over lunches or dinners, adding, "Other courtesies are also extended. For instance, we have invited visitors from federal agencies to sports, cultural, and social events and to hunting facilities, but I believe these would be found to be a minor part of the total."

Such get-togethers, he said, provide an opportunity for people to know each other better and to understand mutual problems. "In short, it is one means of approaching what we are all striving for in our complex society, improved communications." The aim was not to exercise undue influence, Anderson said. The only way to win government contracts, he said, was to be more competent, technically superior and more efficient than the next bidder. "Most of the programs in which we are engaged are complex and difficult, and the government is a demanding and tough customer."

In addition to direct contacts with Pentagon officials and members of Congress, Rockwell set up a committee to coordinate such activities as communicating to the public, to Congress and to its own employees and stockholders its views about the importance of its major defense and space programs, including the B-1. The effort, called "Operation Common Sense," was formally discontinued about the end of 1974. According to the minutes of a January 1974 "Operation Common Sense" committee meeting provided by the company to Proxmire, the group discussed, among other things, "methods for learning the plans of the AFSC and the 'Ban the B-1 Bomber Campaign,' and how to cope with these organizations; developed plans to mobilize support for the B-1 among veterans' and civic groups; assigned research or lobbying tasks to various committee members; discussed possible threats to the B-1 bomber program . . . [and] discussed plans for maximizing public relations impact of Arkansas plant groundbreaking and B-1 bomber rollout."

"Most of our people are doing this as part of their job," Anderson said at the Proxmire hearing. "We expect our plant manager, for example, who's running an axle plant in Ken-

205

tucky, to talk to his local congressman.... So many of these people, particularly in the space area, are doing it on their own time. They are very, very dedicated people."

Supporters' Grass-Roots Campaign

Like the anti-B-1 forces, Rockwell increasingly engaged in an educational campaign to put pressure on Congress where the votes are, in home districts, by pointing out as forcefully as possible that the B-1 would mean money and jobs. An internal company document listed the dollar value of B-1 subcontracts in the home states of 25 key Senate Democrats and 22 Republicans plus 58 Democrats and 40 Republicans in the House. Armed with this information, and with supporting material on the strategic need for the B-1, Rockwell representatives were urged to contact members of Congress personally. In mid-1976, Rockwell executives began an intense lobbying campaign among employees and stockholders. A Rockwell-made film on the bomber was distributed to local Chambers of Commerce throughout the country (Rockwell's name was not mentioned as the producer). The company also bought newspaper advertisements and sent representatives to editorial offices with arguments in favor of the B-1. The appeals were often dramatic. "Why is the B-1 so vital to world peace?" one advertisement asked. "The manned bomber is the only thinking weapon in America's missile-bomber strategic security system. . . . The B-1 can go into action . . . provide time for international negotiations . . . offer the opportunity to prevent war . . . and be called back home."

In an August 1976 letter signed by W. F. Rockwell Jr., the firm's 140,000 shareholders were urged to contact their senators and representatives. Rockwell warned that B-1 opponents were confident that, if they could delay the program in 1976, they could kill it entirely in 1977. Stockholders were told how to telephone or telegraph officials in Washington. A brochure was also prepared entitled "Wake Up, Citizen, Your National Security Is At Stake."

Within the company, an "urgent" internal letter went to supervisors on August 17, 1976, asking them to hand B-1 information packets to each worker and making available stationery, envelopes, and stamps for those who would like to send a letter to a senator or representative. "The B-1," the letter said, "is a program of utmost importance to all of Rockwell and the security of our nation. It is the hope of Rockwell management that all employees who support a strong national defense system, including the B-1, will make their opinions known."

In addition, a special August 1976 B-1 edition of the company newspaper carried an appeal from Anderson, the company president. "Your help is needed to support a program that is vital to the nation," Anderson said. By the end of August, after Congress had voted to continue B-1 funding, a notice went up on the company's bulletin boards that said, "Thank You." More than 80,000 letters had gone out, the notice said.

Throughout the B-1 debate (that is, until 1977), Rockwell was aided by the Ford administration, senior members of Congress, and Air Force officials. Although federal government employees cannot by law lobby Congress, they can answer questions from members, provide information to refute critics and help plot congressional strategy. They can also issue press releases, make speeches and write articles. During 1976, for example, Air Force Secretary Thomas C. Reed travelled around the country pointing out the strategic need for and positive economic impact of the B-1. The Pentagon and Rockwell also provided information to staunch B-1 proponents such as Senator Barry Goldwater, R-Ariz., to buttress their case in Congress for the new bomber.

There were other things the Air Force could do. One was to schedule B-1 test flights to coincide with important votes in Congress. Goldwater actually flew the first prototype of the bomber as the Senate prepared in May 1976 to take up an amendment to delay full-scale B-1 production.

Besides the Ford administration, numerous private military organizations with headquarters in Washington actively supported the B-1 project. (Proxmire estimated that there were 41 such groups with a membership of six million and annual operating budgets of $36 million.) One of these groups was the Air Force Association, with 155,000 members and chapters in every state. In addition, 135 business concerns, including all the major defense contractors, were "industrial associates" of the organization, each paying an annual fee of $450. Since the association is chartered as a veterans' organization, it is not required to register as a lobbyist under the 1946 lobbying act. The association's communications link is *Air Force* magazine, a well-edited publication that strongly supported the B-1 bomber through editorials, articles by Reed and others, and advertisements by subscribers.[8]

On the day before the Senate Appropriations Committee voted on an amendment to delay B-1 funding (in July 1976), the association sponsored a breakfast meeting at which Secretary Reed discussed with a group of Senate aides the merits of the B-1 program. James H. Straubel, executive director of the Air Force Association, said later that "several Senate staff members" came to him suggesting that a briefing on the B-1 would be helpful. "The B-1 had become a confused issue," Straubel said, "and we thought it would be a good educational project."[9] (A similar effort was undertaken by the national anti-B-1 campaign early in 1976, when the group organized a briefing for congressional aides at which representatives from the Brookings Institution and IBM pointed out the merits of the cruise missile as an alternative to the B-1 bomber.)

THE 1976 BATTLE IN CONGRESS

The B-1 was not a decision made on a single occasion by the government. Rather, important congressional actions on the B-1 occurred several times each year, within the framework of annual congressional funding for weapons systems. It takes stamina to lobby a defense budget item; there are numerous critical points in the process each year. First, the Senate and House Armed Services Committees take up the authorizing legislation for weapons proposed by the executive branch (the Defense procurement bill), which then must be passed by both chambers (and where the House and Senate differ, a compromise must be worked out in a conference committee). Then, the House and Senate Appropriations Committees consider and approve the bill (the Defense Department appropriations bill) that actually allocates the funds for the project, which, again must be approved by both chambers.

Thus, throughout the debate on the B-1, the same arguments had to be mustered with the same enthusiasm and certainty at each step of the way. Until Carter announced that he wished to halt the B-1, Congress had appropriated most of the funds requested by the Defense Department for the bomber, in some years voting the full amount requested, in others reducing slightly the funding level. But the congressional decisions were not made unanimously or without significant dissension.

By 1975, the sustained minority opposition in Congress to the B-1 had begun to have some impact. With cost estimates for the new bomber fleet escalating rapidly, the B-1 began to run into increasing opposition on Capitol Hill, particularly in the Senate. The Ford administration had requested $800 million for B-1 research and development, as well as $87 million for procurement of "long-lead" items — parts needed later in construction work. Although no attempt was made to kill the entire project, the House May 19, 1975, handily rejected (164-227: R 23-110; D 141-117) an amendment to eliminate funds for "long-lead" items.[10]

Meanwhile, however, the Senate Armed Services Committee refused to authorize money for long-lead items and recommended delaying all production funding until fiscal 1977, by which time Congress would have decided whether the B-1 should be built. This temporary victory for the anti-B-1 forces was diluted when a House-Senate compromise agreed on an authorization for the purchasing of the long-lead items needed to build the B-1.

The B-1 issue finally came to a head in Congress in 1976, with the Ford administration's request for $1.5 billion for the plane, of which $948 million would fund procurement of the first three regular production planes (by then, four test planes had already been built or were under construction). In the closest vote yet taken on the bomber, the House April 8, by a vote of 177-210 (R 29-103; D 148-107) rejected an amendment to the defense authorization bill by John F. Seiberling, D-Ohio, to delay expenditure of funds for purchasing production-line bombers until after February 1, 1977. However, the Senate once again showed its greater resistance to the B-1. In a key 44-37 (R 7-22; D 37-15) vote May 20, the Senate adopted an amendment parallel to Seiberling's, offered by John C. Culver, D-Iowa. But before adopting the Culver amendment, the Senate rejected, 33-48 (R 6-23; D 27-25), a McGovern move to eliminate procurement funds entirely. Even the halfway step was soon challenged; on May 26, Sen. Robert Taft Jr., R-Ohio, insisting that the Culver amendment had been brought up without previous notice, introduced an amendment that would allow the president to permit B-1 production before Feb. 1, 1977, if in his judgment such action would improve the chances for successful U.S.-Soviet arms limitation talks. When Culver threatened to filibuster Taft's amendment, it was tabled (killed), 47-30 (R 7-25; D 40-5). The Culver (and anti-B-1) victory was short-lived, however, as a House-Senate compromise dropped the Culver amendment in June.

B-1 opponents persisted with their efforts, shifting the focus of the debate from the authorizing process to the appropriations bill. Once again, the House, both in its Appropriations Committee and on the floor, rejected anti-B-1 amendments, offered this time by Addabbo.

However, another partial victory for the plane's opponents came in the Senate. On July 21, the Senate Appropriations Committee adopted a Proxmire amendment delaying production funds until February 1, 1977. The amendment was accepted on the Senate floor. Subsequently, the joint House-Senate conference committee worked out a compromise, appropriating the full $948 million but providing that the funds could be committed at a rate of no more than $87 million a month until February 1, 1977, at which time the new president would be able to review, and possibly cancel, the entire program. The compromise was approved with little debate. Rockwell was awarded the contract to start regular production in December 1976, after Ford, who strongly supported producing the plane, had been defeated in his bid for a second presidential term.

Throughout 1976, the anti-B-1 campaign actively lobbied members of Congress, trying to win at least a delay in the commitment of B-1 production funds, to demonstrate to Democratic presidential nominee Carter that Congress was divided on the issue and that a go-ahead for the B-1 was not a foregone conclusion. Taken somewhat unaware by the growing strength of the B-1 opposition, the bomber's supporters engaged in a holding action — a strategy that proved temporarily successful.

Basic groundwork by B-1 foes for the April 8, 1976, House vote on the Seiberling amendment to delay B-1 production funds was handled by aides in key congressional offices, working with Brammer and Cole of Common Cause. All House offices were contacted and the representative rated according to previous votes or known positions on the B-1. Simultaneously, a "pyramid" telephone system was set up at the grass-roots level: One person would call two others, who would call five others, and so forth — until hundreds of people had been urged to write or phone their representatives.

At the same time, the Pentagon released statistics on a significant Soviet arms buildup that showed the Russians outspending the United States on defense by about 40 percent. There was widespread concern in Congress over the increase in Soviet strength and suspicion about Soviet diplomatic aims. The B-1 became the centerpiece of the debate over the military balance and defense spending. Rockwell representatives circulated around the House office buildings leaving packets of pro-B-1 information stressing national security needs and emphasizing that the B-1 would mean thousands of new jobs throughout the country. The anti-B-1 campaign group responded with a study compiled by the AFSC alleging that the B-1 would represent a significant economic drain in 41 states where millions of tax dollars flowing from the states to pay for the bomber would not be offset by new B-1 business within those states.

On April 7, 1976, the day before the House vote on the defense authorization bill, Seiberling and six other Democrats sent a letter to all House members announcing that he would offer an amendment to delay B-1 production money. In the letter, Seiberling noted that the plane was behind production schedule and had had some structural problems, as reported by the Government Accounting Office (GAO). As the letters were being distributed, Brammer and his associates were counting heads. Those seen as "leaning for" and "undecided" about the amendment were listed by states, each one targeted for a personal visit from a representative firmly opposed to the B-1. At the same time, Pentagon liaison officers set up a command post near the House floor offering information to counter any last-minute appeals of B-1 critics. The vote seemed close at first, but soon the B-1 began to pull ahead. The final tally was 210-177 against the Seiberling amendment.

Attention then focused on the Senate Armed Services Committee. That panel appeared to be in no mood to stop the B-1; in its report sending the defense procurement bill to the floor, it called the bomber "one of the essential measures the country must take to avoid strategic inferiority." The committee rejected Culver's delaying amendment, 6-9. Again, on the Senate floor as in the House, scheduling was critical, and it appeared that the division on the B-1 was close. Aides to Culver, McGovern, and Proxmire worked together with Brammer's group running constant vote checks. There were many absentees. It was an election year and a long Memorial Day recess was coming up. The task was to call for a vote on Culver's delaying amendment when the other side had more supporters away from Washington. The strategy worked; the Senate adopted Culver's amendment, 44-37, on May 20.

On the eve of the Senate vote, Rockwell committed what some thought was a serious blunder. R. J. Watson, a lobbyist, distributing a packet of pro-B-1 information to Senate offices, included a single sheet analyzing the impact of the Culver amendment in blunt terms. In addition to added costs and lost jobs if the B-1 should be delayed, the Rockwell sheet charged that the Culver amendment "furthers USSR objectives." It was that last item that angered many senators and changed the minds of some of them to vote for, rather than against, the Culver amendment.

Although the House-Senate compromise on the defense authorization bill dropped the Culver amendment, B-1 opponents were more successful when it came to the appropriations legislation. A compromise worked out by House and Senate conferees and accepted by both chambers left intact the original request to start buying three production model B-1s, but it limited the amount of money available to $87 million a month until February 1, 1977, when the new president would be able to review, and possibly cancel, the entire program. The Air Force thus retained the psychological advantage no matter how the next administration felt about the B-1. As one B-1 bomber opponent explained, the Defense Department could use the "sunk costs argument," the argument that the government already had spent so many tax dollars developing and buying the first B-1s that it would be enormously wasteful to cancel the program.

Early in 1977, the funding for the B-1 was extended to June, with the Air Force and Rockwell International agreeing to limit expenditures to $87 million per month until that time. After June 30, all remaining funds would become available — $250 million from then to October — if Carter did not decide to halt production. At a February 23 news conference, the president said the Pentagon and National Security Council were reassessing the bomber and that he expected the studies to be completed by the end of May. In his revised budget sent to Congress February 22, Carter called for funding five B-1s in fiscal 1978, rather than the eight proposed by Ford. In April, it was reported that the Pentagon had cut its original request for 244 B-1s to a recommendation for a fleet of 150 planes.[11]

THE B-1 AS A CAMPAIGN ISSUE

Perhaps the most important achievement of the anti-B-1 network and coalition was to make the bomber a campaign issue. Timing was crucial: 1976 was a presidential election year. It was also the year the Pentagon sought funds to begin regular production of the planes. Without the efforts of the coalition, "it is very unlikely that the B-1 would have been an issue, and in that sense they performed a very important function," said Clark McFadden, former counsel to the Senate Armed Services Committee. "They got Carter to take a stand on the B-1 when he knew very little about it, and got him involved in a way that otherwise would not have happened."[12]

Throughout 1976, members of the coalition were reminded that they should be sure to make the B-1 an issue in the presidential and congressional campaigns. Members of groups in the anti-B-1 coalition were urged to attend primary teas, meetings, and so forth, where they could ask the candidates how they stood — it was easier to get them to take a stand at that stage rather than later on, when they would be less accessible to direct confrontation. Representatives from the American Friends Service Committee (AFSC) and the Clergy and Laity Concerned (CALC) lobbied at the Democratic convention, handing out leaflets, while spokesmen for Environmental Action and the liberal Americans for Democratic Action (ADA) worked with the Democratic Platform Committee to produce a plank stating that the B-1 production decision should be left to the next president.

The coalition's high moment in mid-1976 came in the statement made by candidate Carter to the Democratic Platform Committee on June 12: "Exotic weapons which serve no real function do not contribute to the defense of this country. The B-1 is an example of a proposed system which should not be funded and would be wasteful of taxpayers' dollars." The coalition took the pronouncement and ran — to the duplicating machines.

"We really drummed on that statement," said Brammer later. During the election campaign, supporters of the coalition were urged to be there with anti-B-1 signs whenever Carter came to town. They were told to remind members of Congress — and Carter — of his words and to indicate that his integrity and "liberal credentials" were at stake.

By the fall of 1976, Carter edged away from his previously unequivocal position, saying that he didn't "at this point" favor production of the B-1. The period between September and the end of 1976 was a low point for the anti-B-1 campaign: Ford came out consistently and strongly in favor of the B-1, while Carter said nothing about it. But the fact that Carter remained silent on the issue, as well as his apparent lead in the presidential race, was also instrumental in the House-Senate compromise decision that fall to delay a full production decision until February 1977.

1977: FOCUS ON THE WHITE HOUSE

With the decision up to Carter, attention turned from Capitol Hill to the White House. The anti-B-1 coalition urged its membership to telephone the president and remind him constantly of his campaign statement. They also tried to capitalize on a January Harris Survey which found public opinion running 42 to 33 percent against the bomber, with the reminder undecided.

When in February, Carter said the study on options would be completed by the end of May — and with the June 30 deadline for a decision in mind — the anti-B-1 coalition seized on that date to keep the issue alive. Reminders were sent out to activists, and White House rallies and phone-ins were organized, but it became increasingly hard to keep up the momentum and maintain the B-1 on the front pages as a pressing issue.

One reason was a change in the coalition's tactics, once it had won the production delay in Congress in September 1976. Unlike 1976, when the coalition pressed for congressional votes, throughout the spring of 1977, the anti-B-1 strategy was to avoid or delay a B-1 vote in Congress until Carter announced his decision. When Representative Addabbo announced that he would offer an amendment on June 28 to cut all B-1 production funds for fiscal 1978, the anti-B-1 coalition wrote in a newsletter: "Of course, this is our objective — but last winter we considered two *dangers* that convinced us not to pursue this strategy: (1) it would be unwise to divert our focus from Jimmy Carter, and (2) it would be hard to win votes because Congresspeople are waiting for Jimmy

Carter's decision: Congress gave him the choice. . . . Tuesday's vote now brings an even more perilous danger: if we lose the vote, the president may finally say he has an excuse for changing his B-1 position. He may say, 'I couldn't stop the B-1 if I wanted to, since the House just refused to stop it.' "

Although the Addabbo amendment was indeed rejected 178-243 (and the House adopted the defense appropriations bill with B-1 funds June 30, 333-54), the campaign's fears proved unfounded.

After Carter announced his decision to halt B-1 production, the efforts of the anti-B-1 lobby were directed toward protecting the decision in Congress. A great deal of time was spent phoning the White House congressional liaison officers urging them to put more pressure on Congress. The anti-B-1 campaign persuaded the leaders of 25 national groups to sign a letter to Carter telling him the decision was in jeopardy. "The White House didn't do a very good lobbying job," commented Brammer. "Most people, including Speaker O'Neill, didn't believe the B-1 decision was in trouble."

In fact, the B-1 battle was not yet over. Although the Senate July 19 voted 59-36 (R 11-24; D 48-12) on an amendment by John C. Stennis, D-Miss., chairman of the Armed Services Committee, to back Carter and rescind the B-1 funds, and although the House concurred in the decision on September 8, pro-B-1 forces countered by offering an amendment to a catch-all money bill to restore the funds for the bomber. But the House rejected the move on October 20, by a vote of 194-204, with Republicans solidly supporting the B-1 (114-21) and Democrats heavily opposed (80-183). Appropriations Committee Chairman George Mahon, D-Texas, invoked his long record as a champion of a strong national defense to refute colleagues who argued that the B-1 was a strategic necessity. He said: "The only purpose of the bomber is to do the cleanup job. And after the atomic exchange we could probably do the cleanup job in an oxcart." Speaker O'Neill urged fellow Democrats to "stay with the decision of their president. . . ."

CONCLUSION

Up to the very last, Carter's decision on the B-1 remained unknown. When it was announced, it came as a surprise to both supporters and foes of the B-1. Throughout the spring of 1977, the president employed the tactics of remaining silent on the issue while the suspense built up, perhaps perceiving that the strong political passions on both sides of the B-1 issue could be defused by concentrating on the technical aspects and alternatives and by portraying the decision in those, rather than in political, terms.

In June, the president met with both pro- and anti-B-1 members of Congress, many of whom emerged from the sessions convinced that he would favor the B-1, while just as many others said they had no clue as to which way the decision would go.

Observers later pointed out that Carter might have been swayed by a report issued a year earlier (in February 1976) by the well-respected, influential, and independent Brookings Institution. Using a systems analysis approach, the report, prepared by two former Air Force colonels, Alton H. Quanbeck and Archie L. Wood, concluded: "We see no reason to make a commitment to produce the B-1." They proposed that modernized B-52s equipped with cruise missiles be considered as an alternative. Quanbeck and Wood said that although bombers no longer could be called the backbone of the U.S. deterrent forces, they still were valuable insurance against the failure of the more modern missile weapons, the land-based ICBMs, and the submarine-launched SLBMS. However, arguments for retaining an adequate strategic bomber force, the report said, did not present compelling reasons for building an entirely new force at the time. The authors estimated that the cost of modifying B-52s to carry missiles would run about $40 million per plane, less than half the price (at that time) of a B-1.

How much impact did the pro- and anti-B-1 groups actually have on the president's decision? The answer to that remains uncertain. Certainly as a presidential candidate,

Carter leaned against the B-1, but once elected, he had to consider the large contingent of labor and business representatives who supported the B-1. On the other hand, if the administration had felt there was no possibility of gaining congressional support for a decision to halt the B-1, Carter probably would not have decided as he did. But Congress was closely divided and "swing" votes were there to support the new Democratic president, due in part to persistent efforts of the anti-B-1 lobby.

Also important was the fact that alternative weapons systems were available — and that defense experts were divided on the necessity of producing the B-1. Finally, to a president who had pledged to cut the defense budget, the B-1 may have stood out as being just too expensive.

Many of the plane's supporters blamed themselves for not having lobbied harder for the B-1. "Our complaint is not against the [anti-B-1] coalition but against those who sat and watched," said John M. Fisher, president of the defense-oriented American Security Council. An editorial in *Aviation Week* commented that the Air Force had "done a miserable job over the years making its case for the B-1" and said Rockwell's low-keyed efforts "should serve as a good example of where a low profile leads in the defense business...."[13]

The B-1 program was an example of a project initiated by the executive branch rather than by outside interest groups. However, once Rockwell was awarded the contract to develop prototypes of the bomber (in 1970), members of Congress and outside interest groups opposed to the plane swung into action to attack and, they hoped, reverse the administration's decision. Until 1977, the effort focused on persuading Congress to cancel, or at least delay, full-scale production of the aircraft through a two-pronged strategy: activating grass-roots pressures and direct lobbying on Capitol Hill. Responding to the opposition, the plane's proponents, both within and outside Congress, geared up their own lobbying effort, using many of their opponents' tactics.

Not only were the tactics of both groups similar in many respects; rather ironically, their strategies and aims were similar as well. In the end, both settled for a congressional "non-decision" that preserved the options of either going ahead with or halting production, thus resting their case with whoever would be president in 1977. Throughout the B-1 debate, the ultimate decision lay with the executive branch; but both the pro- and anti-B-1 lobby used congressional votes to influence that decision. Until 1977, B-1 opponents had to wage an uphill battle; the strategic advantages were on the side of the B-1 supporters, for, after all, the program was already in operation, thanks to strong backing from a majority in Congress and the Nixon and Ford administrations.

As 1976 drew to a close, both sides of the lobby battle could claim victory. B-1 opponents had won a delay in a final production decision, while supporters had won continuing, albeit month-by-month, funding for the project. The essential ingredient that tipped the scales against the B-1 was the election of Jimmy Carter. As the congressional votes indicated, the anti-B-1 coalition would probably not have been able to secure the votes necessary to override a decision by an administration (such as Ford's) that strongly supported the bomber. Even after Carter in June 1977 announced his decision to halt production, it was not an easy task to win endorsement of that decision in Congress. It was primarily the factor of party loyalty to a Democratic president, together with administration lobbying, that made possible the final success of the anti-B-1 lobby.

NOTES

1. For a general discussion of the MCPL group, see Congressional Quarterly, *Guide to Congress*, 2nd edition (Washington, D.C.: Congressional Quarterly, 1976), p. 618.
2. For background on the formation and activities of the anti-B-1 coalition, see the following articles: Linda Charlton, "The People Behind the Campaign to Shoot Down the B-1 Bomber Project," *The New York Times*, July 25, 1977; James Robison, "How the B-1 Bomber was Brought Down," *The Christian Century*, August 17-24, 1977; Nicholas Wade, "Death of the B-1: The Events Behind Carter's Decision," *Science*, August 5, 1977; Stephen Chapman, "Dump the B-1," *The New Republic*, May 28, 1977.

3. Testimony by executive director Alice Tepper Marlin, U.S. Congress, *DOD-Industry Relations: Conflict of Interest and Standards of Conduct,* 94th Cong., 2d Sess., Joint Committee on Defense Production, hearings, Feb. 2-3, 1976, p. 73.
4. Quotations from Brammer throughout the chapter are from interviews in 1976, 1977 and 1978.
5. Information on these groups was obtained from their publications and interviews with staff.
6. Interview.
7. The following information comes from hearings before the Joint Committee on Defense Production, Feb. 2-3, 1976, "DOD-Industry Relations: Conflict of Interest and Standards of Conduct." See also Congressional Quarterly, 1976 *Almanac* (Washington, D.C.: Congressional Quarterly, 1977), pp. 503-504, 338-340.
8. See, for example, Claude Witze, "Free Speech and the B-1," *Air Force Magazine,* July 1977.
9. John W. Finney, "Air Chief's Briefing for Senate Aides on B-1 Funded by Private Group," *The New York Times,* July 30, 1976.
10. For more detail on legislative history, see the military authorization and appropriations stories in Congressional Quarterly, 1975 *Almanac* (Washington, D.C.: Congressional Quarterly, 1976), 1976 *Almanac* (Washington, D.C.: Congressional Quarterly, 1977), and 1977 *Almanac* (Washington, D.C.: Congressional Quarterly, 1958).
11. William Beecher, "Pentagon Report: Build 150 B-1 Bombers," *The Washington Star,* April 5, 1977.
12. Quoted in Wade, "Death of the B-1," p. 536.
13. *Ibid.,* p. 539.

PART III

Conclusion

8

Conclusion

This book has examined interest groups from a theoretical and behavioral perspective — the nature and types of groups in contemporary America, group resources and their strategies for influencing the political process, the regulation of groups by Congress, and the actual involvement of specific groups in precipitating, amending, or blocking three public policy proposals. We have discussed groups in the light of the ambivalence Americans have felt toward them since the days of the Founding Fathers, which is today reflected in the continuing debate over regulation of lobbying.

We have focused mostly on contemporary groups and their activities. It is important to note, though, that government and lobbying have changed considerably since the nineteenth century. Groups certainly had a significant impact on government in the early 1800s, but it was largely businessmen and mercantilists who organized to influence government policy. Their impact was based, with few exceptions, on their willingness to use money directly to influence Congress, through lavish parties and other forms of social entertainment, or through direct quid pro quos. Their impact was limited, because government itself had a limited scope, concentrating mainly on tariffs, U.S. territories, and patents.

In the decades following the Civil War, industrial and economic expansion of the United States took place along with massive immigration to America from Europe. Government expanded and groups, including broad-based mass movements, began to multiply as well. Farm groups, labor organizations, and a much broader range of economic-oriented groups became active in American society and politics. Groups and lobbies became fixtures in Washington politics, spanning most issue areas.

By the mid-twentieth century, a complex, technologically-oriented government was interacting regularly with a vast number of groups and institutions representing a broad spectrum of interests in the society. Congress particularly, as an institution decentralized by a committee system and based on a detailed division of labor, found that the information provided by groups, and the tendency of groups to sort out issues and set the priorities for the congressional agenda, were useful in overcoming the natural congressional inertia. So, interest group activity in Congress more and more has become a mutually supportive arrangement. Groups turn to Congress as an institution where they can be heard, establish their positions, and achieve their policy goals. Members of Congress in turn rely on groups to provide valuable constituency, technical, or political information, to give reelection support, and to assist strategically in passing or blocking legislation that the members support or oppose. Groups need Congress, and Congress needs groups.

We have seen the growth of another type of lobbying activity in America in the twentieth century — aimed at the executive branch. Bureaus, departments, agencies, and independent regulatory commissions have all expanded in number and size, especially since the New Deal of the 1930s. More agencies have meant more regulatory activity, affecting corporations, unions, farms, and others — and these groups have responded by increasing their contacts with executive agencies. Executive branch lobbying, then, has expanded as well in recent years; its effects remain largely unexamined. This book has concentrated heavily, though not exclusively, on lobbying in Congress, since it is by all odds the most open, massive, and vital of all group political activity. But future research must expand its focus to include more analysis of lobbying efforts directed at the executive branch.

LOBBYING ON SMALLER ISSUES

Just as we have not done detailed analysis of executive branch lobbying, there are a number of other areas touching on groups and lobbying that we have not covered in this book. To begin with, we have not discussed groups or provided in-depth case studies that deal with relatively narrow and insignificant policy issues. In many respects, groups and their representatives may have an even greater impact in moving issues toward implementation if the issues do *not* concern a broad range of citizens. Such issues do not seriously disturb the status quo or activate opposition from other groups. If a group or lobbyist can find a single well-placed "patron" in Congress who will sponsor a narrow bill or limited amendment, the chances for success are strong.

Such issues can affect individuals or groups. Many freelance lobbyists — lawyers, public relations specialists, former congressional staffers — perform these tasks for businesses, or associations, or for private individuals. For example, Congress each year passes several hundred "private" bills, to provide government relief of one sort or another for private citizens. The most prominent type of relief involves immigration; some lawyers and lobbyists specialize in obtaining immigrant status for foreign citizens through private bills.

Other lobbyists concentrate on drafting amendments to the tax code for particular individuals and corporations. Most of these lobbyists prowl the corridors around the House Ways and Means Committee meeting room, hovering around the members during bill-drafting sessions. They achieve success if they can win acceptance of a provision that provides specific tax relief for their clients.

Many lobbyists work for groups that enter the political process infrequently; the issues involved may be insignificant to all except a handful of people. For example, in 1975, the Biscuit and Cracker Manufacturers Association contracted Robert L. Koob to lobby for an end to a five-cent per pound tariff on fig paste imported from Turkey, Spain, and Portugal, which was forcing up the price of fig bars in grocery stores and at candy counters and thereby cutting sales. Koob went to members of the House Ways and Means and Senate Finance Committees, which consider legislation on tariffs, to argue for an end to the tariff.[1]

While issues like the fig tariff or a narrow tax amendment may not seem too consequential when compared to a Clean Air Act or a B-1 bomber, it is this smaller sort of political action which is a more common target for interest groups and lobbying, and their overall aggregate impact on public policy is great. Moreover, seemingly narrow amendments can have a huge impact that is not immediately apparent. An obscure amendment to the 1975 tax reform bill pushed by a tax lobbyist working for industrialist H. Ross Perot was later found to have been worth $15 million in tax savings to Perot.

FREE-LANCE LOBBYISTS

In a related vein, we have not, in this book, made a distinction between lobbyists who are part of a group — employed by the group on a full-time basis, with full loyalty to the group — and those who have several clients, and are contracted by each group on a free-lance basis. Groups like the AFL-CIO, NAACP, Chamber of Commerce and the Grocery Manufacturers of America have full-time legislative staffs as do most of the groups involved in our three case studies. But many companies, organizations and individuals hire lobbyists or lawyers to represent them in the political process. Several of these "guns-for-hire," as they are often called in Washington, are very powerful individuals, more powerful at times than the major full-time group representatives. One of the most prominent is Charls E. Walker, who operates his own lobbying firm. Walker has a Ph.D. in economics, was a lobbyist with the American Bankers Association and, from 1969 to 1973, undersecretary of the treasury in the Nixon administration. He now represents, on tax, energy, and economic matters, such clients as Ford, GM, General Electric, Weyerhauser, Lone Star Steel, and Dupont. A recent profile of Walker suggested that, through his close friendships with Energy Secretary James Schlesinger and Senate Finance

Committee Chairman Russell B. Long, D-La., played a key role, on behalf of his clients, in piecing together a compromise on the major energy bill in Congress in 1977-78.[2]

This distinction, between group representatives and free-lance hired lobbyists, has some implications for group theory. Who speaks for a group? Who legitimately represents a group? Can group representation be separated from the group itself?

The role of free-lance lobbyists is also a question that concerned Congress as it considered regulation and disclosure of lobbying in 1977-78. Congress was careful to include hired lobbyists when it drafted disclosure requirements. This was in part a recognition of the fact that, as government has become more complex, more diffused, more active, the use of highly trained specialists in the government process who have a guaranteed access to decisionmakers, has increased concomitantly. Many such individuals, like Walker, find it more lucrative to become independent lobbyists or join Washington law firms, and take on a variety of clients, than it would be for them to become a full-time representative of a single group. As these individuals become more important in the policy process, the relationship between groups and representatives tends to blur.

TRENDS IN THE 1970s

Finally, we should add a few paragraphs on the meaning of recent trends in group numbers and activity and in governmental structures and behavior, and what they suggest for the future relationship between interest groups and the policy process. The decade of the 1970s has seen a genuine explosion in group numbers and activity that has corresponded to reforms in Congress and change in the presidency. Precipitated in part by Vietnam and the election of an activist Republican president, Richard Nixon, in 1968, a variety of new groups — antiwar, environmental, "public interest" in general — came into the political process. They found a more hospitable environment during this era, since the political decentralization brought on by congressional reforms created more points of access for the groups, through newly powerful subcommittees and increasingly significant junior members of Congress. This new group activity precipitated a corresponding increase in activity from business-oriented groups and spurred the use of more sophisticated methods for communicating group opinions and exerting group influence.

This great expansion of group activity has its advantages. From the Madisonian viewpoint, it means more voices in the society being heard, and being balanced, in the government. Groups previously without organized voices — the poor, consumers, etc. — are now organized and active in the policy process.

But expanded group activity brings several possible negative consequences. Group activity spurs legislative activity, already increased by the growth in congressional staffs and the decentralization of congressional power. Increasingly overburdened legislators become more dependent on group initiatives to determine the legislative agenda; those groups with the sophistication to act and react quickly in the political process hold an advantage regardless of how worthy their goals might be.

In a broader sense, more groups and more legislative and group activity mean more fragmentation in politics. Groups become narrower and more specialized in their interests, and they deal with narrower and more specialized policy units. One of our more perceptive political commentators, Meg Greenfield, has recently remarked on this problem:

> I can't remember a time in Washington when interest-group issues and politics so dominated events. And every day the units of protest and concern seem to be subdividing into even smaller and more specialized groupings.[3]

To Greenfield, this has ominous implications:

> By now, there can hardly be a cultural, racial, regional, economic or professional group for whom the lawmakers of Washington have not fashioned some special statutory blessing — a prerogative, a grant, an exemption, a reimbursement . . . something. It puts a premium on identifying yourself with the special subgroup and helps to thin, if not destroy, whatever feelings of larger national loyalty various citizens may have.[4]

Greenfield's concerns are shared by Kevin Phillips, who calls the problem "the Balkanization of America."[5] Quoting *Roll Call*, a weekly Capitol Hill newspaper, Phillips notes that, with the reform-based decentralization in Congress, "lobbyists have learned to take advantage of this situation by playing one committee against another."[6] This tendency within government, in Washington, merely reflects the broader trend: "Now American society seems determined to pursue smaller loyalties — regional, economic, political, ethnic, and even sexual — rather than larger ones ... it bespeaks a fundamental reversal in the American experience. The heterogeneity of America will become a burden, the constitutional separation of powers crippling, the economy threatened, the cohesion of society further diminished."[7]

This problem points to the lack of ability to get a consensus or to implement comprehensive or *national* policy. In a way, it could lead towards a negative veto, the concurrent majority system recommended by John C. Calhoun where each significant group could veto a policy initiative if it felt threatened.

Of course, the "blame" for the potential problem, as articulated by Greenfield, does not rest entirely with interest groups. Clearly, the weakening of other political institutions which have in the past acted as nationalizing and unifying forces, especially the presidency and political parties, have contributed to the current situation.

But regardless of the causes, legitimate concerns are being expressed about the fragmenting effects of the contemporary explosion in groups and lobbying. The fears expressed by some analysts of these trends are countered by assertions from others that more lobbying, from a wider spectrum of society, is not only constitutionally-mandated, but leads to better, more open, and more responsive government.

The questions have found their way into the debate over regulating and disclosing lobbying activity. Many individuals and groups such as Common Cause feel that increased lobbying activity justifies broadened disclosure of the activities, while others believe that expanded disclosure rules create potential for official interference with legal activities, and

229

threaten First Amendment guarantees. We side with those who argue that disclosure is basically healthy for groups, government, and society. But it is clear that the debate, and the national ambivalence about the proper role of groups in politics, will continue for some time to come.

NOTES

1. Congressional Quarterly *Weekly Report*, May 31, 1975, p. 1141.
2. See "Lobbyist," by Elizabeth Drew, *The New Yorker*, January 9, 1978, pp. 32-58.
3. Meg Greenfield, "Thinking Small," *The Washington Post*, April 19, 1978, p. A13.
4. *Ibid.*
5. Kevin Phillips, "The Balkanization of America," *Harper's Magazine*, May 1978, pp. 37-47.
6. *Ibid.*, p. 44.
7. *Ibid.*, p. 46.

Selected Bibliography

Books and Monographs

Alexander, Herbert. *Financing Politics: Money, Elections and Political Reform*. Washington: Congressional Quarterly Press, 1976.

Bachrak, Stanley. *The Committee of One Million: "China Lobby" Politics 1953-1971*. New York: Columbia University Press, 1976.

Bauer, Raymond A.; Pool, Ithiel de Sola; and Dexter, Lewis Anthony. *American Business and Public Policy*. New York: Atherton, 1963.

Bentley, Arthur F. *The Process of Government*. Cambridge, Mass.: Harvard University Press, 1967.

Berry, Jeffrey M. *Lobbying for the People*. Princeton: Princeton University Press, 1977.

Deakin, James. *The Lobbyists*. Washington: Public Affairs Press, 1966.

Dexter, Lewis Anthony. *How Organizations Are Represented in Washington*. Indianapolis: Bobbs-Merrill, 1969.

———. *The Sociology and Politics of Congress*. Chicago: Rand McNally, 1969.

Eckstein, Harry. *Pressure Group Politics*. Stanford: Stanford University Press, 1960.

Ehrmann, Henry, ed. *Interest Groups on Four Continents*. Pittsburgh: University of Pittsburgh Press, 1958.

Gamson, William. *Power and Discontent*. Homewood, Ill.: Dorsey Press, 1968.

Goulden, Joseph C. *The Superlawyers*. New York: Dell, 1973.

Green, Mark J. *The Other Government: The Unseen Power of Washington Lawyers*. New York: Grossman, 1975.

Greenstone, J. David. *Labor in American Politics*. New York: Alfred A. Knopf, 1969.

Greenwald, Carol S. *Group Power: Lobbying & Public Policy*. New York: Praeger, 1977.

Hall, Donald R. *Cooperative Lobbying — The Power of Pressure*. Tucson: University of Arizona Press, 1969.

Harris, Richard. *A Sacred Trust*. Baltimore: Penquin Books, 1969.

———. *Decision*. New York: Dutton, 1971.

Herring, Pendleton. *Group Representation before Congress*. 1929. Reprint. New York: Russell & Russell, 1967.

Holtzman, Abraham. *Legislative Liaison: Executive Leadership in Congress*. Chicago: Rand McNally, 1970.

Howe, Russell Warren, and Trott, Sarah Hays. *The Power Peddlers*. Garden City, N.Y.: Doubleday, 1977.

Key, V. O., Jr. *Politics, Parties, & Pressure Groups*. 5th ed. New York: Crowell, 1964.

———. *Public Opinion and American Democracy*. New York: Alfred A. Knopf, 1961.

Kingdon, John W. *Congressmen's Voting Decisions*. New York: Harper & Row, 1973.

Koen, Ross Y. *The China Lobby in American Politics*. New York: Harper & Row, 1974.

Lowi, Theodore J. *The End of Liberalism*. New York: Norton, 1969.

Lutzker, Paul. "The Politics of Public Interest Groups: Common Cause in Action." Ph.D. dissertation, The Johns Hopkins University, 1973.

McCarry, Charles. *Citizen Nader*. New York: Saturday Review Press, 1972.

McConnell, Grant. *Private Power and American Democracy*. New York: Alfred A. Knopf, 1966.

McFarland, Andrew S. *Public Interest Lobbies: Decision-making on Energy*. Washington: American Enterprise Institute, 1976.

Milbrath, Lester W. *The Washington Lobbyists*. Chicago: Rand McNally, 1963.

Nadel, Mark V. *The Politics of Consumer Protection*. Indianapolis: Bobbs-Merrill, 1971.

Olson, Mancur, Jr. *The Logic of Collective Action*. Cambridge, Mass.: Harvard University Press, 1965.

Oppenheimer, Bruce I. *Oil and the Congressional Process*. Lexington, Mass.: Lexington Books, 1974.

Peabody, Robert L.; Berry, Jeffrey M.; Frasure, William G.; and Goldman, Jerry. *To Enact A Law: Congress and Campaign Financing*. New York: Praeger, 1972.

Redman, Eric. *The Dance of Legislation*. New York: Simon and Schuster, 1975.

Salisbury, Robert, H., ed. *National Journal Reprints on Interest Groups*. Washington: National Journal, 1975-76, 1977-78.

Schattschneider, E. E. *The Semisovereign People*. New York: Holt, Rinehart and Winston, 1960.

Schriftgiesser, Karl. *The Lobbyists*. Boston: Little, Brown, 1951.

Scott, Andrew M., and Hunt, Margaret A. *Congress and Lobbies*. Chapel Hill: University of North Carolina Press, 1965.

Selznick, Philip. *TVA and the Grass Roots*. New York: Harper & Row, 1966.

Smith, Judith, ed. *Political Brokers: People, Organizations, Money & Power*. New York: Liveright/National Journal, 1972.

Truman, David B. *The Governmental Process*. 2d ed. New York: Alfred A. Knopf, 1971.

Verba, Sidney, and Nie, Norman H. *Participation in America*. New York: Harper & Row, 1972.

The Washington Lobby. 2d ed. Washington: Congressional Quarterly, 1974.

Wilson, James Q. *Political Organizations*. New York: Basic Books, 1973.

Ziegler, L. Harmon, and Peak, Wayne G. *Interest Groups in American Politics*. 2d ed. Englewood Cliffs, N.J.: Prentice-Hall, 1972.

———, and Baer, Michael. *Lobbying*. Belmont, Calif.: Wadsworth, 1969.

Articles

Bachrach, Peter, and Baratz, Morton S. "Two Faces of Power." *American Political Science Review* 56 (1972).

Berry, Jeffrey M., and Goldman, Jerry. "Congress and Public Policy: A Study of the Federal Election Campaign Act of 1971." *Harvard Journal on Legislation* 10 (1973).

Briggs, Jean. "The Countergovernment." *Forbes*, October 15, 1976.

Cahn, Edgar, and Cahn, Jean Camper. "Power to the People or the Profession? — The Public Interest in Public Interest Law." *Yale Law Journal* 79 (1970).

Cooper, Ann. "Mumbling It Through." *The Washington Monthly*, December 1975.

Drew, Elizabeth. "Conversation with A Citizen." *New Yorker*, July 23, 1973.

———. "Lobbyist." *New Yorker*, January 9, 1978.

Guzzardi, Walter, Jr. "Business is Learning How to Win in Washington." *Fortune*, March 27, 1978.

Harrington, Michael J. "The Politics of Gun Control." *The Nation*, January 12, 1974.

Ignatius, David. "Stages of Nader." *The New York Times Magazine*, January 18, 1976.

Levine, Arthur. "Getting to Know Your Congressman: The $500 Understanding." *The Washington Monthly*, February 1975.

Lindblom, Charles E. "The Science of Muddling Through." *Public Administration Review* 19 (1959).

Lipsky, Michael. "Protest as a Political Resource." *American Political Science Review* 62 (1968).

Orren, Karen. "Standing to Sue: Interest Group Conflict in the Federal Courts." *American Political Science Review* 70 (1976).

Pipe, G. Russell. "Congressional Liaison: The Executive Branch Consolidates its Relations with Congress." *Public Administration Review* 26 (1966).

Salisbury, Robert H. "An Exchange Theory of Interest Groups." *Midwest Journal of Political Science* 13 (1969).

Schumaker, Paul D. "Public Responsiveness to Protest-Group Demands." *Journal of Politics* 37 (1975).

Schwartz, Donald E. "The Public Interest Proxy Contest: Reflections on Campaign GM." *Michigan Law Review* 69 (1971).

Sherrill, Robert. "Breaking Up Big Oil." *The New York Times Magazine*, October 3, 1976.

Wellford, Harrison. "How Ralph Nader, Tricia Nixon, the ABA, and Jamie Whitten Helped Turn the FTC Around." *The Washington Monthly*, October 1972.

Williams, Roger M. "The Rise of Middle Class Activism: Fighting 'City Hall.' " *Saturday Review/World*, March 8, 1975.

Wright, Frank. "The Dairy Lobby Buys the Cream of the Congress." *The Washington Monthly*, May 1971.

Index

A

Addabbo, Joseph P. (D N.Y.)
  B-1 bomber funds - 188, 193, 210, 215
Agricultural Groups
  Campaign contributions - 71
  Farm groups - 44
  Farmers' State Right League - 27
  Groups and the Executive Branch - 62, 224
  Initiating government action - 57
  1946 lobby law violations - 102, 103
  Monitoring political activity - 55, 56
  Public protests - 92, 93
  Resources and tactics - 71, 73, 74
Air Force Association - 208
Allen, James B. (D Ala.) - 145
American Automobile Association - 158
American Bar Association (ABA) - 29, 64
American Civil Liberties Union (ACLU) - 49, 64
AFL-CIO
  B-1 bomber support - 194
  Clean air legislation - 158
  Common site picketing battle - 131-133
  Foreign lobbying - 51
  Labor loyalists in Congress - 133
  Membership size - 73
  Political resources - 76

  Priorities, agenda difficulties - 127, 131
  Profile - 24, 25, 26
  Resources and strategy - 131-133
American Federation of State, County and Municipal Employees - 198
American Friends Service Committee (AFSC)
  Anti-B-1 coalition - 193, 195
  Focus on the White House - 215
  Lobbying techniques - 197, 211, 214, 216
American Israel Public Affairs Committee - 74
American Medical Association (AMA) - 29, 62, 70, 71
American Petroleum Institute (API)
  Auto emission standards - 159
  Economic functions - 30, 31
  Membership - 40
  Oil lobby groups - 39
  Resources and strategies - 70, 85
American Political Science Association - 29, 33
American Security Council - 218
American Telephone & Telegraph (AT&T) - 134
American Trial Lawyers Association - 31
Americans for Constitutional Action (ACA) - 32, 49
Americans for Democratic Action (ADA) - 32, 49, 214
Anderson, John B. (R Ill.) - 138

235

G

H

I

J

K

L

M

R

S